A Nun and the Pig

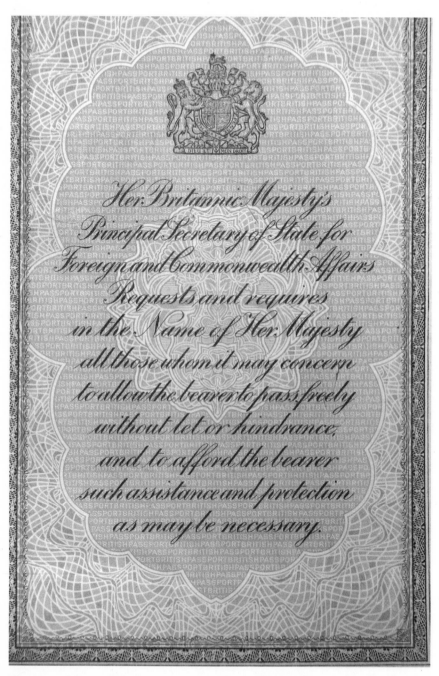

Her Britannic Majesty's
Principal Secretary of State for
Foreign and Commonwealth Affairs
Requests and requires
in the Name of Her Majesty
all those whom it may concern
to allow the bearer to pass freely
without let or hindrance,
and to afford the bearer
such assistance and protection
as may be necessary.

The front of my passport seemed a little pompous, but the bit about 'without let and hindrance' was weirdly reassuring, and exactly what I needed in the months ahead.

A Nun and the Pig

Tales from South Africa

TREIVE NICHOLAS

AMBERLEY

Dedicated to

Sister Mary Paule Tacke
(1932–2014)

and the people of South Africa.

The author and publisher would like to thank the following people/organisations for permission to use copyright material in this book: Steve Gordon at musicpics.co.za for the photograph of the Soul Brothers, Alamy Ltd for use of the image of Nongqawuse and Nonkosi, and Gallo Images South Africa for the photograph of George Matanzima, former Prime Minister of Transkei. Photograph of King George VI in Umtata, 1947, by permission of Royal Collection Trust / © Her Majesty Queen Elizabeth II 2020.

Every attempt has been made to seek permission for copyright material used in this book. However, if we have inadvertently used copyright material without permission/ acknowledgement we apologise and will make the necessary correction at the first opportunity.

First published 2021

Amberley Publishing
The Hill, Stroud
Gloucestershire, GL5 4EP

www.amberley-books.com

British Library Cataloguing in Publication Data.
A catalogue record for this book is available from the British Library.

ISBN 978 1 3981 0677 2 (hardback)
ISBN 978 1 3981 1107 3 (paperback)
ISBN 978 1 3981 0678 9 (ebook)

Typeset in 10.5pt on 14pt Sabon.
Typesetting by SJmagic DESIGN SERVICES, India.
Printed in the UK.

Contents

Acknowledgements		6
List of Maps		9
Introduction		10
1	Nkosi Sikelel' iAfrika	17
2	Ikhwezi	23
3	Peat Bogs and Bagpipes	33
4	Team Transkei	43
5	Buntingville	54
6	Soul Brothers	59
7	The Prime Minister and Me	68
8	Potpourri	71
9	Seventeen Thembu Chiefs	86
10	The Flying Nun	96
11	Blood	102
12	Zipho	111
13	Wild Coast	113
14	A Brief and Incomplete History of Transkei	127
15	The Great Kei River	141
16	Mr Bidla and the Various Mrs Bidlas	154
17	Transkei Heart	163
18	Dignity and Dust (an Adventure in Lesotho)	172
19	Save Water Drink Wine	186
20	Summons to Appear in Court K 504855	200
21	Freedom Fighter or Terrorist?	209
22	Sister Mary Paule Tacke (MP)	229
Afterword: Shadows		240
Bibliography		249
Index		252

Acknowledgements

These *Tales* and all the accompanying photographs would still be locked in my diary and stored in the loft, were it not for Itumeleng Pooe and Garry Buckler. Quite independently, over eighteen months, they badgered, pestered and cajoled me to write about the time I spent in South Africa in 1980. From the snippets of stories I occasionally told, they could see what I could not. I am indebted to them for insisting I start telling my story and for their unwavering support, particularly when my confidence was low.

Life never goes the way you plan, and I certainly did not expect to find Doug Ritchie after thirty-eight years apart. He was my co-conspirator and mischief-maker in Transkei. Besides adding to the momentum created by Itu and Garry, he has proofread each chapter and supplied some wonderful photographs. Thanks, Doug.

On many occasions I have been so focused on the writing of *A Nun and the Pig* that I slid into an impenetrable bubble, where I wasn't fit for normal conversation. I can't sufficiently thank my wonderful wife, Clare, for being so tolerant and understanding whenever this happened. Thank you for the mugs of hot Bovril that miraculously kept appearing on my desk. When feedback on a chapter was needed, she didn't sugar the pill, which was just what I needed.

By chance I found Jane Mqamelo, who lives and works as a freelance editor in Mthatha (previously 'Umtata') in the former Transkei. In addition to sharpening up the whole text, she offered invaluable local knowledge and insight to correct the errors. She helped turn my writing into a manuscript ready to woo the team at Amberley Publishing. Her husband, Simon, was generous enough to open my mind to the world of his Xhosa ancestors.

Acknowledgements

I found the novel *The Native Commissioner*, by the late Shaun Johnson, deeply moving and a source of strength during my moments of doubt. It was a tale I could relate to. So you can imagine my surprise when Shaun called me from Cape Town to discuss his work and encourage me to persist with my stories based in Transkei.

Steve Bowles and Lea were wonderful at reviewing the raw copy and their suggestion that I return to Ikhwezi Lokusa after forty years was inspiring. In the last few weeks of his life I had the pleasure of reading an early draft of this manuscript to my good friend Turkish, who laughed a lot, either with me or at me, I'm not sure which. Michael and Katie Fasosin were invaluable members of the motivational team behind this project and were kind enough to introduce me to Selina Walker. Selina gently guided me through the minefield of the publishing world when I felt like a rabbit in the headlights.

Several years ago, on a very cold Friday evening, at the Richmond Athletic Ground, Steve Tomlin was good enough to let me earwig his conversation about how to get a book published. His advice was worth its weight in gold. I don't think I ever thanked him.

Reading and writing were hugely problematic for me as a boy and a teenager. I hated both and found them frustratingly difficult. It was only the persistence and imagination of my mother that helped me overcome this challenge. Without her love and care I certainly would not have been able to write this book.

On my return trip to the former Transkei, in February 2020, Debbie Eardley was kind enough to provide a roof over my head in Johannesburg, whilst the team at Ebony Lodge in Mthatha went to great lengths to ensure I stayed out of trouble during my time there. Likewise, with Sister Raphael Buthelezi, who safely steered me around Mthatha and provided ecclesiastic protection when I insisted on galivanting about in Ngangelizwe township, contrary to everyone's advice. Their collective care was invaluable.

To all the staff at Ikhwezi Lokusa Special School in 1980, I say a big 'thank you', too. How you put up with Doug and me remains a mystery. To the principal, Archie Gulwa, and the teachers at the school in 2020, I am eternally grateful for allowing me to roam the corridors in search of elusive shadows and precious memories.

Rose Kasumbi, the director of Bethany Home, and her dedicated team were very generous with their time when I went in search of Sister Mary Paule's legacy amongst the region's most vulnerable young children. A warm thank you.

correct mixture of recreation and study. I'm delighted that they are exploiting your journalistic gifts (had you not been so determined to be filthy rich + journalism is the field you could have excelled in — Douglas and I once figured that out for you. (a digression now – 2 weeks ago we had a visit from President Mphephu of Venda, and I assure you that provided material for writing an memorable account) and I'm glad that some of the courses you are doing make you sweat – you'll certainly pass them all, and pass them well, but in the meantime it is right and fitting that you should feel uncomfortable enough to have to exert yourself.

In her 1981 letter to me, Sister Mary Paule and Doug had 'figured out' I should have been a journalist.

To quote Sister Mary Paule in a letter to me in 1981, 'Had you not been so determined to be filthy rich, journalism is the field you could have excelled in. Douglas and I figured that out for you.' Like all good advice teenagers receive, I ignored it. I wish I hadn't. The words 'figured it out for you' resonate very strongly every time I read this letter. So belatedly, I thank her, for her words of wisdom, and I hope this book goes some way to making amends for my failing.

By the way, I didn't achieve the filthy rich bit either.

List of Maps

1   The Bantustans or homelands of South Africa, *c.* 1980   14
2   Transkei, *c.* 1980   15
3   Ongeluksnek in relation to Lesotho, Matatiele and Umtata   173

Introduction

For thirty-eight years, I kept my old personal diary in a bedside drawer, unopened and unread, for safe keeping. The bruised brown cover, embossed with '1980', was bulging and cracked from the letters, tickets and newspaper cuttings jammed between its pages. Inside were my thoughts and recollections of daily life as a teacher at a Catholic mission in Umtata, South Africa. Umtata was the capital of a pseudo-independent country called Transkei, having the status of a

My personal diary from 1980 in Transkei remained shut away, unread, but close by, in my bedside drawer for thirty-eight years.

'homeland' or 'Bantustan' according to the apartheid government of the time. It served as a dumping ground for approximately 2.5 million Xhosa people, considered foreigners in the country of their birth and forced to live in this undeveloped, mostly rural pocket of land on South Africa's east coast.

In 2018 I nervously opened my diary for the first time in decades, read a few pages and closed it again. I repeated this several times until I reached 4 September 1980, the date I left Transkei. Hearing my nineteen-year-old self enthusiastically conveying details about people, places and events that had exerted such an influence on my young mind was unsettling, yet deeply moving; had I really been so brimful of life, so curious, so responsive? I climbed into the loft to haul out the photographic slides that accompanied the diary and was amazed to see that the vibrant Transkeian colours and striking scenes had hardly tarnished over time.

Shortly after the revelation of reading about and viewing my personal world of thirty-eight years ago, I sheepishly opened my laptop. I paused, mindful that I was about to do something significant. After opening a new Word document, I wrote in bold letters at the top of the page CHAPTER 1. I really had no idea where I was going, or where this would take me, but I now had a strong need to write. And so, I started. Three chapters spewed out in only a few hours, my fingers hurrying over the keyboard to start telling a tale that had been subconsciously fermenting in me for the best part of four decades. There was an unfathomable urgency to it. I felt like Forrest Gump, when he couldn't stop running. 'Run Forrest, run!' In my case it was 'Type Treive, type!' I'd quickly built up a momentum that was impossible to stop and difficult to control, and tiring too, with facts and emotions jostling for my attention. Soon, I was quite lost in my own world, or bubble, as the family called it.

I was writing principally for myself; in fact, it soon became blatantly obvious that I *needed* to write my story. Thoughts and feelings about 1980 had been locked away for far, far too long. When I came up for air, so to speak, I'd written the draft manuscript for the book you are about to read.

A Nun and the Pig is a collection of tales based on my personal experience of working and travelling in South Africa, Transkei in particular, and neighbouring countries in southern Africa. They're as true to life as my memory, diary and photographs enable them to be. Doug Ritchie, my work colleague at the time, can vouch for their authenticity. The views and thoughts expressed in this book are those of a naïve teenager, fresh from the UK, unfamiliar with southern African culture and challenged by the intense encounters and situations he experienced each day. This is not a political commentary, but the visceral politics of 1980s South Africa can never be far from the story; the government of the day was omnipotent, uncompromising and brutally racist, and its influence was felt whether one walked the streets of Johannesburg or dwelt quietly in a mud hut on a hillside in Transkei.

To tell my tales I have found it necessary to use much of the language and spelling of names that were prevalent at that time. For example, I write about Umtata, which today is spelt Mthatha. Also, I make frequent reference to people by their race and skin colour – black, white, coloured and Asian. People of mixed race, as an example, were defined as coloured, and treated differently from people defined as black or white. Please excuse me, but this hideous approach was central to everything that happened in this part of the world, at that time, under the laws and culture of apartheid. Race was front and centre. By any standards, it is vile, rude and unacceptable.

My recollections are unfiltered and varied; here are Thembu chiefs, an infant dying from neglect, observations of the brutal consequences of apartheid's laws, a non-racial paraplegic sporting event – a complete anomaly at the time – and an account of my tenuous, vicarious relationship with Nelson Mandela and his nephew, the Prime Minister of Transkei. There were numerous scrapes with law-enforcement agencies, and the challenge of smuggling black liberation literature through border posts into South Africa from the newly independent Zimbabwe. If that's too serious for you, discover how I became Master of Ceremonies at a keenly contested local beauty pageant, and join me for a spot of adventure off the beaten track to the mountains of Lesotho. Forming a constant backdrop to my eight months in Transkei was the stunningly beautiful landscape: the rolling, wooded hills, the vast African sky, the rivers, waterfalls, red dirt tracks and clusters of huts on hillsides, often inaccessible by road.

Transkei cannot be understood without some historical context; it was an ultimately doomed attempt to create a country out of an area traditionally occupied by Xhosa-speaking people, who, generations earlier, had formed part of a wave of migrations of Bantu people from northern parts of Africa to its southern tip. The events that led to the creation of Transkei as a recognised region of South Africa in the 19th century were of truly Shakespearean proportions. War, famine and mystical personalities coalesce to form an epic and dramatic story that could have stepped straight from the pages of the Bard. Some background is provided so that 1980s Transkei may be more or less understood.

In truth, many different clans, tribes and groups, such as the abaThembu, amaXesibe, Gcaleka, Bomvana, amaMpondo, amaBhaca, amaMfengu, amaMpondomise and others, inhabited Transkei. I have used shorthand and called them Xhosa-speaking people. While this was common practice in 1980, I acknowledge that this is a bit lazy on my part, and inaccurate. I tried a more in-depth explanation of the various groups that made up the people of Transkei, but I got bogged down and was worried I might lose you, the reader. Please accept my apologies.

Spelling is another minefield I've had to deal with. Don't be too surprised if a famous Xhosa person's name or place names have spelling variants in different texts. For example, the site of a mystical visitation encountered by the infamous Nongqawuse, the prophetess, is spelt as both the Gxara River and Gxarha River.

To help bring these tales further to life and to show the beauty of Transkei, I've included quite a few photographs of the people and places you'll read about. The majority were taken back in 1980. A handful are from my return trip in February 2020, and there is a sprinkling of stock shots too.

Weaving through all of my experiences during this intense period of my life was the influence of Sister Mary Paule Tacke, my boss and friend, who dedicated her life to the welfare of Transkeians. She was no ordinary person, by whatever yardstick one chooses to measure. Her wisdom, humour, resilience and goodness were legendary in the area and left a huge mark on me. Hers is an influence I and many others continue to feel to this day, so her brutal murder in 2014 was particularly sickening and tragic.

In the final chapter the story comes full circle, as I describe my return to Transkei in February 2020, forty years after my original experience there. I got to see and feel the shadows of my old friends, so I could tie up a few personal loose ends and start to put my mind to rest, at last.

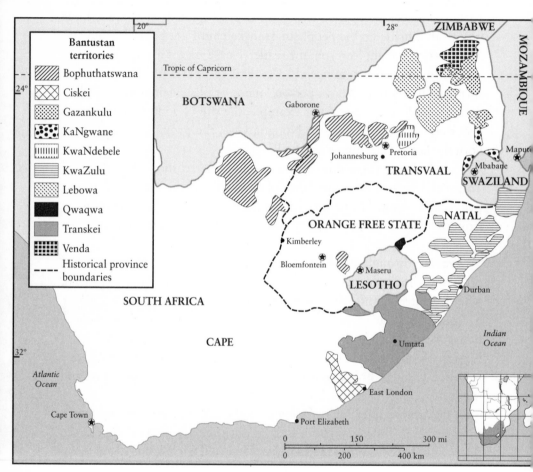

Map 1. The Bantustans or homelands of South Africa, *c.* 1980.

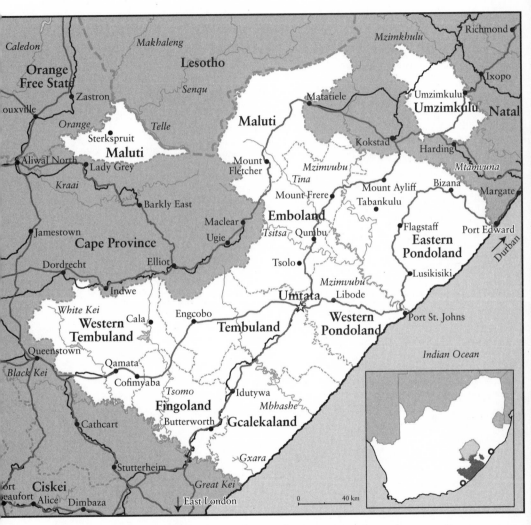

Map 2. Transkei, *c.* 1980. The circles on the inset map show the approximate locations of Durban (to the north-east of Transkei) and East London (to the south-west of Transkei).

1

Nkosi Sikelel' iAfrika

On 4 September 1980, I left Ikhwezi Lokusa Special School, Transkei, South Africa, after eight months teaching art, science and sport to handicapped Xhosa children and young adults. I'd been dreading my departure day for weeks, not wanting any unseemly display of emotion, which would have shown me up. Not the done thing at all for a British teenager.

To ease the envisaged difficulties, I'd started saying my farewells earlier in an easy-going, nonchalant sort of way, giving off an air of relaxation as I thanked the young students, teachers, cooks, gardeners, fathers, fellow volunteers and nuns. In truth, I was feeling far from nonchalant. The bonds of friendship, familiarity and respect forged over the past eight months were stronger than I'd realised. The warm comments and the stack of personal farewell letters, cards and souvenirs I received, all saying such nice things about me, took me by surprise – was this *me* they were talking about? I was overwhelmed, and I hadn't even got to the hard bit – the final goodbye.

One of my roles at the mission had been to support and help supervise the older students, known as the after-care students. Over eight months the students and I had grown close; we'd set them up in their new residential quarters, spent every day together and participated in the South African paraplegic sports championships in Durban. If you add to the mix the pretty severe physical and mental handicaps they lived with, our bonding becomes understandable.

By the morning of my last day at Ikhwezi I'd said most of my one-on-one goodbyes; there was only the final farewell to face, to the students as a group. I dreaded it – who likes goodbyes? I entered the after-care

17

A lighter moment at Ikhwezi with Sisters Genevieve, Mary Paule and Michael enjoying the Easter braai (BBQ).

students' workshop, where Mam, their supervisor, quickly corralled the students together, standing tall and proud amidst the throng. Everything about Mam spoke of pride, integrity and authority. In an army context she'd have been a sergeant major, but amongst the handicapped she was simply firm, clear-headed and compassionate. They all looked at me expectantly. What was I to say to these trusting souls – 'Bye, great knowing you, take care?' How banal.

I'd actually considered sneaking out without a farewell, but that would have been cowardly and rude. Unforgivable. We *had* to say farewell properly, though I knew I'd be awkward. As it turned out, I hardly had the chance to fumble; no sooner had I spluttered out a few words than Mam began to sing, in her powerful, soaring African voice. She led, and her students followed, their words reverberating through the workshop. *Nkosi Sikelel' iAfrika* ('Lord Bless Africa'). Her sincere, booming voice started as a solo, soon augmented by the voices of the group, who plunged in after her. The song was loud and clear. They

Mam and the young women in after-care, outside their brand-new accommodation and rehabilitation centre at Ikhwezi.

were spontaneously singing to *me*, the same way they sang in the chapel each Sunday. Looking me straight in the eye, not flinching a jot, they were united in thanking me through song.

It wouldn't be an exaggeration to say I was knocked sideways, disarmed by the spontaneous generosity of their farewell, and feeling more humbled than I knew possible. It is hard to convey the power of that moment. Today *Nkosi Sikelel' iAfrika* forms the basis of the national anthem and is sung in Xhosa, Zulu, Afrikaans and English, but in 1980s apartheid South Africa it was not commonly heard, nor was it just a song. It was a liberation statement, a symbol of the banned African National Congress (ANC), and outlawed by the apartheid government. It was also the national anthem of Transkei. This was *their* song, something outside the control and remit of apartheid, and it represented hope, identity, dignity and resolute defiance. They were proud Transkeians, not South Africans, and they wanted to express it, without apology or reservation. From the first note to the last, this humble group sang it with such soul and meaning, from so deep down, that it felt like a precious gift.

I had no defences against such a gift and, feeling the tears well up, I thanked them, said goodbye and scuttled off. I simply could not believe that they had sung *Nkosi Sikelel' iAfrika* to me. Feelings of humility, elation and deep sadness swirled about inside me – all pretty

Mam combined an old-fashioned mixture of compassion and discipline when caring for the after-care students. Doug and I were frequently a grave disappointment to her.

disorientating for an emotionally stunted British teenager. It actually caused a reaction of fatigue and confusion as I struggled to cope with the unfamiliar deluge of emotion.

But the hardest farewell was yet to come. That I knew.

Waiting outside the workshop, empathising with what I was going through, stood Sister Mary Paule Tacke, a white American nun, with her trusted companion, a battered white VW Beetle. Dubbed 'the Pig' for its quixotic temperament, this car was akin to Don Quixote's exhausted and long-suffering donkey, Rocinante. On this occasion, the Pig started and so, with my rucksack thrown onto the back seat, we set off for the airport amid the usual grunting, mechanical din. Down the familiar, bumpy, sun-baked road we rattled into Umtata, not running any red 'robots' on this occasion. Robots, as traffic lights are called in South Africa, were almost optional for Sister Mary Paule, who took a girlish delight in rushing through on red. Her curriculum vitae would have listed it as a hobby.

We passed the Golden Egg, a fast-food restaurant of dubious quality that had served as a little escape, a secret bolthole, for my work colleagues Douglas and Babs, and me, often accompanied by Sister Mary Paule. Doug's gluttony had been legendary, the pinnacle being his consumption of two chocolate sundaes in one sitting, egged on by a laughing Sister Mary Paule. Seldom in the history of friendship has such a low-grade fast-food emporium given so much pleasure and generated so much laughter as the Umtata Golden Egg had for the four of us.

Today, however, there was a marked shortage of laughter. Stilted conversation dominated the drive.

'I've left the keys for the vans in the box.'

'Oh, good. Have you got your passport?'

'Yes.'

'Did you pack everything?'

'Yep.'

'Where's your ticket?'

'Got it.'

For two people who knew each other pretty well and had spent the last few months working long hours together, this was a far from normal exchange, all rather staccato in fashion, but it was better than silence, and we were making the best of a difficult situation. Besides, I was starting to sniffle, again.

Arrive at the airport.

Find a parking space.

Park the car.

Pick up rucksack, check pockets for passport and wallet.

Walk silently to the entrance.

Stop. Say goodbye.

Air ticket, passport, Transkei visa – I was ready to leave.

So there we stood, not looking each other in the face, heads slightly dropped to avoid eye contact. I said I'd write soon and I'd best not miss my check-in. Sister Mary Paule said some lovely things and that I'd be missed. But to be honest, I wasn't taking any of it in, with the vortex of unfamiliar emotions turning my inner world upside down and getting worse by the minute. I heard the words but struggled to digest them into anything intelligible. It was like hearing a conversation with cotton wool in your ears or whilst wearing ear defenders. I was doing my level best just to get through this farewell with a semblance of dignity. I was hanging in there desperately, I really was, but not making a very good job of it.

I'd been on planet Earth nineteen years and nine months to the day, and this was, without doubt, the most upsetting moment I'd experienced. I had never been as deeply touched as I was by the events of the past eight months and by the person in front of me, and here I was, leaving it all behind for good.

Finally, she handed me a leaving card and three clay animal figurines that reflected some of the conversations we'd shared over the previous months.

We went our separate ways; Sister Mary Paule walked back to the Pig, whilst I plunged into the melee of expectant air passengers and the somewhat subdued din of the little airport.

There was still time, so I headed straight for the loo, grabbing a handful of tissues, feeling hollow and confused. Leaving Transkei was not meant to be like this. I knew it would be tough, but not this tough! What was happening to me?

I cried myself across Transkei, Lesotho, the Drakensberg Mountains and the highveld of the Transvaal, exhausting my tissue stash before the plane descended into Johannesburg. Some semblance of self-control was restored as I waited to be collected at Jan Smuts airport, and by the time I had disappeared into the blazing Johannesburg traffic, I'd resumed the stiff upper lip of an Englishman abroad.

2

Ikhwezi

Ikhwezi.
Ikhwezi Lokusa.
Ikhwezi Lokusa Special School.
Ikhwezi Lokusa Special School, Umtata, Transkei.

Try saying it out loud. If you're in a public space, the person next to you is hardly going to mind; in fact, get them to join you. Better still, ask the whole bus or train carriage you may be travelling in to learn a few Xhosa words and chant them out in unison.

Me and my Ikhwezi van, lost somewhere in rural Transkei, with no map or GPS to help! Sister Consolata seeks some assistance.

Ikhwezi Lokusa ('the one that shines the brightest', after the Xhosa name for Venus) are among the easier of the Xhosa words I learnt, with none of the clicks that make the language so enticingly musical and bewildering. For 'Ikhwezi Lokusa' you say everything phonetically as you read it; apart from its three distinct clicks, Xhosa has none of the ridiculous tricks of the English language to contend with. Don't be shy, dial up your diction – you're allowed to with the Xhosa language. I'll break it up for your first attempt.

Ikh-we-zi Lo-ku-sa Special School, Um-ta-ta, Trans-kei.

Not too difficult? Now repeat it again with a little rhythm and poetry:

Ikh-we-zi Lo-ku-sa Special School, Um-ta-ta, Trans-kei.

To paraphrase Professor Henry Higgins speaking to Eliza Doolittle in *My Fair Lady*, 'By George, I think you've got it!'

One of the immediate benefits of learning a smattering of Xhosa is that you beef up your enunciation, giving your jaw and tongue a mini gym session. In Xhosa the 'x' is pronounced like the sound one makes when giddying up a horse; 'x!' 'x!' Try it. The click is formed on the sides of the tongue; a sort of sucking sound. The 'q' is formed as your tongue pulls away from the roof of your mouth, and the 'c' is a little sound, as we might make in annoyance, with the tip of your tongue just behind your top front teeth. Have you tried it? I am sure you feel a little uplifted already – I do and I've been practising as I write. Gives you a little spring in your step.

Extremely frivolous and improbable as this phonetic nonsense may sound, it isn't. The Toyota kombi vans I drove at Ikhwezi Lokusa (kombis would be called people carriers or SUVs nowadays) had the name of the school emblazoned on the side, clear to read even when dusty or muddy, as they invariably were. And I drove all over Transkei and parts of South Africa in these vans, sometimes alone, sometimes with a crowd of kids and with one of the sisters, teachers or nurses as a guide. Usually, I was transporting handicapped children from their various townships or rural villages to and from the mission or to various hospitals and clinics. Whenever I pulled up in some village, curious onlookers or family members would surround us, repeating 'Ikhwezi …!' 'Ikhwezi Lokusa Special School …'. They said it loudly and poetically, just like you and your fellow bus passengers did a moment ago.

For many Transkeian families, rural and urban, Ikhwezi Lokusa Special School meant hope, relief and an opportunity for their children, often severely physically or mentally handicapped, to live a relatively normal and productive life. Life in a mud-and-grass-built hut out in the country or in a pokey tin-clad room in an impoverished township was not a good place for many of these children with special needs to live, even if they received the love of a parent, which was not always the case. Ever tried pushing a wheelchair on a muddy, grassy surface with rocks and branches as obstacles? Or guiding a young handicapped girl out of a small, dark township room, trying to avoid ditches and puddles when she can't co-ordinate her limbs, and gets more and more excited and less co-ordinated as she approaches the kombi full of smiling faces? It's tricky. You soon put your own minor gripes and moans to one side. Life and the cards it deals us come quickly into focus when you witness the incredible physical, mental and emotional challenges some people live with.

For these children, Ikhwezi Lokusa was a ray of hope, providing a wonderful opportunity to receive love and care, to be fed, clothed and schooled with other children with similar disabilities. Ikhwezi was a Catholic school and rehabilitation centre, attached to the Glen Avent Convent, and run by the missionary Sisters of the Precious Blood. The rehabilitation centre enabled the young people to learn practical skills like pottery, sewing and woodwork, as well as a normal academic education for those who could manage it.

Rural and urban poverty were common in Transkei and in the many black communities of South Africa at the time. With poverty and governmental neglect came conditions that European countries last faced in the early 20th

Wheelchairs were often a difficult way to get around for students who returned to their rural homes during holidays.

When road and dirt tracks petered out, I had to drive the Ikhwezi van over open fields to reach villages.

century; polio, tuberculosis and cerebral palsy were common among the children we cared for. AIDS had yet to raise its ugly head.

Most of the school's pupils wore steel leg callipers and many carried a walking stick, so the hallmark sound of the school was metal callipers crashing against each other. The sound of colliding callipers grew in direct proportion to the children's levels of excitement. The base-level sound was children in corridors bumping into each other as they went to classes; it cranked up a few decibels on leaving classes; the mealtime rush for a chair saw it ratchet up even further; and the top decibels were reserved for football, when twenty small boys might take on Sister Genevieve and my colleague, Doug Ritchie. Actually, I am wrong; the noise of crashing callipers reached fever pitch when I showed a 'bioscope' (movie) or my photographic slides of Transkei, and a *tsotsi* appeared on the screen. *Tsotsi* is the universal term for a bad guy or gangster in Xhosa, and *tsotsis*, to these kids, came in all shapes and sizes. They included the small-time gangsters I'd met and photographed at Ngangelizwe township nearby, or the German soldiers in *The Sound of Music*. The children could sniff out a baddie or a troublemaker without any difficulty, as reflected on the calliper-bashing Richter scale. The sight of a *tsotsi* projected onto the hall wall occasioned uncontrolled jumping about, yells of *tsotsi! tsotsi!* and the rampant bashing of callipers. The children's carers, known as 'the aunties', tried in vain to restore order and calm, but the only remedy was for the film to move on and for the object of all the excitement to disappear from the wall.

On one occasion I was unable to stand up and subdue the mayhem, as a small boy had curled up on my lap and fallen asleep as I operated the projector. Total madness ensued for a few minutes, with its own built-in mechanism for dissipation; the minute a good guy came on, seats were taken and relative quiet was restored.

The Ikhwezi vans and I travelled thousands of miles without much luxury during my eight-month stay. We covered large portions of Transkei, Natal and chunks of the Eastern Cape, as it is now. Transkei was a Bantustan or homeland, a product of apartheid (separate development based on race), devised by the white National Party government as a place where black people of Xhosa origins would live. Xhosa people were also forced to reside in the neighbouring Bantustan of Ciskei. They became reservoirs of cheap black labour; Xhosa men and women would get temporary 'passes' to work in South Africa's cities, but were expected to return to their Bantustan once their pass expired. Any black person caught in a white area without a pass could be jailed. The government tried to justify the existence of these Bantustans by regarding them as separate countries, with their own little dummy governments and laws, but the idea was a farce; they were as dependent on the rest of South Africa as South Africa was on them.

In 1980, South Africa and Transkei had hard borders with strict passport controls as part of the pretence of independence. At 44,000 square kilometres in size, it was about as big as Denmark or Estonia. As you can see on the map, it was broken into three pieces, one large area and two detached pieces, Maluti to the north and Umzimkulu to the east. It was a weird country.

I couldn't believe my luck that, as a nineteen-year-old, I got to drive to the remotest places of Transkei, sometimes along unimaginable roads seemingly hacked out of the mountainside, to meet traditional people in their villages or towns. During the summer rainy season, roads were a deep, red ochre colour, with the consistency of warm Nutella spread, so that my van and I frequently pirouetted across the surface like a deer on ice, with little or no control over speed or direction. Although petrifying at first, one got used to and even embraced it, as one did with so many unfamiliar sights and sounds in Transkei.

By contrast, in winter, starved of precipitation, the mud roads solidified, cracked and baked to the point where the road surface sometimes glistened with the polishing of vehicle tires. Dust hung in the air, caressed every surface and penetrated every orifice, innate or otherwise. Cars, buses, bicycles and horse-drawn carts would be coated in dust at the end of a short journey, the clouds often obscuring the road as one travelled – especially if the sun was low. The red ochre hues of summer mud turned into a straw-coloured gossamer veil of dust that blended subtly with the drying bush or veld, as it was known. Ever present was the risk of a goat, cow or sheep straying onto the road, quite unaware of a British youth at the wheel, charging along under the illusion of immortality. While I never did collide with an animal, it was touch-and-go on a few occasions. I'll never know why I didn't plough straight into a dead horse, lying in the middle of the road one afternoon as I returned from a student protest at Fort Hare University in South Africa. Perhaps I'm too ignorant or ungracious to accept divine intervention as an explanation.

The places I visited had such exciting and exotic names. There was the Umzimvubu Valley with Port St Johns, Lusikisiki, Cwele (say it like I've taught you, now), and Mkambati over in Pondoland, as well as Bizana, home of Nelson Mandela's wife, Winnie. To the north there were Tsolo, Mt Frere, Mt Ayliff and Maclear. Let's not omit Cofimvaba, Engcobo, Tsomo, Mqanduli, Ongeluksnek and Butterworth. The towns with Anglo-Saxon names were named after 19th-century British military men, missionaries and colonial administrators who had gone to war with the Xhosa or implemented government policy from Cape Town or London,

At a trading station in remote north-west Transkei, petrol was dispensed from a hand-cranked pump.

whose mission had been to contain, control and civilise the 'Natives', as all indigenous people were known.

The nearest city was East London, about 230 kilometres south from Umtata and part of South Africa. How strange, I thought, to be more than 10,000 kilometres from home and at the extreme southern tip of Africa, and be making regular visits to East London. I could have reached East London by train from home in suburban Guildford in less than an hour. The irony was never lost on me.

The Transkeian scenery and wildlife was pretty exotic to my eyes, too; none of it would have been out of place in a David Attenborough documentary.

On the Wild Coast it was not unusual to spot a pod of dolphins playfully surfing in the tumbling, turquoise waves, and a month seldom went by without mention of a shark attack somewhere on the coast. If the British regional papers liked stories about cats stuck in trees, the South African and Transkeian papers just loved a good shark story. They couldn't get enough of them to play on their readers' fears, and I became bored reading about surfer dudes having the backs of their boards bitten off by the men in grey suits. Not surprisingly, swimming in the sea off the Wild Coast felt like a game of chicken or dare; you really never knew what was lurking below the waves. Sharks like colder waters, so as long as you didn't venture out too far, you were pretty safe, or so I was told. Sometimes I'd imagine the menacing cello theme music from *Jaws* emanating from the depths of the Indian Ocean as I cavorted about, way too happy to give thoughts of a sudden shark mauling much shrift.

Transkei was a beautiful part of the world, with enough lush forests and unspoilt golden beaches to occupy a cameraman for weeks. Steep cliffs, chiselled by waves traversing the Indian Ocean, contrasted with the snow-capped peaks of Lesotho, a country just across the Drakensberg Mountains to the north. Here, the rock was sculpted by geological and atmospheric forces to imitate sensuous pieces of modern art.

Most of rural inland Transkei was low, rolling hills and plains, bisected by dry, coarse rills, streams and riverbeds. Open, unowned communal grasslands stretched out for miles. It was a larger-than-life part of the world, best not ventured into by the faint-hearted. The vultures in Engcobo, for example, were the size of small aircraft, constantly scanning the landscape for signs of weakness and infirmity in man or beast. Falling asleep outdoors would not have been a good idea, especially for a small child.

The most distinctive feature of the region was the scattered white huts or *amakhaya* huddled in small groups on the side of a slope, their

Vultures the size of small aircraft would glide over the grasslands, rivers and escarpments near Engcobo.

triangular thatched roofs looking like oriental hats. Close to *ikhaya* (singular) there would always be a kraal, constructed of nothing but stone, with large thorny agave aloe plants growing out of the top as soil settled in the gaps between stones. Cattle, sheep and goats, the wealth of every homestead, were kept safe here at night. When flowering, the agave had a thick stalk reaching several metres high, topped with a large, orange flower like a crown. Silhouetted at dusk and dawn, the tall flowering plants and the little rustic settlements formed an idealised image of rural southern Africa. Little in rural Transkei was really ideal, but I never tired of the beauty.

Ikhwezi Lokusa Special School was located about 2 kilometres up a dirt track from Umtata, the capital of Transkei. It was well known and respected by the great and the good, including politicians, the prime minister, medics, the bishop, the press, wholesalers and civil society; all seemed proud of this little icon of goodness and perseverance in the midst of poverty and injustice. I was proud to be a part of it. In my inexperienced and no doubt incompetent way, I felt I was doing something to make the lives of handicapped children better, and, in the midst of a mad, bad, cruel system, helping to stack the cards ever so slightly in favour of good. I always felt elated to be able to say, 'I work at Ikhwezi Lokusa Special School.'

Mission stations, like this one at Cwele, were often perched atop hillsides with stunning panoramic views.

Amazing as it seems now, even though Umtata was a stone's throw from Qunu, Nelson Mandela's home village, his name was seldom heard then. I drove past Qunu very many times and didn't even know it was his home! It sounds crazy today, but 1980 was a very different time. He was still a political prisoner, hewing stone on Robben Island a thousand kilometres to the south, and there were no civic acknowledgements of him in the form of plaques, statues or museums. He was persona non grata in most of South Africa, feared by many whites and hardly mentioned in the newspapers, so simply never discussed.

What was happening in the world in 1980? In Zimbabwe, South Africa's northern neighbour, Robert Mugabe had just become Prime Minister after a long and bloody battle against the white government led by Ian Smith. In South Africa there was not the slightest glimpse of a multiracial democracy; despite international sanctions, apartheid seemed in no danger of unravelling. P. W. Botha was Prime Minister, although the international face of the country was often the more affable and urbane Pik Botha, who tried to put a positive spin on the country's inhumane policies. Most leaders of the black resistance movement were locked up with Nelson Mandela on Robben Island or in political exile. Just three years earlier, Steve Biko, the leader of the Black Consciousness Movement, had been murdered by the security forces in prison. Almost every form of dissent was banned, so that people in South Africa often knew far less of what was going on in their own country than did the outside world. Recent 'unrests' at black schools protesting the use of Afrikaans as their medium of instruction had resulted in the banning of Pink Floyd's 'Another Brick in the Wall', deemed inflammatory and designed to spark a revolution.

Internationally, the Cold War between the USA and the USSR kept the entire world in tension, with trade embargoes and boycotts of the Moscow Olympics ongoing. Jimmy Carter was the 39th President of the USA and Leonid Brezhnev his communist adversary in Moscow. Margaret Thatcher was shaking up the traditional world of male politics in the UK. In Iran, American citizens had been held hostage in their embassy, while in London, the SAS undertook a high-profile rescue of hostages in the Iranian Embassy. Rubik's cube was a popular brain-teaser all over the world.

On the popular music front there was something for everyone. The angry, pimply punks, with safety-pin piercings and spikey hair, were mellowing or being replaced by the more mundane. My personal favourites, XTC, were still 'Making Plans For Nigel'. (Come to think of it, what *did* become of Nigel?) On the radio stations, it was hard to escape the falsetto vocals of the Bee Gees' disco numbers, while Rod Steward was bellowing at full volume, asking 'Do Ya Think I'm Sexy?'. Blondie were giving it some with 'Call Me' and the ubiquitous Donna Summer was now telling us that she was a 'Bad Girl'. Smoothies like Herb Albert and Billy Joel were keeping the mums and dads happy, while Diana Ross was reinventing herself with 'Upside Down'.

In January 1980, I left the shores of the UK with grandiose ambitions of 'helping Africa', a patronising and bloated ambition based on watching too many black-and-white films about macho European adventurers fighting their way through jungles with famous American actresses in tow. I'd heard various elderly relatives proudly recounting their tales of naval travels across the Empire in defence of the realm. I scaled down my well-intended but ludicrous ambition of 'helping Africa' within a week of arriving and set myself the more modest target of doing what the nuns and staff told me to do, as best I could. Even then I struggled, as you are about to read.

I must have done something right, because by the time I left eight months later, I had been asked to consider becoming a priest and teacher on more than one occasion. My agnostic leanings would have proven more than a trifling problem in a Catholic institution, I felt.

For what it's worth, Transkei did a great deal more for me than I could ever hope to impart to it. If nothing else, I learnt a little humility.

3

Peat Bogs and Bagpipes

Several months earlier, in mid-August of 1979, I found myself knee deep in a peat bog, dredging a well in the Inner Hebrides as a local crofter played his bagpipes on an adjacent hillock. How romantic, how picturesque, I hear you say. Well that's as maybe, but it was bloody cold work. The tea the crofter's wife made was out of this world – brewed from a common tea bag brand, but infused with the earthy, sweet, peat-filtered water from the well we were clearing out.

Assisting crofters on the remote Hebridean island of Coll was one of several tests set by the indefatigable Major Nicholas Verity Maclean-Bristol of Breachacha Castle and his wife, Lady Lavinia Maclean-Bristol, to asses my fitness to join The Project Trust. Along with a number of other teenagers and some posh Oxbridge hopefuls, I was instructed in pseudo-military fashion to perform a range of challenging and unusual tasks as they watched, clipboards and HB pencils in hand. My tasks were mostly child-minding and ceilidh dancing to bagpipes, and a little high-speed seaweed collecting on the blustery beaches of the Atlantic Ocean. All in the name of toughening me up and assessing my fitness and worthiness to work somewhere in the developing world.

Because I'd arrived on the Isle of Coll a day or two earlier in order to recce the place in advance of the assessment, I attracted the suspicions of the good major as someone who might be a little too big for his own boots – someone not quite playing by the rules. How right he was. Yes, I had been doing a recce, climbing hills, traversing beaches and generally getting the lie of the land before the formal assessment started. I'd done

To raise our spirits, a crofter played his bagpipes while we dug out his water well and cleared ditches on the Isle of Coll.

The Isle of Coll, home to The Project Trust, where I was 'noted' by Major Maclean-Bristol for doing a reconnaissance of the island.

a spot of birdwatching, too. He was only too keen to tell me that his spies on the island had been aware of my premature arrival and that my presence had been 'noted'. Noted! This added a little frisson to my Hebridean adventure.

With the assessment over I caught the return ferry to Oban, before traveling in the parcel carriage of the Glasgow to London overnight train. Assorted cardboard boxes and suitcases made for uncomfortable sleeping accommodation, so I arrived in the capital with a strained neck and feeling like a dog's dinner. But there was no time for self-pity as I had a gig to get to, my first at Wembley Stadium. It was a warm Saturday, and Nils Lofgren, AC/DC, The Stranglers and finally The Who played to a raucous crowd of 80,000. Squashed shoulder to shoulder on the hallowed Wembley turf with other sweaty youths, I jostled my way close to the stage and The Who's lead singer, Roger Daltrey. Shedding the constraints of British inhibition, I bounced around with high-octane enthusiasm to the likes of 'My Generation' and 'Baba O'Reilly' as colourful laser rays skimmed over our heads. By the end, my carbohydrate reservoir registered empty and my bladder registered full. Streaming out towards the heavily congested tube stations, small pockets of us could be heard chanting 'We won't get fooled again' and 'Meet the new boss – same as the old boss'. Thwarted by the London transport system, I found a nearby park, climbed into my sleeping bag next to a scrawny hedge and instantly fell into a deep sleep. Even the night rain didn't stir me. So, when I did eventually get home, later that morning, my clothes were damp, I was hungry and thirsty, and I looked like I'd been pulled through the proverbial hedge backwards a couple of times. It was not a pretty sight.

I kept a close eye on the letter box for the next few days, expectantly waiting for good news from the Isle of Coll. It turned out that breaking the rules and being noted by the major was no bad thing in the circumstances, as my application was accepted by The Project Trust and I was assigned to Ikhwezi Lokusa Special School, a Catholic mission for handicapped Bantu children in a region of South Africa called Transkei. While I knew a little about South Africa, this Transkei place was a complete unknown to me. I was excited. As long as I could raise the money and attend the pre-departure briefing, I was going abroad to do something different and useful. My plan was on schedule!

What made an eighteen-year-old so keen to leave for Africa? I think my wanderlust was initiated by childhood experiences of living in Venezuela, where my father once worked for a multinational oil company. I knew there was more to the world than Guildford High Street and Market Jew Street in Penzance, and I wanted to experience it. The pages of *National Geographic* magazine, which I read avidly, also illustrated the wonders that flourished beyond my immediate horizon. I was bored with familiar friends and schoolmates, who seemed way too excited about training as dentists, accountants and pharmacists, vital as these are to the geometry of life in suburban England. Hearing about the career prospects of a profession that involved staring into strangers' mouths all day did not interest me, and nor did their eye-watering salaries or the corporate golfing afternoons associated with this bizarre, halitosis-infused profession. Equally as dull was their premature aspiration for a five-bedroom detached home in the leafy suburbs of Tormead or Horseshoe Lane, or in local villages with quaint names like Peaslake and Abinger Hammer. I'd had enough of being head boy at the George Abbot comprehensive school and the onerous chores of corridor leadership and studying; no more would invertebrate taxonomy and hydroxide molecules hold me captive. I urgently needed a change of scene.

So ... on to the small matter of raising hundreds of pounds to pay The Project Trust to get to me to this place I'd never heard of, Transkei. If I was leaving in January and it was now August, I had better get cracking with building up the bank balance.

A selfie, 1970s style. Photography was my hobby, in between my jobs as a milkman, window cleaner, car cleaner and gardener. I needed every penny to get to this mysterious place called Transkei.

Off I went to the Guildford Co-operative Dairy for an interview, landing a job as a milkman. For readers not familiar with the concept of a milkman, we used to deliver milk and sundry items such as juice and bread to the front door of your house six days a week from a van or electronic float, come rain or shine. It sounds simple, but it was hard work. Not many eighteen-year-olds relish the thought of rising at 4.30 a.m. on a winter's morning; the van would never start first time, the entire journey was undertaken in biting cold and our fingers froze half to death, making it all but impossible to carry the glass milk bottles up a few steps.

I'll stop before I have you in tears. Apart from these toils, the job had other risks peculiar to milkmen.

Risk #1: Randy housewives in Godalming and Cranleigh whose husbands were too busy earning shedloads of money in the City of London to meet their needs, so to speak. It usually started with a seemingly innocent invitation to the milkman to try her bacon sandwich or cupcake. More than one innocent milkman was tempted and went AWOL on these rounds.

Risk #2: Crashing into garden walls, sides of cars and other domestic obstructions with the milk van because it was too dark and wet to see in front of one's nose. The crashing bit was easy and frequent; the getting away with it was a little harder, especially if the wall you hit tumbled heavily and made a loud thump, waking up the household and its neighbours. Somehow, since most people got their milk, most of the time, approximately on time, I kept my job. Just.

After satisfying the daily dairy needs of Surrey I would have a nap before going off to earn a few extra quid gardening, car washing and cleaning windows, where the risks of abduction by desperate housewives and demolishing garden walls were not nearly so high. In my spare time – and there wasn't much of it – I practised my photography. I didn't know it then, but this was to come in handy in the year ahead.

By December I'd amassed sufficient funds to pay for the flight and attended The Project Trust's pre-departure briefing, which covered the dos and don'ts of working abroad. Transkei was just a flight away.

What had I learnt about my eventual destination in advance of leaving the concrete runway of Heathrow Airport? My parents offered a few opinions on South Africa in general, although this Transkei place remained a bit of a mystery. Google, remember, wasn't even a twinkle in Sir Tim Berners-Lee's eye yet. Words like 'internet' and 'search engines' would have been unintelligible to us, gobbledegook. I was struggling to understand why a whole region of South Africa had been put aside by white people for the black population to live in. It didn't make sense from the comfort of suburban Guildford. Apartheid, I guessed, must be

Leaving behind my Co-op milkman's job, I caught the bus to Heathrow, on a wet January afternoon in 1980. My journey had begun.

the answer, but that was all a bit of mystery to me, too. I knew that sporting ties with South Africa had been cut and that there were economic sanctions because of the whites' approach to the non-white population. I was vaguely aware that some chap called Nelson Mandela was being praised by a number of universities in the UK, but I was more than a little confused since I'd been told he was a terrorist. He looked very menacing in any pictures I saw of him. Why would people be championing the cause of a terrorist? Talking back to the referee in a school rugby match was considered bad form where I came from, so terrorism for any cause seemed pretty much beyond the pale.

In fact, terrorism and suchlike was not part of our household vocabulary. At home my parents brought us up on the benefits of science and engineering, home-made chocolate cake, the *Daily Mail*, toast, rugby, golf, the armed forces, more toast, Cornwall, three-speed derailleur gears, well-polished shoes and the pub. Not in that order. Margaret Thatcher, or 'Maggie' as the chattering classes called her, was considered one step away from deity, with the Queen a close second. 'She'll soon sort them out' was a frequent 'Maggie' mantra my mother shared with us whenever an animated union leader with a northern accent appeared on the TV.

I had seen news reports of the Soweto riots on the news back in 1976, but I was fifteen years old at the time and more interested in sport and badger watching than in political strife thousands of kilometres away. The school kids were objecting to learning Afrikaans or something similar – I really wasn't sure. French lessons were a bit of a bore at my school, but not worth rioting about. Anyway, a lot of serious rioting seemed to have been going on.

South Africa couldn't be that bad a place, I reckoned, as my father had made occasional work visits there and so had a lot of other Cornish people over the last hundred years, seeking work in Johannesburg's gold mines. When the price of tin and copper dropped in the 19th century, a lot of unemployed Cornish miners, including a good few of my relatives, emigrated to South Africa. They had been highly skilled and commanded top dollar. It was part of the Cornish diaspora, as academic sorts call it. And then there was Trooper Edwards, a distant uncle I'd heard about whose name was listed, along with many other Cornishmen, on the memorial in Penzance's Morrab Gardens. According to the family, he'd got to know South Africa a bit, courtesy of fighting in the Second Anglo-Boer War (1899–02). During his military sojourn, he successfully dodged enemy bullets only to succumb to disease – Typhoid or dysentery, no doubt.

My first view of Umtata, arriving from Johannesburg.

Feeling a little despondent when there was no one to greet me at Umtata airport. Things soon got better!

Ironically, the first one hundred pounds in my building society account, intended for my forthcoming venture to South Africa, was money left to me in a will by an auntie who'd emigrated to Johannesburg from Cornwall and made a few rand along the way. The money was now coming back to South Africa with me.

Quite inadvertently, I've been a little economical with the truth – I should own up that I actually knew a little more about South Africa than I've let on. I'd seen a trailer for the film *Zulu*, in which Michael Caine and his mates had gallantly protected the British Empire by killing and maiming thousands of angry locals using the latest guns and munitions. The Zulus, armed only with small spears, were objecting to the prospect of being governed by white men with silly moustaches wearing dark suits in a far-away place called Whitehall, overseen by a Queen who relished painting the globe pink for the Empire while pumping out babies to populate the monarchical classes of Europe. The Zulus had been made to appear ferocious and unreasonable in the film, but I could see that they had a point. Anyway, it was a rip-roaring yarn (as I could tell from the trailer), although in truth I couldn't see much further than the blood and guts of the skirmishes. Clearly my horizons were short and narrow, blinkered by a suburban English upbringing.

Oh yes, and I nearly forgot; a couple of years earlier, in London's West End, I had seen *Ipi Tombi*, a musical about Zulu migrant workers leaving their rural village.

That was the limit of my knowledge about South Africa.

For a Christmas present just before I left, my brother and sister gave me a large brown diary embossed with 1980 on the cover. It was this diary, written in most nights, that formed the basis of the tales I am now recollecting. I'm not sure if I ever thanked them properly.

4

Team Transkei

There was nothing subtle about 1980s white South Africa. Nuance was in short supply. I suppose it must have come from all those zealous Calvinist and Methodist settlers in the Cape, many of whom would have been self-righteous, pious and hypocritical in equal measure, by my book. More than 300 years of Protestant-based 'thou shalt not', combined with an unwavering belief in their cultural, racial and moral superiority, had led to a society structured around peculiar rules and norms. There were a lot of rules, mostly based on skin colour and the tightness of hair

A very proud Team Transkei at the South African Paraplegic Sports Championship in Durban. Our after-care students were accompanied by Mam (their carer), Ludwig, Annegret (our occupational therapist), and me.

curls. Normal in South Africa was a little different to any normal I'd experienced growing up in Europe and South America.

Within a few hours of landing in Johannesburg I came face to face with some of these peculiar norms – not always law, but understood as the way things were done. Walking down a wide pavement in a white suburb, I realised that any approaching black person would step off the pavement and onto the road to pass by. It kept happening. At first it bewildered me – why would someone walk on the road when there was ample space on the pavement? It was because I was white and the other person was not – I therefore owned the pavement. Not a law, but an unspoken rule.

My host in the first few days took me to the Eastgate shopping mall, supposedly the largest in the southern hemisphere. It had all the modern retail glitz of escalators, glass and chrome facades, trendy boutiques, polished floors and posters advertising the Bay City Rollers. As a teenage bloke I was no proper judge, but it looked and felt like retail nirvana and you could have been in any modern Western city, except we weren't in a normal city. There were the ubiquitous 'Whites only' signs, most of the serving staff were black and as far as I could see all the shoppers were well-heeled white people, mooching around enjoying retail therapy. Odd, considering that Whites constituted only about 19 per cent of the South African population. At first glance everything looked normal, but one tiny scratch below the veneer revealed that it was all very far from normal by the world's standards.

My helter-skelter introduction to South Africa continued the next evening when my host took me to see a show called *Razzmatazz*. Here, to my surprise, the audience wasn't all white. Surprise must have been written all over my naïve face as my hosts explained that the arts scene in the city took a more relaxed attitude to racial mixing. So, I recalibrated my South African race barometer – the same national laws applied to everyone, but the performing arts scene and the swanky shopping mall just a few kilometres away in the same city had different race rules and tolerance levels, it seemed.

After the show we returned to my host's apartment at St George's School to find two black men wrapped in blankets sleeping on his porch. At first they were anxious and concerned lest the police be called, as under South African law (Group Areas Act and Pass Laws), black people had to be out of this Whites-only area of the city at night. Blacks were allowed to work in the city during the day but were required to return to one of the shantytowns or townships at night, such as Soweto and Alexandra. These were situated some distance from the city, and buses stopped running after a certain hour, so there was no room for messing about. The two men sleeping on my host's porch could have slept on the site where they worked

Eastgate shopping centre, Johannesburg, the largest in the southern hemisphere in 1980. Here I first encountered apartheid rules and a new type of normal.

in the school grounds, but my host said he couldn't be seen helping them break the law, as he'd get into trouble, too. So occasionally he let them sleep on his porch. It was time to recalibrate my race barometer again.

Four months later, as I stood proudly supporting Transkei as a sports coach in the outdoor arena on the Durban seafront esplanade, surrounded by athletes with a wide range of physical disabilities from all over southern Africa and a growing crowd of spectators, my race barometer needed to be recalibrated yet again. My dials were whirling rapidly in different directions as I tried to get to grips with the fact that in this deeply troubled country, with racial fissures blighting every facet of life, I was participating in an absolutely wonderful multiracial paraplegic sports championship, with five-star sports facilities and five-star accommodation, surrounded by heaps of genuine good will. All of Durban's civic dignitaries, including the lady Mayor, were out in numbers to greet us and celebrate the event's opening.

It felt like a mini-Olympic Games opening ceremony, a bit of a jamboree, as disabled athletes and their coaches filed in, grouped by region or country, wearing their respective team colours and proudly holding placards to display who they represented; for example, Natal, the Cape Province, Orange Free State, Transkei and Rhodesia.

By this time, the first multiracial elections had been run in Zimbabwe (previously Rhodesia), with Robert Mugabe beating Joshua Nkomo,

The skyline of Johannesburg looked like many modern Western cities, but apartheid rules made it feel different and alien.

Above: The opening ceremony at the 1980 South African Paraplegic Sports Championship in Durban felt like a mini-Olympics.

Right: Athletes of all races, from all over southern Africa, were welcomed to the Paraplegic Sports Championship by Durban's civic dignitaries.

his principal contender. Independence celebrations were only weeks away, but the Rhodesian athletes, all ex-forces personnel of various races, made a point of stressing that they were Rhodesian. Their missing limbs were evidence of their military efforts, combating what they called terrorists. I don't know what they were like on the battlefield, but they were awesome competitors in the wheelchair basketball event. I had not realised one could be so mobile, aggressive and nimble in a wheelchair, and was bowled over by their performance, as was everyone else.

Our team from Ikhwezi Lokusa, representing Transkei, was far more modest than the numerically and physically large Rhodesian team, but we'd been keenly practising our javelin, shot and discus-throwing for the last two months and felt pretty confident. We comprised eight competing after-care students, Mam, their carer, Annegret, our occupational therapist, and Ludwig and I as trainers. Annegret was originally from South West Africa (now Namibia) and Ludwig was Ikhwezi's resident architect from Switzerland. (Ikhwezi had a lot of new building work happening at that time.) We all wore our dark tracksuit trousers and white T-shirts with TRANSKEI emblazoned in ochre red across the front as we stood shoulder to shoulder with all the other athletes, bursting with pride. It brought on a heady mixture of emotions, especially for the after-care students, none of whom had ever slept a night in a two-storey building, let alone a luxurious, high-rise, seafront hotel like the Elangeni.

The four-star multi-storey hotel on the Durban seafront where we stayed was a far cry from rural Transkei.

They were surrounded by black, white and Asian faces, freely mixing. Even though this was their country, I could see that it was all a huge culture shock for them and at least two were visibly uncomfortable.

We were in South Africa proper now, not a Bantustan. We had crossed the Umzimkulu River in eastern Transkei into the province of Natal, a region traditionally home to the Zulus, rather than the many Xhosa-speaking groups. Most of our students came from undeveloped villages or small-town communities of Transkei, which did not receive a fraction of the investment that went into a metropolitan port city like Durban. The city's highways, skyscrapers, large shipping docks, complex railway systems and sports stadia were all very alien and quite intimidating. Mam had seen South Africa's cities before, so took it all in her stride. In fact, she seemed to like it and flourished. When we went for a ride on the dodgems (bumper cars) on the seafront she laughed and cheered, lapping up the frivolity of the occasion. The students, on the other hand, were cautious and a little afraid – there was just too much that was new, too much to take in at once.

One of the students, Kirri Philiswa Maqume, was processing what she saw, comparing it with life in Transkei and realising the huge inequalities that apartheid threw up. In Transkei you did not see the huge disparities in wealth that were obvious in the big city. Most people in Transkei were poor, while here in Durban, the disparities between the have and have-nots were colossal and conspicuous, the distribution of wealth more

The modern industrial and commercial infrastructure of Durban intimidated some of our students, who had never before left Transkei.

obviously based on race. Whites were on top, then came the Asians and 'Coloureds', and down at the bottom were black Africans. You did not have to be an academic or statistical analyst to work that out.

I didn't raise these issues with any of the students, but I was not surprised when Kirri came to talk to me one evening. The conversation started out as a chat about her achieving a personal best throw in the competition, but this wasn't really what was on her mind. She was trying to make sense of her new surroundings, so utterly different from her home in Transkei and rural Mqanduli. I expected her to express anger and revulsion at the opulent city surroundings, but quite the opposite; she liked a lot of what she saw in Durban – not the race discrimination, but the quality of life and the obviously higher living standards. It was as though she wanted some of it, and so it was no surprise that Kirri was the only student I knew who voluntarily left the security of Ikhwezi Lokusa Special School sometime later to live with a family in Ngangelizwe, a township in Umtata, and later in her home town of Mqanduli.

Not only was Kirri dedicated and motivated enough to perform well in the sports competition, but she was also confident mixing with other coaches and athletes from outside our team. When the lady Mayor of Durban came to introduce herself to Team Transkei, it was Kirri and Mam who stepped forward to engage in conversation. It was wonderful to watch as a young, but proud, Transkeian woman, heavily dependent on callipers and crutches for mobility, grew in stature and confidence in front of us, learning as much as she could from the sports and social aspects of the event, unintimidated by such alien circumstances. I had no right to, but I took vicarious pride in seeing her grow and flourish.

During the opening formalities the lady Mayor, whom I believe was a Mrs Hotz, and her keen entourage of civic dignitaries could not have been more polite to our team, asking questions about Transkei and about Ludwig and myself, who were obviously foreigners. I'd go as far as to say that my conversation with the Mayor and her colleagues was one of the most poignant or ironic of my time in southern Africa.

What struck me was the questions they asked about Transkei. They were not just making small talk or chatting in a banal, detached way; it was blatantly clear they knew very little about their immediate neighbours, but wanted to improve their understanding. I had the feeling that Transkei was as remote as Timbuktu to some of them, which was odd, considering the border was only 160 kilometres down the road.

The Mayor herself was very engaging, charming even, and was fascinated that I'd come all the way from the UK to work in Transkei. She invited me to get to know Durban a little better, and suggested I look her up when I did. She would be delighted to introduce me to other young people at one of the city's suburban tennis clubs. What could be nicer?

I had a strong sense of déjà vu as I realised that in her style, manners, language and hospitality she could have been one of my mother's friends back home. Over the Umzimkulu River only a few miles south of Durban was rural Africa, defined by the landscape, beehive-shaped circular homes, tilled fields and roaming cattle – Kwazulu, as the Zulu homeland was known. Chatting to the Mayor about suburban tennis clubs felt incongruous; I could have been anywhere in an English-speaking metropolitan part of the world.

Despite the apparent sincerity of the Mayor, I did not follow up on her kind offer. I would have felt uncomfortable at a 'Whites-only' tennis club, and my decision was endorsed the following day when a minor incident reminded me once again that this was no normal society.

A coach from another team and I decided to go for a late afternoon jog and swim in the ocean. We left the swanky seafront Elangeni Hotel laughing and joking, running side by side, but as we hit the beach his whole demeanour changed; the smile disappeared, he shook his head and declined to go on. He muttered that he could not swim there as it was a 'Whites-only' beach. I was shocked. A 'Whites-only' beach? I'd never heard of such a thing. I'd assumed the beaches were for everyone, and while I was getting to grips with this absurdity, he sprinted off down the coast. One minute we were two sports coaches discussing common goals and ambitions for our teams, the next we were separated and defined by the colour of our skin. I just stood there disbelievingly as he ran off. I was more than willing to go to the non-White beach, but my colleague was gone, and I don't think he wanted me to follow. Perhaps he was embarrassed and no doubt angry at the situation. He knew the reality he lived with daily, and was seemingly resigned to the ever-present racial barrier, but for me this was a vivid and unsettling incident. In the midst of this wonderful non-racial paraplegic sporting championship, a symbol of tolerance, care and support, the ugly truths of South Africa reared their head, truths he knew and had adapted to, while I had not.

Over the next few days, however, we witnessed black, white, Asian and coloured (mixed race) athletes cheer each other on in a Corinthian spirit that seemed to be vanishing in other sporting arenas the world over. My confidence in the goodness of people was elevated as sports coaches of all races mingled to help the paraplegic athletes pull out their best performances. Watching a blind, black runner being guided carefully

Above: The first-class sports facilities in Durban meant many of our Transkei team achieved personal best performances in their disciplines.

Below: At the athletics venue, our occupational therapist, Annegret Mostert, and our students mixed freely with white, coloured and Asian paraplegic athletes, swapping coaching tips and celebrating successes on the track.

and sensitively around a cinder athletics track by a fully sighted white athlete represented the pinnacle of all that was wonderful about the event. It wasn't just the physical connection between these two athletes that was so touching, but the trust expressed in the synchronicity of their running pattern, their co-ordination as they rounded the bends, and the gentle nudges and whispered words they exchanged. Respect, self-esteem and pride were hallmarks of the event. If apartheid was an omnipotent racial sledgehammer protected by a police state, these paraplegic sport championships were a bit of Polyfilla or grouting, helping to repair, ever so slightly, the gaping cracks that it perpetuated.

Perhaps I was naive and gullible to celebrate this event, as many of the disabilities on show would have been caused directly or indirectly by apartheid. One could argue that if there had been less poverty and a fairer sharing of educational and health resources there might not have been so many disabled black people. Others may point out that a number of the paraplegic athletes were victims of wars the white governments of South Africa and Rhodesia waged against black freedom fighters or terrorists, depending on your standpoint. It would also be fair to say that by holding the event in such sumptuous facilities, the organisers had excluded most black disabled athletes, who could never have afforded to travel and stay in Durban – a sort of economic apartheid. All quite true, I am sure.

All of that would be a fair intellectual or academic argument, but as I stood representing Transkei as a sports coach, cheek by jowl with students and paraplegic athletes from all over southern Africa, I was not thinking intellectually or academically. None of the arguments withstood the reality that this was an iconic, beautiful and moving event that, for those few days, flew in the face of all that apartheid stood for. The athletes and spectators could not have left this event untouched by what was possible, having experienced a whole new way of relating to one another over the course of a few days, and with little political rhetoric. We were a miniature, imperfect, multiracial oasis, and at that moment South Africa was an example to other nations. I know – hard to believe, hey?

5

Buntingville

The Farraghers' marriage was getting very messy, and like it or not, Ikhwezi friends, work colleagues and some of the nuns were being affected. It had been getting worse for weeks, not helped by the fact that Joe lapsed into periods of alcoholic stupor exacerbated by smoking weed. It was dreadful to watch, particularly at close range. Adults losing their dignity and taking metaphorical lumps out of each other wasn't something I'd witnessed before. It was all rather distressing and confusing, and I didn't have the emotional toolset or experience to help. Moreover, I didn't want to take sides as I'd got to know Lynette, Joe and their young children quite well during my stay at Ikhwezi. Of an evening, I'd join them for a beer, a chat and a bite to eat, or maybe we'd watch a sporting event together. When the flames weren't fanned and the verbal shrapnel wasn't flying about, their company was excellent and their bungalow a home away from home.

Lynette was a smart, energetic young woman who knew and spoke her mind, and wasn't intimidated in male company. She was good fun, and she and I enjoyed swapping photographic tips now and again. Looking after three young children, though, was no easy task.

Joe was a bit of an intense character, with a touch of the tortured soul about him. As the head of the pottery department, he was commissioned to create a mural for the new University of Transkei just outside Umtata, now called the Walter Sisulu University. He took me up there one warm afternoon to install part of it. He was relaxed and happy to see his work on public display, and being the nerd I am, I found it exciting to see the wonderful, sparkling new academic facility, knowing that it could be the platform for bigger and better things for Transkei's most able young people.

It reminded me of the new University of Surrey back home in Guildford, with its recently completed campus and state-of-the-art technology. Both institutions had about them an air of brash, youthful optimism, a sense of being able to make the world a smarter place without the stuffiness of an old school campus. I wonder if Joe's mural is still there?

On one occasion, the Farraghers took me for a weekend trip to Port St Johns on the Wild Coast where we swam, made sandcastles and spent a few hours fishing in the Umzimvubu River, beer in hand. I got on well with their young children, so I even did a bit of babysitting too.

Those were the good times. Heading off to a beauty contest on Saturday night with Lynette and Joe felt like it might be a good time too, so I accepted their invitation to join them. Why not? What could be more relaxing than looking at attractive young Transkeians proudly strutting their stuff? I'd already attended one beauty-cum-fashion show in Umtata a few months earlier so I had some idea what I might be in for. I was getting the impression that beauty contests and showing off new fashion were all part of the contemporary Transkeian culture. Why I should be invited to such events, though, was a bit of a mystery as I was a plain-looking hairy bloke, with not one jot of fashion sense or style. I wore wooden clogs some of the time and I had my hair cut only when I couldn't see through the mop.

From the moment we left Ikhwezi for Buntingville, it was obvious that all was not well. Joe had been drinking, and was fractious and argumentative. The atmosphere in the car was tense and a row was only one idle comment way. I'd witnessed it before and all the signs of a matrimonial bust-up were there. And then it happened.

We were nearly at Buntingville, a few kilometres outside Umtata, when the touch paper was lit and Joe exploded. Lynette must have said something I missed, but an almighty row ensued, and before I knew what was happening, Joe had climbed out of the car and was heading off into the veld. It was getting dark. In what little light there was, we caught a glimpse of him staggering about with a grimace, disappearing off to God knows where. Should I get out and find him? Should we call him back? This was supposed to be an entertaining Saturday evening, but my alcoholic friend was now rushing headlong into the wilderness.

To my surprise, Lynette's response was to put her foot to the floor, leaving Joe to fend for himself. We arrived at the Buntingville school where the beauty pageant was to be held. As we approached the brightly lit hall, Lynette explained that Joe was to have been one of the judges and Master of Ceremonies. I understood that, but how did that concern me?

I thought we should explain to the organisers that he wasn't available, so they could select another judge. No. I wasn't reading Lynette's body language or her articulate verbal language. What she was saying was that *I* was to take his place. It was not a point for discussion or negotiation. She was in a tight spot and I was her way out.

Not for the first time in Transkei did I find myself having difficulty understanding and accepting my predicament. I was pretty bewildered. Was she serious? A mongrel and schmuck like me acting as a judge of a Transkeian beauty contest?

No way!

Yes way.

After her bust-up with Joe, she wasn't a woman to be trifled with. 'No' wasn't part of her vocabulary at that moment. My protests had about as much chance of success as black person becoming President of South Africa in the next five years. If I thought I could grind her down with persistence, my strategy was severely flawed. We entered the large school hall, packed to the rafters with excited young people and pulsating with loud music from a record or tape player. It was a happening place, no doubt about it.

Surveying the room, I hoped to see Joe turn up to save me from my forthcoming torture. Not a chance.

You could feel the excitement and anticipation in the room, heightened as, pair by pair, one of the boys and one of the girls would gyrate their way to the centre of the room, meeting and cavorting suggestively as their fellow students cheered them on. After a few seconds, another couple would take their place as the first pair sank back into the crowd. It was explicit and sensual, and some of the dancers were very popular, judging by the yells of approval from the crowd. A couple of the adults looking on were slightly flustered but unwilling to disrupt the obvious fun leading up to the main event.

Ah, yes, the main event. Joe still hadn't turned up. Accordingly, I found myself sitting behind a long table at the head of the hall, with a senior teacher on one side and a Transkeian woman who lived in New York on the other. The latter was immensely proud of her metropolitan home and cosmopolitan connections, but not much interested in me, it seemed. She was obviously a good judge of character. In front of us lay a sea of young, expectant faces and some beautiful and handsome contestants, men and women.

I was told that the contestants would be invited forward and we should note their appearance and ask them three questions. Questions? That was a new one on me. Apparently, with the aid of a microphone, we needed to ask them questions to assess their character and intelligence so that this was not a looks-only event. We hurriedly devised three questions for each, such as 'What is your greatest achievement?' 'What are your interests?' 'Why would you like to win the competition?' I was uncomfortable and the main event hadn't even started. I felt such a fraud, even with the microphone in hand. Who was I to judge these beautiful people in front of an audience?

And, yes, they were beautiful. Senior students, young Transkeian men and women, took it in turns to parade confidently before us, the panel of judges. Evidently they were having a fabulous time, enjoying their fifteen minutes of fame and keen to shine in front of the panel. They had all the confidence and beauty of youth, modesty not being their principal trait – and why should it be? Each contestant had a strong, sculpted bone structure, a complexion to die for and hair as black as the cover of the old Methodist Bible my family kept locked away in a drawer at home. To add icing to their performance, some of them included a bit of a choreographed strut as they arrived at our table to present themselves.

We were required to score each contestant, which felt rather bewildering, but it was made much easier by my fellow judges 'guiding' me to the correct score – and if that failed, the volume of the cheering generated by the excited audience served as a barometer of the popular view, much as the crowds had at the Coliseum when Caesar was ever in two minds. We were not in Rome, and these fine young people weren't gladiators, but the competition was still fierce and the stakes seemingly high. Thank goodness I wasn't required to use a thumbs up or a thumbs down to indicate my preferences.

After a while I forgot about Joe and the pre-event shenanigans, being in no doubt about the importance of the current challenge. Hiding my feelings of being a fraud and an imposter, I soldiered on, doing my best to impersonate someone who knew what they were doing. Finally, we met and questioned the last of the beautiful, ebullient people. It was time for the judges to retire and confer.

You could feel the tension in the hall as the climax of the evening approached. Who was to be crowned? Who would be the chosen ones? Our scorecards were collated, the numbers totted up and the winners agreed upon. I went with the flow. I wasn't going to argue, that's for sure. All eyes were now on us, the judges, and it was time for the results. No one could wait much longer. The microphone was poised and crackling in anticipation. To much fanfare and exuberant shouting, cheering and clapping, the winners were called out over the loudspeakers and ceremoniously decorated for their success. The smiles of the winners were so broad and radiant they could have adorned any TV beauty product advertisement as they waved enthusiastically to their many adoring admirers. Even though my knowledge and experience were decidedly on the light side, it felt like a real beauty pageant. The beautiful and intelligent young people of Transkei had been ranked and were now being openly celebrated.

Most importantly, the end was in sight for me. I was not needed anymore in the capacity of a judge or master of ceremonies – or was I?

I wasn't escaping that easily. The show wasn't over, not a chance. I clearly hadn't read the non-existent job description at my non-existent recruitment interview for the job. There was even *more* to come – the crowning moment of the whole evening, in fact.

The winning contestants, now in their triumphant regalia, were lined up in boy-girl pairs in descending order of merit to form a procession. Who was at the head of the procession as the celebration music started up? My fellow female judge and me. Me, at the head of a beauty pageant procession – have you ever heard of anything so preposterous and incongruous? I wanted to curl up and disappear, to evaporate into thin air. But there was nowhere to hide, not at the front of a beauty procession in the middle of a large hall of cheering onlookers. My fellow judge could now sense how ill at ease I was. My forced, fixed smile and stiff movements must have radiated discomfort as we marched around the hall in time to the music, our proud winners following our synchronised steps. My fellow judge had to virtually coax me around the room, literally step by step to the end as the cheering continued unabated. I reached the end by the skin of my teeth – relief! I had not let the side down.

I was too shell-shocked to remember much after that, except that Joe, having found his way through the Transkeian bush, turned up at the end and we all drove back to the sanctuary of Ikhwezi in relative peace.

I don't suppose beauty pageants like the one in Buntingville feature in the textbooks about Transkeian culture, but despite my fear and feelings of inadequacy, I felt I had participated in a worthwhile, memorable event. Beauty contests, fashion shows and the like don't appear in my hierarchy of interests, but I was left in no doubt about how important the evening was to the audience, the judges and the contestants. It united and elevated the mood, giving people a chance to shine and show off, opportunities which were all too rare for black people in South Africa at the time. Strange as it may seem, I felt I had witnessed and participated in a genuine bit of contemporary Transkeian culture, even if I was in no hurry to repeat it.

6

Soul Brothers

On 10 December 1993, Mr Nelson Mandela received the Nobel Peace Prize after actively resisting apartheid as a leader in the African National Congress (ANC), including its military wing, Umkhonto we Sizwe ('Spear of the Nation'). Despite imprisonment for twenty-seven years, he preached racial tolerance and fairness as the foundation of a new, multiracial South Africa. Along with other black leaders like Archbishop Desmond Tutu, he promoted forgiveness for those who were prepared to admit to their crimes and immoral acts, including murder and torture, during the

The Soul Brothers in the late 1970s. They were hugely popular with South Africa's young people, as well as Nelson Mandela. [Photo thanks to Steve Gordon at musicpics.co.za]

decades of white dominance. He won the respect of most of the world and many of his traditional enemies in the white community with his statesmanlike behaviour and integrity, as South Africa lurched unevenly out of apartheid, jolting and undulating perilously close to complete anarchy as myriad factions fought for their place at the top table.

The man who stood humbly in the Oslo City Hall to receive his prestigious award may well have reflected on his childhood and youth growing up in rural Transkei as a member of the Thembu community. Many of the skills he had used to help broker peace and facilitate forgiveness in South Africa were honed in the patriarchal village settings of Qunu and Mqhekezweni, near Umtata. This is where he had watched and listened to his uncles, brothers and village seniors administer traditional Xhosa governance with its emphasis on fairness, consensus and inclusivity.

Also standing in the Oslo City Hall on 10 December 1993 was Mr F. W. de Klerk, President of the Republic of South Africa, and co-winner of the Nobel Peace Prize with Nelson Mandela. On the surface you would say they were chalk and cheese. F. W. de Klerk was white, an Afrikaner, politically conservative and leader of the National Party, the founding party of apartheid. He was shaped and guided by his deep-rooted Calvinist beliefs. To all intents and purpose, he was the white face that represented apartheid, both internally and internationally, and might have been considered Mandela's enemy during the latter man's years of hard labour and incarceration.

So, why was Mr de Klerk having his big day in Oslo courtesy of the Nobel Committee? Had de Klerk had a Damascene experience and decided that apartheid was wrong? No. Did he start to believe in racial integration? No. Was he wracked with guilt for the excesses of apartheid? No. Had his Calvinist faith started to lead him to new pastures? Maybe. I believe he was there because he was a pragmatic and skilful political operator, at a time when the white community in South Africa had its back against the wall.

Unlike many in the white community, de Klerk was smart enough to realise that white, privileged South Africa simply could not withstand the intense adverse pressure it faced on multiple fronts. Active internal protests, sabotage and disruption from the black population, particularly the urban young, was growing. It could not be ignored or hidden, as increasing media coverage was unavoidable, even in such a heavily censored country. On the global scene, the country stubbornly maintained a top-ten place as an international pariah, crippling them economically and offending their self-perception as an advanced Western country with strong European roots. With the victory of Robert Mugabe's ZANU-PF and the creation of a free Zimbabwe in 1980, the financial costs and loss of life from military activity on multiple borders began to seem just too high.

Mr de Klerk bore the brunt of the anger and frustration of people in his own country and from the international community. While he ruled, he had to use skill and diplomacy to avoid total anarchy and uncontrolled attacks on the minority white population. It was an all but impossible task. Strange as it may seem, Mr Mandela, former leader of the armed wing of the ANC, was his saviour, and he was smart enough to realise it, even if his faith in Mandela wavered many times. In de Klerk, Mandela had a representative of the white ruling class with whom he could negotiate, even if his faith in de Klerk wavered many times. It was an unlikely alliance, and one that only just survived the 'slings and arrows of outrageous fortune'.

In the eyes of the Nobel Committee, the distinguished Thembu leader and the white Afrikaner president were the principal facilitators of a relatively peaceful transition from white-led apartheid South Africa to the so-called rainbow nation, with election plans already underway for the first ever non-racial democratic election.

I have summarised monumental achievements here and entirely skipped the pain and bloodshed of the anti-apartheid struggle, waged both in South Africa and internationally, to which thousands dedicated their lives. But I hope you get the point – the final resolution needed two skilled political operators with just sufficient trust and willingness to bend in order to broker an end to the struggle. They were the men of the hour. Both sidestepped saboteurs of their plans at every crossroad, fork and roundabout from within their respective parties and from outside. Theirs was no ordinary task, and these were no ordinary men, as the Nobel Committee recognised.

While the awarding of the 1993 Nobel Peace Prize to Mr Mandela and Mr de Klerk is common knowledge, perhaps few are aware that to celebrate the occasion, the Soul Brothers, one of South Africa's most popular musical groups, had been invited to perform in Oslo City Hall. With their vibrant rhythms, uninhibited performance style and street lyrics, they would certainly have livened up what might have been a rather formal, stuffy affair in a northern European setting.

Now I, sadly, was not present in Oslo that day, but I was already a big fan of the Soul Brothers, having watched them perform thirteen years earlier in the less salubrious surroundings of Umtata Town Hall, not too far from where Mr Mandela began his life. No prizes were being handed out that day, but if ever I'm up for a prize, Nobel or otherwise, the Soul Brothers would be my choice of musical back-up.

My after-care students at Ikhwezi first introduced me to the band during our Thursday and Friday evening Sports Club get-togethers. Elsewhere we might have called it a youth club, or something similar. Next to the apartment Doug and I shared was a social room with a table-tennis table and a record player, and I would bring along my cassette tape player. In addition to a bit of ping-pong, we'd play cards, chat and listen to popular music, African, American and European. Naturally that included the Soul Brothers. And of course, no one stood still while the Soul Brothers played – it was impossible. Irrespective of callipers, walking sticks and wheelchairs, we'd all start dancing the moment the first note belted off the record player. The girls would lead the way, and then the lads, even the shy ones, would get going. Lennox M. Mdawe (Scout Master) smiled on in approval from the confines of his electric wheelchair with all the gravitas of a local chief. These were golden moments.

In a country where a great deal of culture was dictated by white values, Afrikaans or British in origin, and where European and American musicians were held up as the pinnacles of musical taste, the Soul Brothers were one of the most exciting popular music bands to unite black South Africans, particularly in the urban areas. They spoke to young people in their own language, literally and metaphorically. *Mbaqanga* was a type of street music enjoyed and understood by working people, particularly the young, who were dealing with everyday challenges and emotions, and wanted to let their hair down come payday. *Mbaqanga* resonated with migrant black workers in the industrial and mining complexes of South Africa's cities, and with students and their families in the townships and homelands.

The Soul Brothers tapped directly into people's feelings and aspirations with their lyrics and beat, and dazzled with their names and personal style, like American Zulu, always cool on rhythm guitar, and Moses Ngwenya, with his distinctive electric organ sound.

If you're not familiar with the Soul Brothers, then please –! Put down this book and listen on YouTube, Spotify or iTunes. If the digital world has passed you by, they have plenty of CDs or LPs to choose from. You're in for an unexpected treat, and unless you are catatonically stiff, or have little or no feeling, you'll find your foot tapping and more probably your whole body cavorting about the room, propelled by the amazing zest and life in the songs. Explain to snooty onlookers that you're having a 'Soul Brothers experience' for five minutes and invite them to join you. You'll win friends and the admiration of many; you'll be enhancing their lives in incalculable ways. If the Soul Brothers were good enough for Nelson Mandela and F. W. de Klerk at their Nobel Prize ceremony, they are good enough for everyone else.

If you still haven't actually listened, you may care to know that they had huge amounts of energy, expressed through animated band members and luscious rhythms, and that their songs were sung in local languages, not a European word among them. If you're more aware of European and American genres of pop music, then the closest comparison I could draw would be with Malcolm McLaren's 1983 hit 'Double Dutch', or parts of Paul Simon's *Graceland* album – which, by the way, he recorded with another black South African band, Ladysmith Black Mambazo. Neither of these comparisons really captures what they had, though.

Anyway, as luck would have it, the Soul Brothers were playing in Umtata in March 1980, generating huge excitement and anticipation amongst my after-care students. Their pop idols were in town and they wanted to go! So, with Sister Mary Paule's permission and Mam's approval, it was agreed that I take them to the gig – which seemed a good idea at the time.

The big day arrived, excitement mounting all morning and reaching fever pitch by late afternoon. Finally, eight or so of them dressed in their finest partying clothes piled into the Ikhwezi van and off we rattled to the city hall in town. We'd planned to arrive early to ensure front-row seats, and were soon waiting in our hard-backed chairs, soaking in the energy and mounting excitement of the crowd.

What a sight it was. Umtata's young and trendy were swelling the hall to capacity, dressed in their most fashionable clothes and smelling of various heady colognes, aftershaves and perfumes. Young men with large, open collars and flared trousers gathered in small groups, and young women in bright colours and tight skirts huddled amongst the comfort of their friends, shooting suggestive glances at each other, whispering, chatting and giggling in secret. Occasionally, one brave, flirtatious individual would leave the security of their cohort to chat up the members of another group, register an interest, or play the fool. As the beer began flowing, the volume of excited voices dialled up and I found myself looking on at what had become a cauldron of flirtation. In dating terms this gig had already turned into a target-rich environment. It was

Friday night, everyone was having a good time, and the band hadn't even stepped on stage yet.

I was simply observing this boy-meets-girl, girl-meets-boy theatre, quite enjoying the alchemy of hormones, perfumes and beer as it worked its magic, loosening inhibitions and providing courage where none existed before. It was all very interesting from a distance; but that cool, detached tone vanished in an instant when I caught the eye of the young woman from the local Barclays bank – someone I had long admired and before whom I had already made a fool of myself. What was she doing here? I hadn't considered for one second I'd bump into this gorgeous Xhosa woman, but there she was, and she'd clocked me, and I'd clocked her. It was one of those intense moments, when for an infinitesimal fraction of a second time stands still. Our glance across the room was over before anyone could have noticed, but it was a glance that penetrated, holding steady just a fraction longer than normal. It was that fraction that left a whole lot unsaid and yet slightly said. She continued laughing and chatting with her friends ... and then she looked over a second time.

Should I do something – go over and talk to her? No, Treive. Not a good idea. I was the only white person in a hall full of trendy young black people, so any clumsy amorous moves on my part would have been scrutinised and commented on by hundreds. Who would be more embarrassed if I attempted a casual saunter-over to make polite chitchat – her or me? My previous attempt to win this girl of my dreams had been notably unimpressive; it could register as a 'crash and burn' chat-up disaster, a lesson in how not to try to impress someone you fancy.

I'd been banking a cheque, exchanging cash or something equally mundane and had misguidedly attempted to be witty, cool and interesting. What a disaster. When I opened my mouth to speak, I instantly became all fingers and thumbs, lost the ability to speak English and appeared exceedingly uncool. Although, to be honest, I never had one iota of coolness to begin with. I can't remember what I said or attempted to say to this attractive young woman, but it was all an incomprehensible mumble as far as I recall. She could tell immediately I was trying to be suave, and wasn't going to be easily impressed by this bumbling fool who seemed incapable of engaging in a normal, banking-related conversation, or any conversation for that matter. I'd been a complete twit, tongue-tied and feckless, and so I retreated from the bank counter, my ego somewhat dented, conceding that the woman of my desires was too classy for me. Hardly an auspicious start. Approaching her at the Soul Brothers gig seemed foolhardy and asking for trouble.

David Masondo, lead
singer of the Soul
Brothers. He soon got
the audience gyrating
in the aisles of Umtata
town hall. [Photo
thanks to Steve Gordon
at musicpics.co.za]

However – affairs of the heart flew out of the window as the heroes
of the hour plus their entourage stepped onto the stage. The crowd
erupted. A small army of musicians began tuning up guitars, keyboards
and drums, the PA system gave a short high-frequency squeal, and the
gig began. The crowd roared their approval. The Ikhwezi students at
my side were more excited than I'd ever seen them, their faces shining,
their joy erupting in whoops and laughter. It felt great. I was doing
some good, making the little world I knew and cared about just a tiny
bit better.

As the only white person, I'd felt conspicuous in the hall before
the band even started playing, and was clearly conspicuous to David
Masondo, the lead singer, as he did a double take on seeing me in the
front row. To make matters even more embarrassing, he came over and
sang one of the songs to the Ikhwezi students and me.

As the evening progressed the energy rose. David Masondo was sweating profusely, gyrating with more slick hip moves than Mick Jagger in his heyday. The whole hall was dancing, seats forgotten, every available space filled with bodies going nuts to the beat. It was a sensation. The reincarnation of Elvis Presley would have had less impact. So when the band took their final bow, my ears still ringing with their powerful sound, I was ready to round up my charges and get us all home quickly. We'd chalk the evening up as a success and get out of there fast.

But the night wasn't over yet. No, sirree.

Outside the hall a huge crowd lingered, flirtations now intensified. Some of the young men stood around in groups posturing next to their prized possessions, their cars, confident of catching the eye of any passing young woman.

I hastily got the after-care students into the van and started reversing. Visibility was bad once the van was full, and I felt the kombi scraping the side of the car in the adjacent bay. Immediately I knew this was trouble with a capital 'T'. So, reluctantly, I climbed out of the van to inspect the damage.

The scrape was small and easy to repair, but I had not scraped any old car; I'd had the misfortune of scraping the car of Umtata's Mr Big. His clothes, his confident demeanour and his entourage of cocky mates told me instantly that he was one of the young big shots in town. Of all the people whose car I could have scraped, I had to have chosen him.

I went over to apologise, but knew at first glance I was in for a rough time. He was hostile even before I'd offered to pay, and what's more, he seemed to be enjoying the conflict, which worried me. While I was trying to calm the situation down, he seemed bent on escalating it. Nothing I said improved matters; my words seemed to inflame him, and he stressed that I was going to pay for what I'd done, and not with money. My adversary had enjoyed a good evening at a gig, was drinking a few beers and mixing with the girls and now some rookie from Ikhwezi Lokusa Special School goes and scrapes his pride and joy. I'd spoilt his evening, and I could tell that, in his eyes, there was only one satisfactory remedy – beating me up. A small crowd was gathering, relishing the thought of another home-grown form of entertainment to round off the evening.

My thoughts switched from placating the irate chap opposite me to how I might get to the Accident and Emergency ward at Umtata Hospital after receiving a beating. In the next instant, I concerned myself with how the after-care students might get back to Ikhwezi if I were debilitated. I wasn't too proud to run away from an impending beating, but I was surrounded and trapped, so I braced myself for the inevitable. I could see no other possible outcome, and neither could Mr Big. Getting beaten up in Umtata seemed the most likely ending to what had been a lovely evening.

And then – a miracle. I couldn't believe my good luck. Just as Mr Big was about to exact his price for my driving misdemeanour, one of his entourage stepped forward, urgently addressing the big man. I recognised the guy. He was one of several bricklayers who had worked at Ikhwezi, helping to build the new workshop. As I went into work each morning I'd stop and chat to the lads and we'd built up a bit of banter, a bit of rapport – nothing much. It wasn't like he and I knew each other well. Yet here he was, forcefully telling Mr Big that I was a good bloke and how he knew me from Ikhwezi, and Mr Big should leave me alone. The verbal exchange was frenetic and not easy to understand, but after a short dialogue he'd persuaded my angry adversary not to punch my lights out.

In short, a daily acknowledgement of the local Xhosa builders at Ikhwezi and a bit of chitchat had saved me.

Sensing that hostilities had abated for a moment, I didn't hang around – I was back in the driver's seat and heading out of Umtata before Mr Big had a chance to change his mind. The incident provided material for hilarious conversation all the way from the city hall to the gates of Ikhwezi; I don't know when my students had last been treated to such an entertaining evening. I was amazed at my good fortune and eternally grateful to the young man who had saved my bacon just when I was running out of hope.

Had I been the beneficiary of Transkeian diplomacy and skilled negotiation? I also wondered if I'd have got off so lightly had the incident occurred in a British city, late at night after a boozy gig. Probably not.

7

The Prime Minister and Me

Where would you expect to meet a Prime Minister, if indeed you were to meet one? It's probably not a question you're asked often, but ponder it for a moment. No doubt you'll be thinking of some highfalutin' function, a civic engagement or something of that sort. The official opening of a new hospital or some prestigious awards ceremony might be an appropriate place to meet a bona fide PM. Well, I've only met one and that was the Prime Minister of Transkei (1979–87), George Matanzima, who funnily enough was the brother of Kaiser Matanzima, the President of Transkei (1979–86) and the Thembu Paramount Chief.

Kaiser and George played a major role in creating and leading the Transkei National Independence Party, facilitating the 'independence' of Transkei as a Bantustan in 1976. They both fell from grace following accusations of corruption in 1986–87, with Kaiser choosing to retire whilst George's exit was forced. Their uncle, none other than Nelson Mandela, was detained on Robben Island at the time courtesy of the South African government and had nothing to do with either of them, nor their involvement in the creation and running of Transkei. As we know, he saw things very differently and preferred to fight for a united, multiracial South Africa. Separate Bantustans based on race and tribal groups were anathema to him and the ANC, as they perpetuated the principles and gross injustices of apartheid.

Now, I'm stretching the truth just a little when I say I had a meeting with George Matanzima. No high-level meetings were held between the PM and me. A more accurate way of putting it is that I bumped into him – or … OK, *nearly* bumped into him, at a petrol station one fine

Prime Minister of Transkei
(1979–87) George Matanzima,
whom I bumped into one day
at an Umtata petrol station.
[Courtesy of Gallo Images, South
Africa]

morning in central Umtata. So, an encounter. We shared the same air. He
may or may not have glanced in my direction.

Sister Mary Paule and I were replenishing the Pig with fuel before it had
another reason to complain and malfunction, which was happening a fair
bit at the time. A white youth panting profusely while pushing a nun in a
petulant VW Beetle was not an uncommon sight around town, especially
in the Ngangelizwe township close to Ikhwezi. It could have been listed
in the tourist guide as a local feature, for all I know – it was common
enough and quite appreciated by the locals. Sister Mary Paule couldn't
help giggling as her human starter motor was rewarded for his efforts with
a face full of oily exhaust fumes. Small boys and other passers-by would
enjoy the sight, too, especially at the end when the engine kicked in and
Sister Mary Paule disappeared over the horizon, forcing me to charge after
the car and clamber in while she revved furiously. It was pure slapstick.

Anyway, on this occasion, once the Pig was replete with fuel, I went
over to the petrol station shop counter or something similar, and as
I turned to go, the esteemed and impeccably dressed Thembu gentleman
strode across the forecourt. I noticed him; I doubt he noticed me. That

The petrol station where Sister Mary Paule, the Pig and I had our encounter with the smartly dressed Prime Minister of Transkei. [Photo taken in 2020]

was the limit of the encounter. But he was the Prime Minister! Where else in the world does one bump into a Prime Minister filling up his car and paying for his petrol? Of course, I had no idea who he was until Sister Mary Paule told me. Indeed, MP, as we called her, had spotted the PM. I was amazed, and turned to gaze none too discreetly, suddenly recognising him from the papers. In a small 'country' like Transkei, things like this happened. There were no bodyguards, no hangers-on – just an ordinary-looking bloke in a smart suit and a slightly fancier car than was commonly seen around town.

I believe things have changed in South Africa now. No one high in government ventures out of their house without a complete security detail, several high-profile cars and flashing lights, often accompanied by motorbikes and hooting. A big splash is mandatory. Millions are pumped into keeping parliamentarians flush with cars and luxury homes, and, while living standards for many have risen, most of the former Transkei remains poor. Lavish lifestyles and corruption play their part in keeping many ordinary people in similar circumstances to those they endured in the 1980s.

8

Potpourri

Ikhwezi Lokusa Special School was a real potpourri of people, languages and cultures – Transkeian, Basotho, Zulu, South West African, South African, Austrian, American, Swiss, German, Dutch and British. We were the modern-day equivalent of butchers, bakers and candlestick makers. Our wire-fenced oasis on a hillside outside Umtata included aunties, teachers, the laundry team, cleaners, physiotherapists, cooks, gardeners, architects, potters, priests and miscellaneous nuns, black and white, with a broad canvass of skills and personalities. Xhosa and English were the two main

View of Ikhwezi Lokusa School and Rehabilitation Centre from the main road into Umtata.

languages for general communication. I never heard Afrikaans spoken in the mission, although it was one of the official languages of South Africa.

In addition to this regular line-up, Ikhwezi was an absolute magnet for visitors. We sucked them in from all over. Some would stay for an hour or two, others for days, even weeks. There were large tornadoes with less pulling power. In fact, that was one of the delights and challenges of working there; from one day to the next, you never knew who was going to turn up. One day it could be the world leader of the Girl Guide movement, the next a zealous student from Durban. Ikhwezi was a good place to be seen if you were on the way up in the world. Visits from local chiefs, ministers, chief architects, ecclesiastical bigwigs, field doctors and building contractors were all taken in our stride. We offered hospitality to all. Even my father turned up for a couple of days.

By the time I left, I was on regular speaking terms with the Bishop of Umtata, The Most Reverend Andrew Zolile T. Brook. Like most people, he knew, I think, that I was a cynical agnostic, but I was still fair game for a conversion attempt. In his eyes he was saving me from purgatory, which I have to admit is a place I'd rather skip, even though I like warm weather. An intellectual and moral football match played out between us, closing with a score of about two-all, if I recall correctly. Extra-time and a penalty shoot-out may have been needed to determine the final winner of my soul. Sister Mary Paule was on his side, of course, so the Catholic Church had

Ikhwezi attracted dignitaries from all over southern Africa and the world. Here, Sister Dolorata welcomes the world leader of the Girl Guide movement.

Many students would arrive at Ikhwezi on buses from Transkei's small towns at the start of term.

both superior resources and scholarly advantage. One of the benefits of hobnobbing with the ecclesiastical big cheese was the occasional invitation to take tea, where a superior biscuit was served – most of the time.

In addition to bourbons and custard creams, I even got to have lunch with the Bishop at his town residence. Here, I learned about his deep disapproval of communism. It was sweeping through Africa, he explained, and was more than likely doing no good – no good for Africans and no good for the Church. I listened politely, but with one eye on the dessert trolley.

What really made the mission work well, and what bound this large, transient team together, was a desire to make life better for the children. In our own way, big or small, most people wanted to do some sort of good for the young people in our care, whom life had handed a raw deal.

Considering the daily suffering of our charges, the mission was a happy place, not in some idyllic, other-worldly way but in the daily experience of laughter, fun, caring and kindness. We were idealistic, but our idealism was contained and channelled by a sound structure that kept everything ticking over like clockwork. Without our efforts, the lives of many of these children would have been dreadful. I knew that from seeing some of them outside of term time in their rural or urban homes, where living conditions and domestic facilities were often poor at best. Out of term, back at home, the physical condition of many Ikhwezi students visibly regressed.

Some reading this will interpret our actions as a low-key form of colonialism and accuse us of seeking only to assuage our white guilt. Fact is, whatever the motivations may have been – and I would not judge

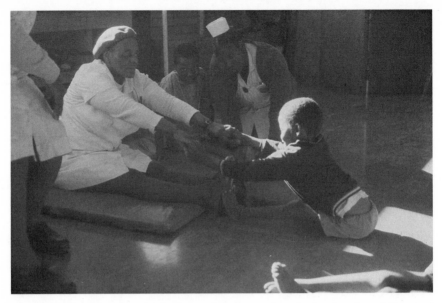

The physiotherapy team worked wonders improving the students' mobility and confidence.

them – the children benefitted. Those who came to help were sincere, and their willingness to help was not assessed or categorised by either the nuns, the children or their employed carers. We were welcomed, and I know that our being there made a positive difference in the lives of some very vulnerable people and their families.

With so many high-profile cases of child abuse by the Church and its institutions having been reported in the press in recent years, I have had to consider whether anything of that kind happened at Ikhwezi. I can honestly say that until I read about the scale and severity of Church-related child abuse, the matter had never crossed my mind. I never heard, saw or sensed any ill-treatment or unkindness by anyone towards the young people in our care. Quite the opposite. Kindness and care were the principal traits I observed in and around the mission.

Ikhwezi was an oasis, and society needs oases. Transkei certainly did. Physically, the mission school was fenced off from Ngangelizwe township lower down the hill, where there was considerable deprivation and violence. Roads there were rough and dwellings flimsy, makeshift and tightly packed. We were not exactly rural, but nor were we urban. In the township, women would walk long distances with buckets on their heads to fetch water from the river. Inside the fence of Ikhwezi we had running water, cleanliness and a strong sense of order, even of aesthetics. Gardeners cared for the grounds, while outside there was wild veld and low bush. We had small, tarmacked roads between buildings, while outside roads were dusty mud tracks. The school buildings were modern, made of cement and brick, sometimes whitewashed and with solid roofing. New buildings with modern amenities were going up every few months; hence the frequent arrival of government ministers and the bishop to give their various blessings.

The sense of being an oasis was also defined by our working and social relationships, which were quite different from outside the mission.

Just down the road in Umtata, and even more so in neighbouring towns and villages, a white face was seen infrequently. This meant that when we came into contact with Transkeians for any ordinary purpose it was often an unusual experience for many of them. We were white, and our skin colour in 1980s South Africa carried a huge amount of baggage with it, or should I say privilege, and I was for the most part painfully ignorant of this. Our skin colour defined us even before we'd opened our mouths, got out of the van or walked through the door. Not only were we white, but also it became clear to people quite quickly that we weren't from these parts. If our accents weren't a giveaway, our mannerisms and behaviours were. We tried to behave like we did in Ikhwezi, which was not the norm.

While white people stood out in Transkei, there were a high number of local people who were albinos; black people, but with an absence of dark pigment in skin and hair. My heart went out to them as I had the impression they were outcasts, always seen alone. Their predicament was another one of those uncompromising, harsh realities of life in Transkei that smacked you in the face. People could be so warm and embracing, and so matter-of-fact and seemingly unfeeling about certain aspects of life. No doubt there was more to the matter of albinos than I saw. I just witnessed lonely, outcast people, weaving their way through a crowd on Umtata's streets and speaking to no one.

In Transkei, Blacks ruled the roost officially, but it seemed they were still looked down upon by many Whites. Those employed by the hospital and university seemed a little different, seemingly motivated by ideology or compassion to teach, heal and make a difference. The dedication of white doctors and nurses working alongside their black colleagues in challenging circumstances was often truly inspirational. The cooperation, care and expertise shared in these mixed-race medical teams often significantly changed the quality of a local person's life, as many serious diseases were rife. People without hope were given a lifeline.

However, over the border, a couple of hours drive away in South Africa, race relations took a dive; there, one would find absolutely no pretence of equality or what you and I might regard as normal. From start to finish, every aspect of life was defined and structured by law to ensure that white people enjoyed a multitude of privileges and opportunities and black people enjoyed few. The quality of education, healthcare, accommodation and jobs was far lower for Blacks than for Whites. Most draconian of all were a set of laws known as the Pass Laws, restricting the movement of Blacks and requiring a pass (permission to be outside of a homeland) to be carried on their person at all times. Increasingly, the Pass Laws were flouted, with 300,000 black people per annum arrested in the late 1970s. The state and at least one denomination of the Church promoted this race-based discrimination, using the Bible to justify it. Protecting this odious system was a huge security infrastructure that started with informers in the townships and spread as far as the battlefields of Angola and Mozambique, where armed forces fought against the military wings of black liberation movements. The Russian and Chinese governments supported many of these black liberation armies, enabling the National Party to frame the 'war on terrorism' as a godly battle against the dark forces of communism.

All this tension and injustice was a far cry from life at Ikhwezi, where in our imperfect way we tried to treat everyone with respect. We were all aware of our differences in ethnicity, nationality and gender, but unlike much of the world outside Ikhwezi, which was often racially toxic, these things did not define how we behaved or worked together. Personality clashes existed, as they would in any workplace, but differences and behaviours based on ethnicity, nationality and gender were not prominent.

In fact, our potpourri of races and cultures gave the place a real diversity, one that most people valued. It made working together richer and more interesting, and it meant that the students got exposure to many different worlds, including traditional Xhosa culture and Western culture.

Interestingly, because of the gender imbalance of the core Ikhwezi team, there was a very strong feminine influence in the ways we related to one another. However, I had the impression that many aspects of life in neighbouring white South Africa had a strong male bias, with traditional masculinity featuring prominently. This was one aspect of life that seemed to traverse the racial divide – patriarchy reigned supreme in black and white society.

Ikhwezi was a happy place, run efficiently by women – nuns, teachers, nurses and 'aunties'.

The aunties at Ikhwezi had high standards in everything they did and reminded me a great deal of my Granny Phyllis, who was a house cleaner in Penzance, West Cornwall.

Thwarted though they were by an international sporting boycott, white rugby and cricket stars enjoyed iconic status. The senior politicians and clergy I read about were predominantly white and male, except for the lady Mayor of Durban whom I met. All white men had to serve in the armed forces for two years, with the country under growing pressure from armed resistance both inside and outside.

In Transkei many of the black men of working age were forced to migrate to find employment in the mines and industries of white South Africa, to pay their taxes, among other things. They would return once or twice a year to be with their families. This was particularly obvious in the country villages, where women predominated. The Bantustan of Transkei was simply too small and undercapitalised to offer adequate employment for so many young men.

Although many men were away from home working, Transkeian society remained strongly patriarchal. One picked this up from customary laws, where women had considerably fewer rights than men. Most of the roles of visible authority were still held by men: the chiefs, the ministers, the clergy and civic leaders. The President, Kaiser Matanzima, and his brother, Prime Minister George Matanzima, were conspicuous in the media, as was Gatsha Buthelezi (now Mangosuthu Buthelezi), the leader of the neighbouring Bantustan of KwaZulu. At the time Desmond Tutu was enjoying a meteoric rise through the ecclesiastical ranks on his way to winning the Nobel Peace Prize in 1984 and later the top job as Archbishop of Cape Town. While he was the doyen of the international scene, the South African state ensured he had a very much lower local profile, and one that courted controversy. Steve Biko and Nelson Mandela were seldom mentioned.

Anyway, as a result of the male migrant labour system, many of the Transkeians with whom I came into contact were women, or else younger or older men. I had the impression that despite their seemingly lower status, women were the backbone of society, the engine house of the country. When we drove among the villages to collect or return children, we were always greeted by womenfolk, young and old. Women did much of the work in the fields, preparing, weeding and harvesting crops; they also fetched water and firewood, while the few remaining men took care of the animals, particularly the cattle herds. In the hospitals most of the medical staff except for doctors were women, as were nearly all the teachers I met. While men supervised the banks, wholesalers and shops, young women took the clerical and administrative functions, doing the legwork.

The local fruit and vegetable wholesaler was a middle-aged white chap with a walrus moustache who sat at his desk with a vantage point over an open warehouse. He was old school. I supposed he'd been in Umtata all his life; he exuded a sense of having seen it all.

At this wholesaler, battered trolleys, sacks and cardboard cartons of aromatic produce, often from the Cape or Natal, created a cascade of colours, sounds and shapes. A heady wave of exotic aromas wafted around the warehouse: onions, apples and the fragrance of ripe pineapples, damp earth and exhaust fumes. The cocktail assailed you as you walked in.

Running the show, mercilessly bossing the porters and van drivers about and seemingly having her finger on the pulse of every operation in the warehouse was a woman who looked no different from my mother or Auntie Monica after a few days in the sun at Long Rock in Cornwall. According to the perverse system of the day, she was 'Coloured' – not white, not black, but belonging to a group that fell somewhere in between, status-wise. Coloureds tended to speak English or Afrikaans, and lived in designated coloured areas in South Africa, but were freely dispersed among Blacks in Transkei.

Ikhwezi was liberal in some ways and quite a bastion of progress in being run by a sisterhood of fine women, black and white. Ninety per cent of the top roles were occupied by women, both black and white. As far as I could make out, Sisters Dolorata, Mary Paule, Ignatia, Mirriam, Consolata, Maria Corda, Genevieve, Reginald, Michael *et al* were senior management, in modern corporate parlance, running a tight and expanding ship in choppy waters. No one took advantage of these fine women. They could smell and deal with trouble before most people could see it. They were quick and accurate judges of character. Between them they were able to balance tenderness, kindness and care with pragmatic operational effectiveness to ensure that jobs were done on time and within budget, and that everyone pulled their weight. There was no room for slouchers – a category Doug and I slipped in and out of depending on whether or not our deceptions were detected (they invariably were).

The aunties who cared for the children were the foot soldiers of the whole operation. There were eighteen in total, from Ms Banyo to Mrs Zibi. Under their caring stewardship the children were washed, dressed, fed and ferried to classes, physiotherapy and extracurricular activities like Guiding and Scouting. They were fine people, for whom I had much respect.

The aunties reminded me of my Granny Phyllis, a housecleaner in Penzance, West Cornwall. She wasn't just any house cleaner; she was

Above: Under the eucalyptus trees, everyone at Ikhwezi joined in cooking meat and mielies on the braai to celebrate Easter.

Below: In contrast to Ngangelizwe township, some parts of Umtata had lovely modern houses – the 'posh' houses, as Doug and I called them.

the best in town, and she chose her clients, requiring local doctors and teachers to register their names on a waiting list for her services. But her background was humble. As the youngest of seven children, raised in a poor Cornish mining village, she had lived in cramped conditions, collecting water for her mother from a stream for drinking and cooking. But she had high standards. The aunties had high standards, too, just like my Granny Phyllis. Things had to be done properly, on time and without fuss. In Cornwall, my gran would have used the word 'pop-an-towse' for fuss; 'What a lot of pop-an-towse – too much fuss!' was her maxim. Granny Phyllis and the Ikhwezi aunties appeared to have many similarities.

Bearing in mind that outside Ikhwezi the world often ran to the irregularities of Transkeian time, the aunties ensured that the lives of the children ran like clockwork. Thankfully, they were patient when Doug and I were slow at doing a job they could do blindfolded. Individually and collectively, they exuded real pride and fun. I always viewed them as an informal union, or better still a family of their own. If Ikhwezi were a Russian doll with concentric units forming the whole, then the aunties were at the heart of it. If you upset one of them you had the whole group to deal with.

The teachers, all seventeen of them, considered themselves higher in the pecking order than the aunties, being conscious of their professional status. What shone through most was their belief in education as a means of escape. They believed passionately that getting a proper education would afford their pupils and their own children a shot at a better future. They made it clear on more than one occasion that they had very little tolerance for not achieving in school. Whatever educational opportunity came their way or the way of their family was going to be firmly grasped. Every homework assignment, every class test and every exam was a stepping stone to self-improvement, irrespective of the constraints of apartheid. I visited some of them in their very cramped homes in the township, while others were upwardly mobile and living in newer housing in Umtata.

On the surface, it would be fair to say that Doug, my colleague and roommate, and I had nothing in common. He was blond and slim; I was dark and stocky. My family originated from Penzance in Cornwall at the south-west tip of the UK; his family came from the opposite end, Aberdeenshire in the north-east corner of Scotland. He had a gentle Scottish burr; I had a mongrel English accent. He was so relaxed he was almost horizontal; I was serious and far too earnest. I planned

The head of the Ikhwezi laundry back in her home village with her mother and extended family.

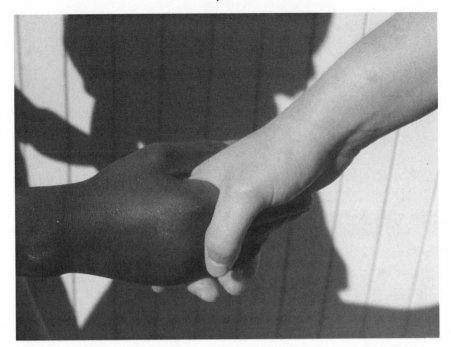

If racial difference and separation were front and centre in apartheid South Africa, everyone at Ikhwezi tried to march to a different tune. For the most part, it worked well.

ahead, thinking in weeks and months; Doug's time horizons focussed on the next mealtime or bedtime. All my clothes were unfashionable and functional, whereas Doug had a cool denim jacket that I coveted. I'm not a covetous person, but I did covet his snappy denim jacket. If sleeping were an Olympic sport, he'd have won a rostrum place every time. I was often concerned about spending too much time in bed for fear of missing something, although I didn't know what. Doug's end of our room was decorated with posters of young women in bikinis and a comic image of Father Christmas. My end had *National Geographic* maps of southern Africa, annotated with distances, altitudes and other geographical parameters in order to plan my end-of-term trip. He was in Transkei because his dad thought he should do something useful with his time. I was there because of a personal desire to see and work in the developing world.

We shared a bedroom, bathroom and kitchen, which we may have been sharing with a snake, too. After one of our many guests saw a puff adder slithering under the external door towards our bedroom, I made a search of the room a couple of times but avoided looking in some of the obvious snake hiding places, like behind the fridge. Drawing a blank, I could only assume that the curious reptile had found our room so offensive it had beat a hasty exit, or, alternatively, was living there still, keeping a low profile. I kept my suspicions of our reptilian guest to myself to avoid unnecessary concern. Snakes weren't uncommon in Transkei, so the idea of one sharing our room wasn't too absurd. Funnily enough, at round about that time, the local paper printed a story about a patient who had woken up screaming in bed in Umtata Hospital as a four-foot snake slid out from under her pillow.

We were chalk and cheese, oil and water. Except we got on famously. I don't think we argued once, and if we disagreed we let it pass, mumbling a few expletives under our breath for a couple of minutes. Our first point of similarity was how much we both loved, indeed needed, a hearty breakfast. I can extend that to include any food or beer – cold, warm, light or dark. Secondly, and much to the frustration of everyone else in Ikhwezi, we hated keeping our lovely new room clean. It looked like a tip and smelt of sweaty male youth – T-shirts, stale *dagga* (marijuana), and work boots. Chaos was king.

Doug and I worked with the aunties and teachers daily, trying to share their load. The day started early, getting the young students up and dressed for breakfast before classes. We both hated early starts to the day, especially as the mornings grew colder. In winter, icy winds from the Drakensberg Mountains and the highlands of Lesotho often wrestled with the tepid warmth of the rising sun as we set off for the dormitories, bleary eyed. The trouble was that to get to the dormitories we had to walk through the main reception area, where Sister Dolorata, the Head, tapped her wristwatch and dispatched a few sharp motivating words. Tiptoeing through reception didn't help. Once Sister Dolorata was on to us, she got the bit between her teeth and watched us like a hawk. We were amateurs against a woman who could smell slovenliness a mile off. Remember the Child Catcher in *Chitty Chitty Bang Bang*, who could sniff out children and catch them? While the good sister didn't share any of his physical attributes or nastiness, she had olfactory powers of equal stature, capable of sniffing out people shirking their responsibilities, being foolish or acting in a work-shy manner – us.

Neither Doug nor I could qualify as intellectual giants, so we had to pool our limited brainpower to overcome our formidable boss, who was clearly a whole magnitude smarter than us. It was to Doug that the brainwave fell. He realised we could get to the dormitories without going through the main reception area if we were prepared to tackle a wire fence. We organised a recce that very day, hatching a fail-safe plan to deceive Sr Dolorata. Next morning, at a time when we should have been hard at work dressing the kids, we were sneaking around the side of the main building and crawling commando-like under the wire fence. Deception complete, or so we thought. Day after day, maintaining our tardy timekeeping, we took the long route to the dormitories, crawling with great stealth under the fence in the mistaken belief that we were brilliant.

Little did we know that our failure to saunter through reception each morning had not gone unnoticed. Suspicions raised, Sister Dolorata, with Sister Mary Paule at her side, made it her mission to find out how she had been foiled. It didn't take her long to work out. Thirty years after these events Doug learnt from Sister Mary Paule that she and Sister Dolorata had watched from a window as we slid beneath the perimeter fence. Our wheeze was discovered, but they said not a word. Month after month we executed our long-winded and torturous arrival to work, under the wire fence, in the mistaken belief that we had beaten the system.

But who had the last laugh? The moral of the story is that you could never outsmart a nun from Ikhwezi.

9

Seventeen Thembu Chiefs

I subscribe to the view that the dance and rhythm gene in most white males is removed at birth, assuming they were blessed with any such DNA in the first place. This is not a vulgar prejudice, but a carefully deduced, scientifically analysed conclusion, drawn after watching white European and North American men strutting their stuff at any function where they attempt to interact with rhythmic music.

I'm sad to admit I include myself in this disadvantaged category. While I flung myself about with great enthusiasm to Saturday Night Fever, Chic and other disco music back home, it was not a pretty sight and should have been banned under some Protection of the Realm or Emergency Proclamation. This rhythm gene deficiency could be camouflaged in your local village hall disco in the UK, but not so easily in Transkei where most people had more timing and rhythm than Aretha Franklin and James Brown put together.

On the odd occasion, and by invitation, I joined some of the nuns to play the marimba (a kind of wooden xylophone) in the music room of the convent. It was slightly strange to watch, as four or five of them would play the marimbas with a rhythm and grace that perfectly reflected the landscape and culture of Transkei while I tried their patience by playing along, struggling to maintain the tempo they attained with ease. But it was such uncomplicated fun and I felt so at home with these very caring, sensitive and generous women that I enjoyed every moment. They were appreciative of my efforts and so full of humour and delight that one just got swept along.

Occasionally the nuns would spontaneously break into dance. And boy, oh boy, could those nuns dance. Sister Ignatia in particular. Their

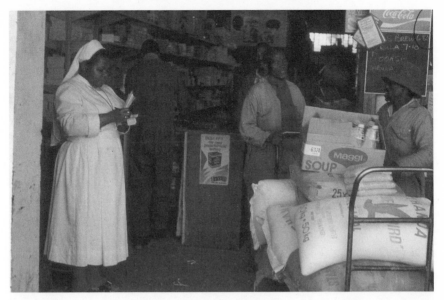

Sister Ignatia, the best dancer in the world, holding court at the wholesaler in Umtata.

dancing to the rhythmic, pulsating music contrasted with the stiffness of their clean, starched habits and their usual calm, unassuming demeanour.

Sister Ignatia was special in many ways, not just on the dance floor. Firstly, she was in charge of the school's catering, providing hundreds of meals to all the staff and kids every day of the year, in term and out of term. As a teenager with a voracious appetite, I thought it prudent to get to know the Head of Catering. I need not have worried about trying to get to know her, as I was frequently called on to ferry her between wholesalers to stock up on provisions in one of my trusted Ikhwezi vans. And this sister didn't do things by halves.

We pushed the van's suspension flat as we loaded it to the ceiling with sacks of mielie meal (ground maize), cartons of tinned sardines, boxes of apples and enough bread to feed the proverbial five thousand. None of the wholesale managers, burly men of all races, messed with the good sister. When Sister Ignatia turned up with her British flunky in tow, they all but stood to attention and addressed her requests like new recruits on a military parade ground. I couldn't help noticing that when I turned up alone at these places I was not afforded the same respect, and quite rightly so. But I *was* the good sister's flunky, and that was good enough for me. As a reward, she often made sure I enjoyed an extra breakfast or similar culinary bonus.

Managers of the wholesalers jumped to attention when Sister Ignatia turned up. Her teenage lackey was not afforded the same courtesy.

At other times Sister Ignatia was my navigator, or perhaps I should say I was her driver. Anyway, let's say we were a good combination, driving to the remotest parts of the Transkeian countryside to collect children. North, south, east and west we travelled on rough dirt tracks, to places so remote they were not recorded on the map. Sometimes the settlements didn't even have a track; we just rode across open fields. The tops of rondavels and herds of livestock would serve as our SatNav when the topography disorientated us.

Our working partnership flourished in and around Ngangelizwe township, too. When the new, purpose-built brick homes for the Ikhwezi staff were completed, just outside the school grounds, we were the Ikhwezi home removal service, ferrying furniture and belongings from their old shacks to the new bungalows. Sister Ignatia coordinated us, helping the aunties and teachers to empty out their often squalid and cramped staff homes in Ngangelizwe and transporting them up the hill to their new, modern homes. As you can imagine, this was a job with a great reward, with staff expressing disbelief and delight at this significant improvement in their quality of life. Some actually seemed a little daunted and disorientated in their relatively sumptuous new surroundings.

Above: Sister Ignatia's lackey loading an Ikhwezi van to the roof with provisions to feed the large and growing number of students and staff.

Right: Working with the nuns from the Glen Avent convent was often a lot of fun.

Above: Two Ikhwezi gardeners vacating their home in Ngangelizwe township in order to move into their new house, supplied by the school.

Below: I acted as a furniture removal service, with Sister Ignatia, to relocate the two members of staff into their new home adjacent to the school.

Once the staff had settled into their new homes, Sister Ignatia would do cookery demonstrations with a low-tech invention called the Wonderbox. This simple thermally insulating pair of cushions in a cardboard box enabled the staff to cook using far less fuel, saving them money. Things were improving for the staff in small but discernible ways. I think that such interest shown by an employer in their employees' domestic comfort and welfare was certainly appreciated.

I got to know Sister Ignatia so well that one day I plucked up the courage to ask her why she had become a nun in Transkei. A little impertinent, I know, but I asked anyway, and she took great delight in telling me that she had faced the choice of two marriages: marrying a man or marrying God. I wasn't expecting that answer. She explained, without one inflection of doubt, that dedicating her talents to God and the needs of unfortunate children was much better, in her view, than hitching herself to any man. In a rather disdainful voice, she explained that men's various and many shortcomings had not impressed her, and she was not a woman easily impressed. God, on the other hand, had never let her down. There was absolutely no wool pulled over the eyes of this fine woman.

When I'd first met Sister Ignatia I'd been more than a little intimidated; she seemed so serious, far less humorous than any of the other nuns at Ikhwezi. When I relayed this to Sister Mary Paule she chuckled, as she did to many of my shallow pronouncements, telling me that Sister Ignatia was one of the nicest and most caring people I'd ever meet. I concluded that Sister Ignatia was more serious than the others because of the responsibility of feeding a small army every day. More telling, she really didn't fall for the blatant malarkey and laziness that Doug and I dished up daily. She was way too savvy to have any truck with our youthful nonsense.

I forgot to mention her stature, which is important, especially as I've already told you she was a great dancer. Sister Ignatia was short and stout, but with an upright posture that accentuated her air of authority and reliability. Because of her demeanour and the seriousness with which she went about her work, one would never have imagined that she was the world's best dancer, but *Strictly Come Dancing* would have been a breeze for this wonderful, caring, no-nonsense woman. I discovered this one evening in the music room.

The older children were playing about on the marimbas and drums, which they often did, but on this occasion they were really letting rip and the music was flowing. Some of the nuns started dancing quite spontaneously to the infectious Xhosa rhythms and soon Sister Ignatia, normally so solid and earnest, was on the floor in a world of her own, so light on her feet, so perfectly blending her movements with the music that she was a joy to behold. Responsibilities seemed to roll off her shoulders as she ebbed and flowed, gracefully and rhythmically. There was nothing overt or ostentatious about her style; her movements were understated, her footsteps small, but they were completely in time to the beat, which was complex and rich. Watching her dance that evening left an indelible impression on me. I can still see her vividly, caressing the rhythms of the music, losing herself and mentally drifting to a place beyond our view.

I don't know what the collective noun is for a group of dancing nuns, but to add to this mesmerising occasion, Sister Ignatia beckoned me to join them, and for five minutes, not a second more, I, too, could dance to the luscious tribal music of southern Africa. I wasn't in the slightest bit stiff, out of time or overly self-conscious, as Sister Ignatia gently and generously led me through the dance. When I'd finished I watched, thankful for that very special moment with the world's best dancer.

I'm pleased to say that wasn't the last time I was invited to dance in Transkei, but the next two occasions had none of the grace and splendour of my first, my only dance with Sister Ignatia.

8 May 1980 was as ordinary an autumn's day in Ikhwezi as you could imagine. I'd done a bit of teaching, I'd transported a few of the after-care students to the local hospital and helped at the infant school in Ngangelizwe with Sister Mary Paule. It was late afternoon, the sun was low in the sky, and I was ready to take a shower, eat and hit the sack. But that is not how things turned out. Seventeen Thembu chiefs were about to scupper my simple domestic ambitions. And these weren't just any old Thembu chiefs. They included none other than the Paramount Chief of West Thembuland and the Deputy Minister for Agriculture.

Sister Mary Paule caught me in full stride as I left one of the classrooms, heading for my room at the top end of the school. She wasn't her usual, relaxed, witty self, and instead of asking what I might have planned for the evening, she said that seventeen Thembu chiefs had come from Transkei's parliament to look at the school and would I please help. We needed to make a good impression. Before I could utter a whisper of resistance, she asked me to get out the oil drums and grills, fire up the braai (BBQ to the rest of the world) and get some meat cooking for the chiefs. I was reminded that they were very important and that one of them was President Matanzima's close relative, therefore even more important. I would have to put my shower on hold while I flexed my culinary skills in the interests of Ikhwezi-governmental diplomacy.

As a bona fide alpha male, I couldn't turn down an invitation from Sister Mary Paule to braai, but honestly, I wasn't keen because of the rushed way it had to be done. I wished we could have been informed of this a little earlier. We were running around like headless chickens at the end of a full day's work because, it seemed, these seventeen chiefs had spontaneously decided about ten minutes ago to pay us a visit and take supper. To do a great braai you need time, a bit of planning, due consideration for all sorts of things. But time wasn't what we had. The political honchos were already there, had finished their inspection and were ready to eat.

Out came the oil drums and grills. Wood was quickly collected and loaded into the drums and lit. Right, we were started. Sister Mary Paule was flustered and kept asking, 'Is the meat on yet? When are you going to start cooking? They're getting impatient to eat, can you speed it up a little?' In a huddle, a few metres away, were the chiefs, chatting with some of the nuns. After a little while, with the lack of food, out came their hip flasks and all began to take a few nips of whisky. They were restless. In fact, we were all getting restless. I could feel the pressure to deliver something from the flames sooner rather than later.

I had hoped for a little help from Doug, but he was way too busy flirting with our Swiss colleague Babs, which I thought was fair enough. The pressure was on to get the meat and baked maize (mielies) dished up to our honourable guests. Finally, with a flourish, the chiefs no doubt faint from hunger, the meat was served. It was a basic meal, not my best braai, but good enough, all things considered. Most importantly, the chiefs devoured it in seconds. Ah! Now for some rest. I'd achieved grumpiness and job satisfaction in equal measure, and I needed to get back to my room, kick off my working clothes and have that well-deserved shower. Ikhwezi Lokusa Special School had got its pound, or kilo, of flesh from me that day. But apparently my working day was not over.

As I packed away the braai, the chiefs were guided into our large, well-appointed rondavel that served as a music room. Nuns and teachers followed, including Babs and Doug. To my surprise, Sister Mary Paule asked me to join them. My mild protests and the mention of a much-needed shower did nothing to dissuade her, and I was soon corralled into joining part two of the evening's chieftain charm offensive. Did I have a choice? There was no way I could say no. But I was still a bit grumpy.

Older students often played marimbas, drums and guitars for their own amusement or to entertain visiting dignitaries, such as Thembu chiefs!

Moses wouldn't have received this much attention if he'd turned up unannounced.

So, we all took our places, chiefs on one side, sipping their hip flasks more boldly now. I noted that the President's close relative didn't indulge. He was dressed in a slightly snappier way than his colleagues, seemingly conscious of making a good impression.

On the other side of the rondavel sat miscellaneous nuns and an assortment of volunteers from Europe like Babs, Doug and me. Between us was a band of senior students giving their all on the marimbas, drums and guitars. Most evenings I would have enjoyed the music, but my mind was with my shower and I really did not want to be there. Out of respect for our guests, the school and Sister Mary Paule, I kept my seat, listening and smiling and hoping it would all end soon.

But the room's dynamics were changing rapidly. As the music warmed up and the whisky took effect, the chiefs took to the dance floor, responding to the beat exuberantly in a uniquely African style, rhythm coursing through their bodies. The charm offensive was proving a huge success. However, from the corner of my eye I could see Sister Mary Paule, and I knew her well enough to sense she was hatching a plan.

Something was brewing. What was she up to? Sure enough, moments later she glided over and whispered in my ear.

She explained that it was embarrassing for only the chiefs to be dancing and none of the white folk to be joining them. I had to admit this hadn't escaped my notice, but despite my deep respect and admiration for Sister Mary Paule and the chiefs, I wasn't going to be the one to buck the racial dancing trend. Not me. Not today. I'd done my bit for community relations by cooking; dancing in front of Thembu dignitaries was at the bottom of my to-do list.

Sister Mary Paule's plan was to slink over to the chiefs and have a quiet word in their ear. The next thing I knew they were pointing at me. Oh, no – a faultless plan! Sister Mary Paule was smiling, suddenly the picture of calm and relaxation, with a hint of mischievousness. She resisted the temptation to chuckle.

There was no escape. One of the older chiefs came over and cordially invited me to dance. I couldn't refuse. I simply couldn't say no. These were important people after all. I had to comply. It was a slam-dunk for Sister Mary Paule. And as I got up to accept the gracious invitation, I caught a glimpse of her, a cheeky smirk of satisfaction on her face. She'd got me, as she knew she would. As though I was ever going to be able to avoid her cunning plan.

So there I was, dancing away in my stiff, incompetent style while the much more adept Thembu chiefs gave themselves to the music, dancing with real feeling and power. I'd left suburban Surrey to do something different and this felt very different. My absolute ineptness on the dance floor was on show for all to see. I'd have given anything for the dancing gene to be reinstalled. The only good thing about my predicament was that the chiefs seemed happy. In a minuscule way I was enhancing Anglo-Thembu relations.

Onlookers giggled at my predicament, but their giggling was soon stifled as the chiefs got everyone up on the floor dancing. It was a great evening in the end, closing only when the seventeen Thembu chiefs went laughing to their waiting cars. Sister Mary Paule was beaming. As far as I was concerned, that was all that mattered.

I nearly forgot to tell you – I never did get a shower that evening.

10

The Flying Nun

One afternoon, across the grassy quadrant between classrooms, Sister Genevieve went flying past as a bright flash of white, in pursuit of two errant small boys. Have you ever seen a nun fly? That's what it looked like, as her sandaled feet careered over the ground and her bright, immaculate habit billowed out behind her. Her wimple did not fare well; it flew off her head and onto the grass, much to the shock and amusement of the boys and girls looking on. A nun without her wimple! It was unheard of.

The wonderful action-orientated Sister Genevieve, who saved my bacon more than once. I adored her contempt for the South African authorities, white and black.

The crowd of children gasped, and Sister Mirriam put her hands over her mouth to hide her horror and laughter. Undeterred, Sister Genevieve restored the wimple to its rightful place and continued in hot pursuit, disappearing from our line of sight. We resumed our lesson.

This was Sister Genevieve to a tee.

Sister Genevieve was one of the black nuns, a handsome, strong woman with a sturdy frame and high cheekbones. When she spoke, she used her hands and arms to reinforce her point as a Spaniard or Italian would, but in a slightly more subdued, less choreographed way. In conversation, she held your gaze with a frank, open countenance and held nothing back. Diplomacy was not her strong suit – she said what she felt, directly and without unnecessary concern for how her words might be received. But what she lacked in social grace she made up for in sincerity, reliability and zest. Like me, she was earnest. Perhaps we were both a little too earnest, but we got on famously.

Sister Genevieve was a bit of a tomboy, seeming to enjoy the company of men – not in any improper way, but for general rubbing along with and getting work done. Perhaps she needed a break sometimes from the all-female environment of the convent. If there was a BBQ to be lit, she'd be there, managing the flames. She loved running the Scout troop and enjoyed a bit of hearty banter. Like most of us, she was not as confident as she appeared to be, needing affirmation and the occasional word of praise, especially for her sterling work with the Scouts.

I found out that when you were in a tight spot and needed help, she was utterly dependable. My bacon was saved on more than one occasion by Sister Genevieve, even when I didn't know my bacon needed saving. A case in point was the day I nearly got arrested for what I thought was (and in any other country would have been) an innocent activity.

A couple of times a month I had to get up in pitch darkness at 4 a.m. to drive one of the vans over the border into South Africa to the city of East London. The drive took about three and a half hours each way and involved a thorough passport check at the Great Kei River border post.

East London was the nearest major South African city, lying to the south-west on the coast. Even in 1980 its early 20th-century architecture and wide, straight high street through the city centre gave it a distinctively colonial feel. The shops and the way things were done felt as a city in Europe might have felt a couple of decades earlier. Its beachfront was lined with graceful old hotels, pristine sands and a busy harbour just off to the side; its suburban gardens, overflowing with tropical vegetation, were neat and elegant, the neighbourhoods quiet and clean. Black

I drove to East London from Umtata so frequently I knew where many of the speed traps were set.

people were hardly seen in town, coming into the city to serve mostly as maids, gardeners and petrol station attendants and returning at night to townships far from town. Many homes had live-in domestic staff sleeping in servants' quarters without their spouses or children, whom they might see once or twice a month on their day off.

For us in Ikhwezi, East London offered the opportunity to access specialist medical services for the children and to buy things we couldn't get in Umtata, from electric motors to certain food items. Arriving in the city early in the morning, my first task was normally to drop off the children and their accompanying nuns, nurses or teachers at the hospital for non-Whites where an orthopaedic medic would attend to their disabilities, often fitting them with new callipers and prosthetics. I was there so often I ended up on speaking terms with the orthopaedic medic, a caring, mild-mannered chap of Cypriot or Lebanese origin, I think. While he saw to their medical needs I would do my rounds in East London, sometimes accompanied by Doug, a teacher or another member of the eclectic Ikhwezi community. Sister Dolorata or Sister Mary Paule invariably gave me a comprehensive to-do list.

While the early start was a challenge to a callow youth, I did get to see lots of the wonderful Transkei and Cape Province landscape, and a huge spectrum of East London life, including the insides of various hospitals, the shopping areas, the harbour, townships, factories and coastline. I hardly met a single black person in the city – although they were the large majority – but I did meet a variety of white people.

I'd be talking to a member of the liberal white elite in charge of a charity (in this case Cripple Care) one minute, and deep in conversation with working-class dockworkers, factory supervisors and shop managers the next. All wanted to know what in God's name a British teenager was doing living in Transkei, and, even more, what motivated me to work in a church mission for disabled black people. Some were flummoxed, if not a little suspicious. In the world of apartheid this behaviour just didn't follow the script. Transkei, for many, was a no-go zone, a foreign and dangerous place for Whites. Some would consider taking a holiday on the Wild Coast, but for the rest this was a place to avoid, or at best just to drive through en route to Durban. Even though these were English-speaking people, many of British heritage, I felt culturally distant and struggled to reconcile their perceptions of Transkei and its people with my lived experiences. Invariably, there was a huge gap between us.

It was strange and unsettling to cross the border from Transkei into South Africa and to adapt to this weird world of separation based on race. The atmosphere, culture and expected behaviours were so very different here from what I had grown accustomed to in Transkei. Here the law and signs on doors and walls saying 'Whites only' told us unambiguously that white people and black people were irreconcilably different and should stay apart. How humiliating and restrictive it must have felt for my black colleagues, the nuns and teachers, and for the children. I thought this often, but I seldom mustered up the courage to ask about their thoughts and feelings on this madness, a cowardice I regret. Crossing the Great Kei River border into South Africa changed drastically how they were regarded and what they were allowed and not allowed to do by law.

We all took the view that we would do what we came to do in East London and head home to Ikhwezi as soon as possible. East London was not a comfortable place for us to be in. Besides, it was always a long and tiring day's travel.

Wherever I went, my trusty Olympus OM-1 SLR camera went too, so that I could capture people and places at unexpected times. The camera was precious to me, considered advanced for its time, and served me

In 1980, my Olympus OM-1 was the height of modernity, a compact SLR camera, using 35mm film. Digital cameras were still the fantasy of sci-fi books. [Photo taken in 2020]

well from Zambia to Cape Town, and in many out-of-the-way places in between.

On this occasion I was accompanying Sister Genevieve and Sister Mirriam to one of the 'Non-white' hospitals. While the two sisters were busy inside, I noticed a long queue of people standing patiently in the sun, many of whom would have been sick and weak. The queue was hardly moving and the sun was blazing, and I became more and more concerned that they were being made to suffer in this way. White people would never have been subjected to this. I did what any photographer would have done; I took out my camera and began taking shots, perhaps to show people back home what went on.

I was clicking away when suddenly a loud, heavily accented white male South African voice came over the public address system. It was the police or hospital security announcing that the white man taking photographs should stop immediately, stay where he was and await the arrival of the authorities. It wasn't a polite request. It was an order.

I'd had an inkling I was being watched by someone in security, but had chosen to take the risk anyway. Now I was unsure what to do. Worse still, I was unfamiliar with this hospital so didn't know where to go or what to do. But staying put, waiting for some burly security guy – or, worse, a whole gang of them – didn't sound like a smart plan either.

At times like this you quickly find out who your friends are.

As the announcement on the PA system was being repeated, Sister Genevieve appeared at my side, looking distressed. I tried to explain that I'd better wait and at least speak to these guys, but she hurriedly told me, in short gasps, that this was a very bad idea, grabbed my arm and led me down a couple of corridors to the exit gate. Her urgency, firmness and directness conveyed that this was not a jolly caper. I'd crossed a line. We were in some danger. We needed to get out ASAP, before we were all hauled off by the security people. I had no choice in the matter. She was in control.

Sister Mirriam, one of the most mild-mannered nuns I worked with, had heard the PA system messages too and, anticipating what would happen, was waiting at the parked Ikhwezi van, the door already open. I was bundled into the back seat, the door was slammed, the two nuns vaulted into the front seats and off we sped, not waiting a second longer to be interviewed by the security personnel. The sisters' urgent and united response had taken me by surprise, and their reaction conveyed volumes about the reality of life for Blacks in South Africa. Sister Genevieve turned to explain that what I had done was a very irresponsible thing and leaving was our best and most necessary course of action.

Later, of course, on our homeward journey to Ikhwezi over the Great Kei River crossing, there was much laughter about this little incident. I'd caused enough of a fracas for one day, and had learnt first-hand how terrifying a place South Africa could be for black people who broke the law and for anyone who sympathised. More personally, I had discovered what great allies Sisters Genevieve and Mirriam could be. And as it turned out, I would need that strength again only a few weeks later, again while venturing into apartheid South Africa.

11

Blood

Transkei could be pretty challenging, emotionally and psychologically. You needed to be a piece of plasticine or elastic to cope in a place like Ikhwezi, because you were frequently being pulled in different directions, both positively and negatively, and sometimes at the same time. Some of the experiences were so profound and intense that they were beyond the processing ability of a nineteen-year-old more accustomed to delivering pints of milk than witnessing the peaks and troughs of daily life among the very poor and disadvantaged. In Ikhwezi, emotional resilience meant learning to deal with whatever came your way, as there was very little

Sister Mary Paule, Doug and the Cool Gang on the way to class.

let-up during term time. The delights and pains were numerous and varied, and presented a huge learning curve for me.

There were times when I'd quietly make my way back to the room Doug and I shared just to take a breather and have some space to myself. I needed to enter my own little bubble for a while, to build up my emotional strength and perspective. I was helped by being able to share various challenging moments with Doug, who was similarly affected at times. At weekends I'd often spend time in conversation with Sister Mary Paule in the school library, where her experience and tender probing would help me tackle the merry-go-round of emotions. Getting away now and then to the Wild Coast also served as a kind of tonic, where the simple cocktail of sun and swimming massaged the emotional bruises and strains. And if I'm honest with myself, the evenings Doug, Babs and I spent smoking *dagga* (weed or marijuana), sourced from the infamous Mr Bidla, the head gardener (more of him later), were a bit of a release valve, too.

When I first arrived, I was an all-purpose gofer, driving all over the place, running errands in Umtata, fixing water filter systems and on one occasion, in response to a screaming teacher, fixing a classroom tap that had exploded in a fountain, drenching all within a three-metre radius and creating puddles across the room. There was an expectation that I could do a whole lot of things, and to my surprise I found out that I *could* do many of them. Back home, the family thought me incapable of putting a spanner to good use, but when a crisis arose at Ikhwezi, those preconceptions were put to one side. I might not have been saving Africa, but I was doing some good, if only for the fretting and damp teacher.

I was happy in my jack-of-all-trades role, but it was only a matter of weeks before Sister Mary Paule decided I might be put to other uses and asked if I'd like to do some teaching. The word 'asked' is a polite euphemism when it came to Sister Mary Paule, because there was only ever going to be one outcome. Over tea and biscuits or tinned fruit, after being charming and chatty and getting my guard down, she'd approach with, 'How would you like to ...?' or 'I think you'd be very good at ...' or 'Is it right you can ...?' It was coercion and stealth of the highest calibre, because the answer was always affirmative; something along the lines of, 'Of course I will,' or 'When do you want me to start?' Resistance was futile, and besides, by then I'd be full with fruit or biscuits from her personal stash, so guilt came into play, too. And most of the way through this seduction she'd chuckle and smile in her infectious, girly way. You simply didn't stand a chance. The West's secret services could have learnt a lot about interviewing suspects and interrogation from this charming woman.

Members of the Cool Gang were always full of beans and not easy for a novice teacher to manage.

So it was that, by virtue of a tin of fruit and Sister Mary Paule's nunly charm, I found myself standing in front of a class of excitable small Xhosa boys, with only a teacher's desk to protect me from their guile and wit, with which they were amply gifted. My first task was to break up calliper fights that had erupted in several areas. It was a battlefield. Think of a Star Wars lightsabre fight scene, but involving a variety of callipers, wielded by ten- and eleven-year-olds. If Luke Skywalker had owned a set of these crude prosthetics he'd have seen Darth Vader off by the end of the first film, saving us all the tedium of numerous sequels of intergalactic bish, bash, bosh. The only downside is that George Lucas would have ended up on the dole queue before moving on to a new career as a TV chef or as a social worker for sci-fi fantasists.

I digress – but note that in my first five minutes in the classroom I might have welcomed the support of Mr Vader or a couple of stormtroopers to calm the class down.

Once the fire had been doused I noticed that my classroom included the Cool Gang. These were normally part of Doug's class. He and Sister Mary Paule had identified and named the gang because they were just so cool. They were a very cheeky cohort of four or five boys, all aged eleven-ish and suffering a range of quite serious physical and mental handicaps, although none of them used a wheelchair and not all needed callipers. Because of their frailties they walked slowly, with gaits like that of a new-born calf, but always as a group. Two of the boys had brain conditions, possibly cerebral palsy, which resulted in poor coordination of the limbs and head, and slurred speech. Some had to wear heavy glasses. Even today, these little guys bring a pang to the heart when I recall the burden they carried every day. When you stopped and thought about their dreadful afflictions and the impact on basic things like mobility, it would fell you emotionally. What made it all so hard to process was the tragedy of their conditions coupled with their incredible resilience and cheerful nature. These were the happiest and most mischievous people in the whole mission. Crazy Gang would have been an apt name.

It was humbling to see how they used their collective range of abilities to get the most out of each day. They didn't dwell on what they couldn't do, but turned adversity on its head. Those with stronger linguistic skills talked on behalf of the group, while those with lesser physical challenges helped those more constrained. Everything for them was hilarious, a delight, a reason to laugh and have fun. It was an irony that never ceased to challenge me.

Wherever Doug went, the Cool Gang were never far behind, often laughing and playing practical jokes.

One day I found myself the object of their ridicule, for reasons I cannot now recall. Vuyo, one of the youngest, teased me about something and the rest of the Cool Gang joined in, verbally pulling me this way and that. The classroom laughter and ridicule I endured must have been audible in the corridor outside, but I couldn't scold them because I was in awe of them! Here I was, a privileged young man with all my mental and physical faculties intact, and the Cool Gang were running rings around me. You couldn't quantify my admiration for them.

On another foray into teaching I was slightly less in need of protection from the Death Star or other celestial sci-fi heavyweights, for I had Doug at my side. The class loved Doug. He was gentler than I was, more easy-going. I might have been able to impress the boys by climbing to the top of a eucalyptus tree or by traversing a narrow plank of wood in a clown-like fashion, but these skills paled in comparison with Doug's warm heart, laughter and generosity of spirit. In fact, he might well have been the leader of the Cool Gang, as he was so often in their company and enjoyed creating havoc just as they did. If not the leader, he was the Pied Piper. Wherever Doug went, the Cool Gang were not far behind, lured by his comical ways and entranced by his sensitivity to their physical and mental challenges.

On this occasion the weather was fine and we agreed to take the class outside, overlooking the lush rolling Transkeian landscape, where we could read stories, draw pictures and suchlike. We all sat down in the grass, huddled in a circle, the small boys propped against my shoulders and sides. Apart from the occasional dig in the ribs from a stray calliper, the afternoon could not have been more pleasant, and I doubt if anyone was more content at school than this small group. Doug was holding court and the kids listened. After a while, I began to sense a strange tingling on my leg and in my hair. What I had naturally assumed to be the work of an insect or spider was in fact small boys taking turns to feel my skin and hair. I was wearing shorts and they wanted to know what white skin felt like, and they rolled their fingers in my hair to find out what white person's hair felt like. They spoke in quiet voices comparing observations, intrigued by the novelty. I'd turned into an exhibition piece representing white people.

Once again it was one of those so very poignant, memorable moments in Transkei where several worlds, cultures and backgrounds met for a disorientating instant. We hadn't prepared for this, and just for a fraction of a surreal Transkeian second, sitting on that hillside, Doug and I were thrown off balance as we realised that white skin and hair was something very alien to these boys. Once we realised what the boys were doing, they hesitated, and we laughed, allowing them the freedom to satisfy their

On warm days we might take lessons outside.

curiosity. It seemed that feeling our hair and skin was as good a lesson as we'd get to teach that day.

I can only suppose that in today's world we'd have had so many rulebooks thrown at us for this that we'd be climbing out from under them for months to come. But it was simple curiosity, nothing more, and a relaxing of barriers seemed the appropriate and natural response to their innocent prods and strokes.

This wasn't the last time that issues around race and background were to come to the fore in the classroom. I must have done some things right as a teacher – although I don't know what – since Sister Mary Paule soon had me teaching older children, the fifteen-and sixteen-year-olds. This was more suited to my serious nature, and enabled me to get my teeth into some science and art.

I liked art history and knew enough to follow the syllabus and teach it. But I felt uncomfortable teaching these Xhosa children about European schools of art and famous pieces and artists. Why on earth did I have to convey to them the nuances of Picasso's Cubism or the Dutch masters when southern Africa was bursting with stunning artwork visible in the caves of the Drakensberg, in patterns on the walls of people's houses and in soapstone carvings, just to mention a handful of everyday examples? The paintings of Durant Sihlali, Gerard Sekoto and many others reflected realities of apartheid South Africa and were totally worthy of study – but completely ignored by the syllabus. Of course, I did not know of these artists at the time, but would have taught them with enthusiasm had any information on them been available.

After the first lesson, I shared my frustration with Sister Mary Paule at this cultural farce. It felt insulting to be teaching about European art when we were at the far end of southern Africa, surrounded by artwork of equal merit, but different. In fact many of the so-called European masters had spent the last few hundred years pinching ideas for their art from far-away places and cultures, including Africa. Modigliani, Gauguin and others owed much of their success to studying the art and methods of non-European cultures. Sister Mary Paule was more than sympathetic and patiently listened to my low-key idealistic rant. But the syllabus won the day, as I knew it would. So I was soon back to explaining the radical nature of the Impressionist movement and why an artist might feel the need to cut off an ear. I was put off Monet, Seurat and that narcissistic bunch of tortured bohemians for life. Don't ever talk to me about water lilies and poppy fields.

Science classes were a different cup of tea – or test tube full of hydrogen sulphide to be more apt. They were great fun to teach to an attentive class, covering a bit of this and a bit of that. And if the class wasn't interested I was going to do my best to bring some fun and whizz-bang into the lessons.

I had been one of those nerdy keen kids who'd had a chemistry set at home as a child, eager to make potions, stinks and mini-explosions. The combining of molecules to make heat and sparks floated my geeky boat. Besides, my best friend, Paul Williams, understood all the complex bits which I failed to grasp, so that I was able to make sense of it all, which, to a curious boy, is really quite a joy. I'd also had a microscope at home with which to examine dragonfly wings and leaf structures, and I loved nothing better than to compare my findings with what I found in insect and mammal anatomy books. While healthy and testosterone-fuelled friends of mine chased girls around the village, I was at home dissecting roadkill and annotating their various organs. Badgers, foxes and pine martins killed on the local roads all found their way onto my desk to satisfy my curiosity and enhance my anatomical knowledge.

So when the Transkeian science syllabus touched on the subject of amphibians I was ready to get out a scalpel or two, a handful of pins and show the class the delights of frog anatomy. A poor frog was found and elected as the object of scientific wonder. The class had never had science taught this way before and there was a buzz of excitement mixed with bewilderment as Mr Frog became an annotated, splayed display. The squeamish remained at the back of the class, while the rest plied me with questions. Where was the stomach? Why did the muscles shine? What was this organ, and that one? Mr Frog didn't say a word, but he had done his job. I'd done my small bit to lift anatomy from the page and make it come alive, if you get the irony.

Next, we moved on to human biology and the composition of blood. Once again the textbook was boring us all senseless, explaining this cell type and that cell type, why we needed them, and so on. We were in nodding-off territory. What we needed was blood – real, human blood. I voiced these thoughts without really thinking, and before I knew it we were in action.

We located the microscope, the glass slides and a pin, and one of the girls at the front volunteered to supply her blood for analysis. That was one problem solved. The particular volunteer came as a bit of a surprise. The wheelchair-bound young woman in question was normally the one obsessing about Queen Elizabeth II and her latest photo spread, eager to know which of the royal family I had personally met. I explained that I had once walked past Prince Charles, at close range, in Windsor Castle, but the Queen was a bit out of my social circle. Perhaps my enthusiasm for science would make up for this obvious disappointment and failing with the royals.

So, within minutes, the pinprick of blood was transferred to a glass slide and after a bit of jiggery-pokery I had some cells in focus. The class filed past to have a look and the whole subject took off; they were fascinated to see the outline of red blood cells, and many asked to have a second look.

Then came one of those very special Transkeian moments, when the bigger picture broke through the little machinations of our day, and hearts and minds were changed. I stressed that apart from a few exceptions, like sickle cell anaemia, everyone's blood was quite similar, with different cells doing different jobs to keep us going. I was thanking the blood donor when it became obvious that while I stressed the universality of human blood composition, I hadn't demonstrated it, and more to the point I had every opportunity to do so. In this racially sensitive sphere of southern Africa, where race was front and centre, I was saying that under the skin we were all pretty much the same. I thought I should prove it.

Although the practical class was all but over, I gave my thumb a jab and set out to show that my blood was just like theirs. On this important topic I wasn't just Treive, the teacher, I was the *white* person. Everything about South Africa yelled that I was different to them, and I wanted to show up the lie that this was. If I'd been concerned that minds had wandered to the approach of the lunch bell, I need not have worried. As I prepared the slide, they clustered eagerly around to check it out. They saw through the wonders of the microscope that both sets of blood, one from a black student and the other from their white teacher, were indistinguishable.

I'm not sure how much science was conveyed that day, but I believe a deeper lesson in humanity may well have hit the mark. Collectively we heard the penny – or should I say the rand – drop.

12

Zipho

Comparing the blood cells of a black student and a white teacher wasn't the last of these poignant and deeply moving Transkeian moments. They seemed to crop up when you were most unguarded. 'Jolting' would not be an exaggerated way to describe them. I guess that's why these moments are so vividly etched in my memory, more than four decades later. So it would be remiss of me not to share with you another of these mind-shaking moments, where an ordinary event, probably long forgotten by the others involved, left an indelible impression on me.

While teaching and spending time with the older students became an increasing part of my duties, I still had to help with younger kids in the evenings, when it was a case of all hands on deck to get everyone fed, bathed and ready for bed.

One evening I was asked to help in the boys' dormitory, as one of the new children to Ikhwezi needed bathing. He was about nine years old. Because of his physical constraints, getting into a bath was difficult for him. Added to this challenge was the need to be sensitive, to maintain a sense of independence for him, and not to embarrass him.

Zipho, one of the Cool Gang, joined me. He was about to teach me a life lesson in caring, tenderness and kindness – all that Ikhwezi represented.

The new boy didn't understand a word of English and my Xhosa was shameful, so the task of bathing, drying and teeth cleaning was proving to be an awkward and torturous experience for both the new boy and me. We had a clear language barrier. But I had not counted on the invaluable role of Zipho. And therein lies the lesson – a lesson for life.

I'd formed an inaccurate impression of Zipho. His limbs were uncoordinated, his head was held at an unnatural angle, his speech was slurred and he wore thick glasses. I am eternally ashamed to admit that up until that moment I had assumed he saw, heard, felt and communicated little. I'd always done my best to help and encourage him but had not the slightest idea of the care, tenderness and intelligence that were locked up inside him. As I struggled to communicate to the new boy how to climb into the bath, wash himself with soap and rinse off the suds, Zipho stepped in and acted as the translator. To my complete amazement, Zipho understood and spoke Xhosa *and* English, and was a splendid go-between. And his caring extended further; rather than just passing on instructions, he tenderly washed the new child, rubbing on the soap and rinsing it off. He squeezed toothpaste onto the boy's toothbrush and gently showed him how to clean his teeth. I was totally disarmed. These were everyday moments to Zipho, but to me they were a lesson in humility.

All of Zipho's frailties faded as I saw a whole new person, one defined not by his disabilities but by his abilities, so cruelly masked. For a moment, my thoughts drifted to one of my favourite songs by the folk singer Ralph McTell. While he was most famous for his song about lonely people living rough in London, I'd always loved 'Michael in the Garden'. I'd borrowed a Ralph McTell album from the library earlier in my teens and been mesmerised by his song about Michael, a person seemingly blighted by brain damage and unable to communicate normally, trapped in a different world. The song explained that although everyone around Michael assumed he saw and understood very little, he actually perceived, saw and felt a great deal; more, in fact, than the rest of us and in different, more vivid, ways. This was how I felt about Zipho. My perception of him underwent a total reversal in minutes. It was jolting for me to realise that *he* was Michael, not in some imaginary English garden but right here at my side, caring and communicating, making life better for those who needed care.

This was one of those days when I needed to spend time alone in my room, simply reflecting on how wrong I'd been in my assumptions and prejudices, and adjusting a world view that had been overturned in an instant. It was the weakest, the smallest, the most overlooked who taught me the most valuable lesson.

13

Wild Coast

In 1969, eleven years before I arrived in Transkei, we lived near the oil refinery in coastal Venezuela, where my father worked. Cardon was a wonderful place for an eight-year-old boy to grow up. I would disappear for hours with my slightly older Venezuelan friend, Oscar, chasing lizards in the bush (*monte*) and fishing at the beach. Fishing was our special delight – we would spend all day on the rocks, armed with rudimentary kit and a pocket of Bolivars to buy Fanta and empanadas (local pasties) for lunch, if we could find the time. Fishing absorbed us completely.

While I was out fishing at Hole-in-the-Wall we were joined by local Bomvana women harvesting shellfish.

Our kit consisted of two empty motor oil cans, each wrapped with fifteen metres of tatty fishing line, and a crude lead weight and hook, knotted at the end. Our bait was from my mother's fridge or pinched off the local fishermen. Together, we would dangle our feet over the jetty and repeatedly cast our lines into the Caribbean, or hop over the decks of moored boats and rocky outcrops in search of better fishing spots. When we had exhausted our bait we'd jump off the jetty and swim to shore, or go and prod the rotting whale shark carcass marooned slightly further up the coast.

By late afternoon, the fishing boats might return to land magnificent sail fish, marlin and tuna. Invariably, we'd race each other to get to the weighing-in scales as these silvery marine beauties were manhandled off the boats and ungraciously strung up by their tails for display, like a public gallows. Congealed blood, flaking scales and glistening entrails were all essential parts of the visceral performance. The smell of rotting fish hit the nostrils and a squadron of rapacious flies swarmed in Brownian motion, anticipating a treat. Sea water quickly crystallised into salt patches on the pitted jetty floor. While proud fishermen stepped forward for their trophy shot, Oscar and I would jostle with each other and the growing crowd of admirers to get in the photograph. We were photo-bombing, 1960s style. After all, we considered ourselves fishermen, too.

So you can see that fish and fishing have played an important part in my life since childhood. The tatty condition of my copy of Hemingway's *The Old Man and the Sea* is a testament to how many times I've read it, and each time I wish the old fisherman better luck. Boy, what a fish that must have been! I still feel his elation as he slowly hauls in the beautiful marlin from the depths, and then his pain as it is violently ripped apart, leaving nothing more than an ugly, fleshless carcass.

In 1980, as I stood on an exposed rocky outcrop on a deserted beach, the waves from the Indian Ocean breaking on three sides and encroaching on the fourth, my fishing ambitions were a little more modest than a monster-sized marlin. Once again, I was using a battered old oil can wrapped in fishing line with a hook and weight coarsely secured to the end. I thought I'd try out my Venezuelan technique at the Wild Coast. Using a large pebble, I dislodged a couple of mussels from their rocky base and used the oozing, bloody innards as bait. It was just like old times. Now I was ready to cast the line and test myself against the Transkeian elements and the fish. All I needed was Oscar with me; he had been the brains behind our childhood enterprises.

There was little time to dwell on the past, however, as the present demanded full attention. First I had to keep skipping across the rocky outcrop to avoid the frothy waves swirling about my feet, and then, completely unexpectedly, there was a tugging at my line. Fish! The line was tight only minutes after I'd cast, and I could feel that distinctive vibration on my index finger of a fish desperately fighting to escape the hook. Not a chance. Childhood memories kicked in, as if by instinct. Hand over hand, controlling my excitement, I slowly and deliberately drew in the taut, wet nylon, avoiding contact with the sharp rock edges. The silvery flash of a fish darted left to right, up and down, visible in brief glimpses through the translucent green waves. The glimpses became more frequent and the flash of scales became brighter, and soon the beautiful fish was landed, still flexing its plate-shaped body in the shallow, warm pools of water at my feet.

By now, I had reverted to my eight-year-old self. A crude fishing expedition on the Wild Coast at the age of nineteen wasn't so very different from one in Cardon, Venezuela, eleven years earlier.

Urgently, another mussel was prised open for bait, the line repeatedly rotated through 360 degrees to generate momentum and then released by my now bloody fingers. The weight and baited hook splashed into the waves some ten to fifteen metres out in the open sea, before vanishing under a trail of bubbles. This time I had a tingle of excitement and

Using flotsam and jetsam, the Bomvana women made a fire to cook some of the shellfish they'd collected.

anticipation. Before the gnarled old weight hit the bottom of the ocean, the line strained again and another fish sent vibrations to my finger as a signal to start drawing in. Bingo! I landed another silvery beauty. Fish number two kept fish number one company, and I cast off again.

My fishy exploits briefly caught the attention of a group of ten to twelve local Bomvana women and girls, who were harvesting sacks full of shellfish, using only a steel pole and similar rough tools. Out on the damp rocks, framed by the beach, the cliffs and the sea, the Bomvana women looked striking in their traditional dress, dyed in colours typical of the area, mostly red ochre. I admired their traditional dress and the picture they formed, but they were far too engaged with their task to pay much attention to a callow white youth reliving his childhood, courtesy of an oil can and a couple of fish. Once my luck ran out on the fishing front, I gingerly made my way over the rocks back to the beach to show off my catch to Doug, Babs and Ludwig.

Soon afterwards, the Bomvana women slowly ambled onto the beach from the rocks, bearing their harvest in heavy sacks on their heads.

Above left: We were generously offered cooked shellfish, but the Bomvana women weren't interested in the fish we offered in exchange.

Above right: After eating shellfish, the Bomvana spontaneously started dancing, framed by *EsiKhaleni*, 'place of thunder', as they called it. We knew it as Hole-in-the-Wall.

On the way they collected dry flotsam and jetsam to make a fire. They used large metal cans to steam open some of their shellfish, which they shared amongst themselves and generously insisted on offering to us, too. I tried to reciprocate their Transkeian hospitality by giving them my fish, but they declined.

This was the distinctly odd thing about the Wild Coast, something almost unnatural. Apart from these Bomvana women who harvested shellfish, I never saw a single Transkeian fishing community – not one. Now and again I'd see a few white guys from South Africa with long rods casting off on the beach or a rocky headland, but never any Transkeians. There were no fishing boats or canoes, no hanging nets and no drying fish. In fact, there were few fish to be seen at all. Today, you could imagine Rick Stein, the TV chef, pulling his hair out at this travesty. The occasional beach vendor might have a handful of crayfish or lobster to offer, along with a pouch of *dagga*, but that was your lot. We already had more *dagga* than we knew what to do with.

As for real fresh fish to eat, Transkei was bit of a no-go zone, despite there being plenty of fish just off the coast. Strange as it may sound, you've probably seen them yourself. If you've watched natural history documentaries with shoals of migrating sardines being chased by waves of dolphin, tuna and shark, then the footage may well have been from this neck of the woods. Big fish, small fish, silvery types, brown types, fast ones or slow ones, the Wild Coast had the lot. My amateurish fishing attempts proved that.

So why were there no fishing boats or fishing communities in Transkei? I couldn't figure it out. Every coastal location I have ever visited has had a fishing tradition, from the trawlermen of Cornwall to the spear fishers of Cape Verde, from Costa Rica to The Gambia, and all coasts in between. In an impoverished region like Transkei, you'd have thought that cheap, locally sourced fish would have been a wonderful addition to the diet. But there was one problem. As far as I could tell, most local people just did not like the taste of fish. They were much more accustomed to meat from cattle, which is why, I suppose, my offer of fresh fish to the Bomvana women wasn't taken up.

The 250 kilometres of Transkei's Wild Coast was aptly named. It looked and felt wild. Shipwrecks littered the coast, reminders of many hapless mariners who had fallen victim to the ocean currents and rocky snares above and below water. Coffee Bay, for example, was named after the spilt cargo of a wreck, while Port St Johns, the largest town on the coast, was mistakenly named after the *São João*, a Portuguese vessel that had fallen

Mkambati Nature Reserve in Pondoland where monkeys watched us eat breakfast.

From the late 16th century, shipwrecks were a common occurrence along the Wild Coast. Many Europeans survived the trauma and integrated with local clans.

victim to the sea in 1552. The vessel, with an expensive cargo of Chinese porcelain and spices, had actually been wrecked further up the coast.

From the 16th century, villagers along the Wild Coast became accustomed to seeing desperate people of European, African and Asian descent washed up on their shores from shipwrecks. The currents, storms and reefs of the Indian Ocean had no regard for rank or title. Slaves and gentry were treated with similar contempt and severity by the elements. Sometimes local clans helped survivors while other times they attacked them, often depending on how they had been treated on previous occasions or how they were faring with the encroaching Dutch and British colonists.

Depending on their circumstances, some of the fugitives preferred to start a new life in a local village, take a wife or husband, and raise a family. This could be considerably more appealing than trekking hundreds of kilometres in the vague hope of finding a Dutch or British settlement. These risky ventures might even lead to cannibalism among the trekkers themselves. For the lower-ranking maritime survivors, a return to a life under the thumb of European masters would have been very unappealing compared to a rural existence amongst the local clans of the Wild Coast.

So many wreck survivors settled locally that parts of the coastal area were known to have villagers with particularly light skin complexion,

Mlengana Rock. Steep river valleys, lush vegetation and spectacular rocky outcrops were typical features of Transkei's coastal landscape.

long hair and features more associated with people of European and Asian descent. One coastal clan even became known as *abeLungu* or 'the Whites'.

The most famous story of these shipwreck survivors tells of Bessie, an English girl of seven, who was found abandoned on the beach in the 1730s by the local clan. They brought her up as one of their own and later she married a local prince. Her great beauty and wisdom soon became well known, and she went on to start a Xhosa dynasty.

Much of this stunning coast wasn't easy to access, as nearly all the roads were dirt track, although the scenery to get there could have graced any Kuoni travel brochure. Rivers large and small formed numerous deep valleys, brimming with dense, lush vegetation. In places, rocky outcrops soared from the river's edge to form spectacular mountains, such as Mlengana or the scarily named Execution Rock. Elsewhere, gently rolling hills and valleys supported scenic Transkeian villages, with their huts, kraals and cultivated fields.

Close to the sea, the ragged sea cliffs often gave way to undulating, golden sand dunes and endless deserted beaches, where occasionally cows wandered, straying from nearby hills. They seemed to love the cooler air of the sandy shore. There was ample space for us all to get along, even if our bovine companions looked a little incongruous plodding along the beach.

Many of the rivers – some very silty, others clear – meandered to the coast where they merged with the mighty Indian Ocean over a large

Cows were frequent visitors to the beaches of the Wild Coast. [Photo taken in 2020]

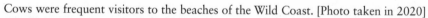

sandbar. These bars, running parallel to the coast, were conspicuous at low tide. Other rivers terminated abruptly as cascades and waterfalls, spilling their fresh water directly into the ocean or close to the shoreline.

Accommodation along the coast was very limited and mainly quite crude. I'm pleased to say that there wasn't a multi-storey intercontinental hotel branch anywhere. A hut or shack in Pondoland, for example, may have been a touch on the rough-and-ready side, but the pleasure of having monkeys entertain you over breakfast more than compensated for this.

The Wild Coast was also host to young couples of different races. Occasionally, you might meet a white guy and his black girlfriend enjoying a beach holiday together, which in South Africa was a definite no-no. Well, it would have been outright illegal. Apartheid even regulated what went on between consenting adults in the privacy of their own bed! There were several Immorality Acts, starting in 1927, that were unambiguous and prohibited 'illicit carnal intercourse between Europeans and natives and other acts in relation thereto'. In Transkei, and on the coast in particular, such Orwellian rules did not apply.

One of the most distinctive and attractive places along this sensational coastline was Hole-in-the-Wall, where we were now. An isolated island of tall, sheer rock at the mouth of the River Mpako had a large hole eroded right through the middle of the rock – hence its name.

Because of the thundering sound sometimes made by waves crashing through the hole, the Bomvana people called it *EsiKhaleni*, or 'place of thunder'. Xhosa folklore had it that the hole in the rock had been created by the much-revered sea-people, with the assistance of a large fish. A beautiful young woman had fallen in love with a sea spirit, and the fish had created the hole so that she might escape her landlocked life and join the sea-people who lived beneath the waves. Who knows? Perhaps this is how the hole in the rock was created, or maybe it was the more familiar interaction of wind and water with geological structures. I'll let you decide. One had to be there, gazing at this massive wall of rock jutting out of the sea, with its hole right through it, to be swept up in the more romantic version of events.

That Sunday afternoon, after basking in the beauty and solitude of the rugged coastline and catching all we could, Doug, Babs, Ludwig and I prepared to leave Hole-in-the-Wall beach and head back to Ikhwezi. The nuns had been very generous in allowing us to borrow an Ikhwezi van, so the least we could do was return it on time. The van wasn't the only thing we had borrowed. Sister Michael, like all the nuns, did not

Above: Babs, Ludwig, Doug and I set up camp for a weekend at the famous Hole-in-the-Wall.

Below: Crossing the Mpako River in front of Hole-in-the-Wall at low tide was easy. At high tide things were a bit trickier.

have many personal possessions, but she did have a camera, which she lent to Doug for the weekend. Aware of how valuable the camera was to the good sister, he knew he had to take great care of it. But now we had a problem – of a watery nature.

In the morning, when the tide was out, we had waded across the mouth of the River Mpako, with the mighty Hole-in-the-Wall an imposing backdrop. The merging sea and river water came up to our waists. Sister Michael's valuable cargo was transported across without a moment's thought. It was a piece of cake. By the afternoon, the moon and the sun had exerted their gravitational pull on the sea, so the river was now considerably wider and, as we now discovered, a lot deeper, too. As we surveyed the scene from the riverbank, Doug looked worried. In fact, all four of us were quite concerned. How would we get back? We hadn't factored in the incoming tide. Babs and Ludwig were from landlocked Switzerland and could be excused, but Doug and I ought to have known better. A plan of action was needed to get us, and the good sister's camera, safely across the swelling river.

We formed a line, each of us spaced about two metres apart. Ludwig led, Babs was second, third came Doug with the camera and I was last. It all started so well. We snaked across to the middle of the river, each of us on tiptoes as the water rose to our necks. Doug, looking a little fraught, giggled nervously and held the precious camera above his head, out of harm's way. There wasn't much leeway, but as long as we followed the cautious Ludwig, we would all be OK, wouldn't we? Well, what do you think?

Ludwig and Babs ploughed ahead, keeping their heads above water – just. But when Doug followed, seemingly on the same path, he started to sink. The riverbed dropped away, and he was literally up to his nose, bobbing like a cork, with the camera held desperately aloft. Our Swiss colleagues, who were always a touch more serious than we were, looked worried. My reaction was to start laughing out loud at Doug's predicament. The humour of the situation proved infectious, and Doug started laughing, too, while flailing about in the river trying not to inhale mouthfuls of brackish water. Worse was to come as his toes lost contact with the riverbed and he began drifting downstream, camera held vertically above his head. It was pure farce! In a scene that could have come from a 1920s Buster Keaton movie, the rest of us splashed after him, frantically cajoling and pushing him across the river until he made contact with terra firma. Not a drop touched the camera. What a responsible guy! As we landed on the other side we

When the tide had come in, the Mpako River swelled, making it considerably harder to cross for gullible visitors from Ikhwezi.

fell about laughing – especially Doug and I, who were schooled in that peculiar strain of British humour that sees near disaster as hilarious. Our Swiss colleagues were a little shaken. Not us. We still laugh about it today.

With our precious cargo, we made our way up the grassy slope to pack up the tent and leave. From our panoramic vantage point we could gaze down at the beach, the dunes, the cliffs and the majestic Hole-in-the-Wall. Everything was calm. The Bomvana women had drifted away into the wooded landscape with their hoard of shellfish, the rocky outcrop I'd used for fishing was now submerged below the tumbling surf and the River Mpako had yielded to the incoming tide. The Hole-in-the-Wall looked magnificent against the vast Indian Ocean, with lively waves crashing through the central archway. It was a scene of great beauty.

As we turned to go, I scoured the horizon, taking it all in. I did not observe any of the revered sea-people of Xhosa folklore, but I now wonder … had they been watching us, as we made our minuscule mark and then disappeared up the dirt track to Umtata?

14

A Brief and Incomplete History of Transkei

The backdrop to these absorbing tales is a sweep of land and coast with a fascinating past, born of a country that was always a site of contention – as most countries are at some point in their history. *A Nun and the Pig* would be incomplete without a gaze into the past, particularly as Transkei's creation was epic, tragic and messy. A great deal of blood was spilt and painful sacrifices made in the process of birthing this oddity; even after its re-absorption into South Africa it remains a unique and largely hidden place, still rural and isolated in parts.

Transkei, the entity I knew in 1980, was created by the pressure of diverse and competing external forces, some global and some regional, as well as by geography, hereditary connections, culture and language. Over centuries, larger-than-life African and European characters and historical events shaped it, including the apartheid system, the engine house of South African political governance in the 20th century. In many ways, the history of Transkei reflects broad changes that were to impact most non-Europeans all over South Africa.

The Bantu peoples of southern Africa, including the Xhosa speakers of the Eastern Cape, originated in equatorial Africa, starting in what is modern-day Cameroon and then in the area of the Great Lakes. Over millennia, one branch of the Bantu migrated slowly south, down the eastern side of Africa, through many different habitats, arriving south of the Limpopo River in what is now South Africa in about AD 300.

The Xhosa branch of the migrating Bantus went on to inhabit mainly the modern-day Eastern Cape, never moving as far south as Cape Town. By at least the 18th century they had reached as far west as the area near where Port Elizabeth now stands. They were pastoralists and small-time farmers, keeping large herds of cattle and cultivating maize, pumpkins, sorghum and beans. Apart from skirmishes among themselves, often settled without much loss of life and limb, and occasional fights with the Khoikhoi (previously called Hottentots) and San (previously called Bushmen), there was a degree of stability or managed tension between the various indigenous peoples. The Xhosa had a tradition of absorbing other captured groups into their own society, which led to the adoption into their own spoken language of some of the pronounced clicks used by their neighbours, the Khoikhoi and San. The word 'Xhosa' is itself thought to have been derived from their neighbours, the Khoikhoi. It means 'angry men'.

The area the Xhosa occupied had a lot going for it, making it a source of conflict with visiting Europeans, who started appearing on the ocean horizon in the late 15th century. Much of the land was well watered, traversed by many rivers and receiving a good summer rainfall. Malaria and sleeping sickness, a plague in many parts of Africa, were quite absent, and grassland was plentiful, enabling the survival of huge cattle herds. Wood, mud and grass provided the materials for shelter, and game was abundant, supplying the Xhosa with additional food and clothing. Topographical features provided further benefits; the Indian Ocean to the south and east gave them a strong boundary, while the mountains and highlands of the north and west prevented likely attack from those areas.

Xhosa society at this time was well structured and hierarchical. Paramount chiefs ruled the roost, supported by hereditary chiefs and headmen who ruled over loose associations of families known as clans. Their organised social system, strong sense of identity and culture, military capability, deep traditions and resilient civic institutions gave these people a status that was instantly recognised by the European settlers who came into contact with them. Compared to the indigenous people inhabiting land near the Cape, they were darker in complexion, taller and physically stronger. Their reputation as a distinct and formidable group reached the corridors of Amsterdam and Whitehall, where plans for Dutch and British global expansion were coordinated. Often, they were referred to as Kaffirs by white settlers and their colonial masters. From the very beginning, the energetic and strident European colonialists were aware that the Xhosa were not going to be corralled, exploited and eliminated as easily as the Khoikhoi and San people, who were almost destroyed as a culture during the 18th century, their tribes dismantled and pushed to the geographical margins of southern Africa by a combination of disease, displacement, forced labour and assimilation.

The trouble for all the indigenous people of the southern tip of Africa, including the Xhosa, was that from the late 15th century onwards, the area now known as the Western Cape was a geopolitical hotspot, even though it was so far south. In fact, it was significant *because* it was so far south. Several prosperous peoples, including the Portuguese, Dutch, French, British and Johnny-come-lately Americans, were on a global mission. They all wanted to control large swathes of the world, which meant commanding the high seas. The Far East, in particular, had riches galore to delight European monarchs, merchants and the growing middle classes, who found themselves with more than loose change to spare for rare luxury items such as silks and spices.

Indigenous Cape populations first got wind that something was afoot when they saw a Portuguese sailing ship off the coast around 1488, captained by the intrepid Bartolomeu Dias. Ominously, this brief initial encounter led to the first killing of an indigenous southern African by a European. The indigenous people had hurled stones; Dias retaliated with a crossbow. Already, a pattern was set.

The frequency of these strange marine sightings increased over the decades, as did the number of half-starved, half-drowned white people washing ashore from shipwrecks. At first, these vulnerable travellers received traditional Xhosa hospitality so they could recover and make their way to back to their home countries on the next passing ship. Some wreck survivors stayed with their hosts and integrated into Xhosa society, where a number prospered, starting a whole new dynasty. But there is evidence that this hospitality towards the maritime stragglers diminished in response to the hostility and avarice of the relentlessly encroaching white settlers.

If you could teleport yourself back a few centuries you'd soon realise that getting to Ceylon, Malaysia or Indonesia from Europe was a touch harder than wrestling with crying babies on an overcrowded Boeing 747 jumbo jet out of Lisbon, Paris or Amsterdam. Even the best mariners took months to reach these trading nirvanas, in ships made of timber, tar, rope and cloth, and powered only by the vagaries of winds and currents. These adventurous trips were so gruelling that many sailors would die on the journey, and those who survived could end up in pretty poor shape. It was not a venture for the faint-hearted. So, the mariners and their European investors established Cape Town as a 'refreshment station' – a place to break the colossal journey to the Far East in order to manage the sick, take on provisions and make repairs. The Cape of Good Hope, originally called *Cabo do Boa Esperança* by the Portuguese, grew in strategic global importance, with control shifting to the Dutch (via the Dutch East India Company) and then the British.

The problem for the Xhosa-speaking people of the Eastern Cape was that Europeans not only settled in the vicinity of Cape Town but by the late 17th century were starting to expand outwards and eastward towards Xhosa territory. Moreover, it became clear to the Xhosa that the white man wasn't leaving; he had no intention of going back to his home across the sea, as they'd first hoped. While there was trade between the Xhosa and their new white neighbours, it became obvious that the white man operated on a different set of rules, many of which conflicted with Xhosa tradition – none more so than the attitude towards land occupancy and stewardship. By 1702, some of the first clashes between Europeans and Xhosa had started.

The value and importance of cattle to Xhosa society at this time cannot be overstated. This bovine currency was the equivalent to modern-day cash, equity investments, stocks, shares, bitcoin, secured loans and credit cards. More cattle meant more milk, meat and leather for the family. More cattle meant more wives. Cattle was a ubiquitous symbol of wealth and success, and a means of securing the support and influence of others to protect you. In fact, without cattle it was difficult to even acquire, let alone maintain, power. Cattle, and therefore land to graze them on, was absolutely pivotal to Xhosa society. But land was never owned; it was not something you traded in, it simply existed for the common good. As long as everyone's cattle had enough grazing and water, there was never any need to buy or sell land.

Conflict between the colonialist Europeans and the Xhosa really started to heat up in the late 18th century, intensifying when the British took control of the Cape Colony in 1806. The new colonialists not only wanted administrative control and occupancy of the expanding Cape region by Europeans, but were prepared to import boatloads of assorted British people to achieve it – most notably in 1820, when about five thousand hopefuls from the British Isles made the epic journey to seek their fortune, finding a piece of Africa to own, farm and expand.

Trouble was brewing.

At a similar time, numerous evangelical missionary groups, such as the London Missionary Society, financed from the major cities of Europe and North America and led by larger-than-life personalities such as Jon van der Kemp and James Read, started to scatter far and wide through the Cape region. Many missionaries were driven by a zealous desire to save souls and usurp local culture, with their uncompromising notions of Christian values and Western civilization. They had the Bible in their hands and Protestant notions of God to back them up.

There began a lengthy period of vigorous evangelicalism and Western liberalism, the missionaries sometimes offsetting the worst excesses of the

Cattle have been at the heart of Xhosa society for centuries. They represented wealth and are still used symbolically in marriage negotiations. [Photo taken in 2020]

settlers and their colonial masters in the Cape by reporting the cruelties and injustices they witnessed on farms and in the newly settled towns. They were well connected, with direct access to politicians, newspapers and philanthropic groups in Europe that could influence policymaking and the governance of the region.

The pressure on the resident Xhosa people from settlers, colonial administrators and high-minded missionaries was increasingly broad and intense. All aspects of their culture came under attack, from how they dressed – nudity being frowned upon by the colonial and evangelical powers – to the seasonal movement of their cattle herds. The authority of the chiefs and diviners was systematically challenged and undermined, new colonial taxes were levied, the abundance of game to hunt declined due to overkill, family structures based on polygamy were roundly condemned, and even access to red clay for painting the body was restricted.

Many of the Dutch-speaking inhabitants of the Cape and its hinterland, who were called Boers, were none too chuffed at being pushed about by the British either, as they implemented new laws, abolished slavery and generally spread their Anglo-Saxon ways wherever they went. By the 1830s, many Boers became *voortrekkers*, and were literally upping sticks and moving north and east en masse to find new lands beyond the reach of their unwanted British masters. This seminal period of Boer history is known as the Great Trek, and it, too, was to add to the pressure on many tribal groups, including the Xhosa, as the *voortrekkers* advanced into Xhosa, Sotho and Zulu territory, provoking numerous bloody clashes.

The Xhosa people had no intention of going anywhere. They stood their ground. In their eyes, they had rightful custody of the land around the east coast and deep into the Cape region, for cattle grazing, crop production and building homes. What right had the white man from over the water to enter or control land lived on and administered by generations of Xhosa? And so, a tragedy of theatrical dimensions unfolded as local settlers of Dutch heritage and then British colonialists from the Cape, governed by London and supported by the machinery of empire, fought the Xhosa people in nine ugly wars, from 1779 to 1879.

The brutal Cape Frontier Wars or Xhosa Wars, as they are called, were increasingly racist and indiscriminate. They would prove catastrophic for the Xhosa people and their way of life, ultimately leading to the formation of Transkei. Relentlessly the settlers, the military and administrators moved east from Cape Town, occupying more and more Xhosa land, capturing more and more cattle, and reinforcing their dominance by naming traditional Xhosa lands Albany, Victoria, Crown Reserve and British Kaffraria.

Apart from having to defend themselves from the invading Dutch and British, from the 1820s the Xhosa people also had to deal with waves of aggressive intruders fleeing from the carnage and human turmoil of their north-eastern neighbours in the Zulu Kingdom. Here, King Shaka and his successors let loose repeated violent waves of ruthlessly efficient armies in the pursuit of power, land and cattle. These desperate, displaced souls, often called Fingo or Mfengu, disrupted and split the Xhosa tribes before some eventually became absorbed into Xhosa culture, forming part of the emerging Transkei. Others chose an opposite course of action, forming an allegiance with the British and fighting *against* the Xhosa in the later battles of the century-long conflict.

By the early 1850s, the Xhosa were already severely battered and demoralised, weakened by the relentless grind of an invading global empire and the modern machinery of war. Infighting among the various Xhosa royal families and chiefdoms played a part in their demise, too. Add to this the traumatic murder of the revered Paramount Chief Hintsa by British troops in 1835, the impact of a fatal cattle disease (bovine pneumonia), drought, spiritual, political and economic crises, and the Xhosa people in many areas were literally and metaphorically on their knees, seemingly defeated and without hope.

Loss of hope is a dangerous state to be in, as you are about to read.

This brings us on to the infamous Cattle Killing of 1856–57, a defining moment in the history of the Xhosa people and the eventual formation of the Transkei as a recognised administrative region.

In April 1856, a teenage girl, Nongqawuse from the Gxara River area, just inside the western boundary of Transkei, prophesised that the wretched British, their settlers and other enemy tribes (e.g. the Mfengu) would be defeated and driven into the sea for good. Healthy cattle would rise from the underworld to replace diseased herds, crops would be plentiful, and people would be furnished with the things they needed for a better life. Help to achieve this would come from their ancestors and the Russians, who, they heard, were giving the British a good run for their money in the Crimean War.

The prophetesses Nongqawuse and Nonkosi, who promoted the fatal Xhosa Great Cattle Killing of 1856–7. [Courtesy of Alamy Ltd]

The pool on the Gxara River where Nongqawuse heard her ancestors telling her that the Xhosa had to kill all their cattle in order to get rid of the European invaders and the Fingo, their enemy clans. [Photo taken in 2020]

According to Nongqawuse and her growing legion of supporters, called believers (*amathamba*), all the Xhosa had to do to rid themselves of their enemy, to recover their land and their healthy cattle and to prosper again with their ancestors was to kill all their own existing cattle, renounce witchcraft and destroy all their *own* crops by the appointed time. She had received these seemingly strange messages of hope from the ancestors while bathing in the Gxara River, near the Great Kei River. Her prophecy formed a heady and dangerous mixture of traditional and Christian beliefs, assuring a bright and prosperous outcome for true believers. Because they jeopardised the certainty of the millenarian prophecy, unbelievers (*amagogotya*) – those who refused to kill all their cattle – were castigated, their property, crops, livestock and persons physically attacked. Xhosa society quickly became divided between believers and unbelievers. Should you kill all your cattle and refuse to cultivate crops, as the teenage prophet instructed, or not? Deep, long-lasting schisms erupted between fathers and sons, wives and husbands, siblings and even across whole clans.

The appointed times for great tumultuous events came and went, and of course, the white people did not meet their watery end as promised, nor were the desperate Xhosa furnished with masses of healthy cattle and maize. This became known as the Great Disappointment. In fact, the consequences of Nongqawuse's prophecies and the believers' loyalty were brutal.

During the Cattle Killing of 1856–57, some 400,000 cattle were slaughtered, leading to the deaths of up to 50,000 Xhosa from starvation. Some survivors reportedly even turned to cannibalism. Human skeletons, particularly of the old and young, lay scattered along roadsides, alone and in family groups. Many died where they dropped, unable to walk one pace further. Dogs and vultures grew fat on the easy pickings.

Those who did not starve to death crawled into colonial settlements begging for food and help. The Cape authorities, led by Governor Sir George Grey, seemed to exploit the human suffering by failing to offer anything like adequate relief to tackle the mass starvation. Instead of supporting the charitable efforts of more humanitarian-minded souls, he took advantage of the starving Xhosa by forcing them into labour and service miles away in the Cape Colony, on low wages and meagre rations. In fact, you could argue that Sir George Grey used the tragedy of the Cattle Killing to tighten his grip on the region and undermine the authority of Xhosa chiefs. Some people even think that Grey instigated the Cattle Killing movement.

As the full scale of the tragedy emerged, a small group, led by the Xhosa chiefs and headmen, travelled further north and east, away from the Cape Colony, to escape the settlers and their military minders, joining their kin across the Great Kei River and up to the Mbashe River. These lands were already known as the Trans-Kei by a decree of the Cape administrators

Some experts believe that the Xhosa prophetess Nongqawuse spent time at the Gxara River waterfall. [Photo taken in 2020]

Mist near the Gxara River might have evoked images of the ancestors and Russians rising from the sea to save the Xhosa people from the British. [Photo taken in 2020]

who had set the Great Kei River as the border between the Cape Colony and the Trans-kei. Many Xhosa chiefs were hastily captured by Grey's men for their part in the Cattle Killing. He'd repeatedly warned them against the mass slaughter, concerned it would lead to civil unrest, uncontrolled population movements and another war against the settlers. The Cattle Killing was seen by Grey and his men on the ground as a dangerous catalyst to unite the Xhosa against colonial authority. He desperately wanted firm control of all aspects of Xhosa life, so a spontaneous mass slaughter of livestock, led by a teenage girl with maverick tendencies, was most certainly not part of his colonial plan. For their part in this colossal loss of human life and livestock, many of the believer chiefs were imprisoned for years on Robben Island, a desolate rocky outcrop off Cape Town. As you probably know, this hostile island was to serve as a place of incarceration in the 20th century for many leaders in South Africa's black liberation movement, including several high-profile Transkeians.

Nongqawuse, too, was arrested and sent to Cape Town as a prisoner, partly for her own safety, as she was vilified and vigorously denounced by her own people. Her name and the events she ignited are still matters of huge controversy in modern Xhosa culture, but that is a story for another day.

Chiefs Sarhili and Sandile, the last great independent chiefs of the Xhosa, and their followers, made a last-ditch attempt to defend the traditional Xhosa territories by fighting the Wedding Feast War, but by 1878 they had no choice but to throw in the towel. The Cape Frontier Wars, lasting one

The prophetess Nongqawuse convinced her followers that an army of Xhosa ancestors would rise from the sea at the mouth of the Great Kei River, among other places, to replenish their cattle and expel the white settlers. [Photo taken in 2020]

hundred years, could not continue a day longer. The damage to Xhosa culture, and the loss of land and cattle, had been colossal and irretrievable.

And so, by 1894, with the annexation of Pondoland in the east, all the Xhosa-speaking people between Cape Town and Natal, including the area known as 'the Trans-Kei', were under the administrative control of the Cape Colony, lock stock and barrel. The backbone of the chiefs' authority and their traditional rule had been broken. Military resistance was now futile and from the 1870s, Umtata, the future capital city of Transkei, was being established close to the Mthatha River as a military and magisterial post for the Cape administration.

It would be another one hundred excruciatingly long and torturous years before South Africa's first black president was to take office. Is it coincidence that the first black person to hold this great office of state, Nelson Mandela, was born and brought up in Transkei, the member of a distinguished Thembu family? Is it coincidence that Transkei was to be the birthplace of Thabo Mbeki (from Mbewuleni), the second president of a multiracial democracy in South Africa? In fact, Transkeians were to be absolutely integral in the leadership of the African National Congress (ANC) and the military wing, Umkhonto we Sizwe (Spear of the Nation), in the fight against apartheid, racism and the subjugation of the non-white population, leading to eventual multiracial democracy. Other notable anti-apartheid activists from Transkei included Oliver Tambo (from Bizana),

Govan Mbeki (from Nqamakwe), Walter Sisulu (from Engcobo), Winnie Mandela (from Bizana) and Chris Hani (from Cofimvaba), to name just a few. Steve Biko, the leader of the Black Consciousness Movement, who was murdered in prison by the South African security forces in 1977, was also a Xhosa-speaker, originally from the Eastern Cape (then still known as the Cape Province) close to the border of Transkei.

Growing racial segregation, race-based discrimination, reduced political power, land expropriation, a brutal security apparatus and waves of draconian legislation leading to the formal policy of apartheid after 1948 were the hammers and tongs to violently and uncompromisingly shape much of Transkei in the 20th century.

So, for example, with the introduction of a 'hut tax' from the late 1800s, many Transkeian men were forced to seek paid work or to sell their produce. A further and more significant consequence was the start of the mass migrant movement of black people, over long distances, to seek work in the emerging mining, agricultural and industrial businesses owned by white South Africans. Many women eventually also left their homes and children in Transkei to work for white people in domestic service. For decades, this dislocation of young people was to be a crucial factor in the disruption and disintegration of traditional Xhosa family structures, leading to a range of crippling social ills that had not previously existed.

The Transkei, as a region primarily for Xhosa-speaking people to live in, complied nicely with the Whites' enthusiastic implementation of apartheid (separateness), demonstrating, in their minds, how Blacks and Whites could live separately, each shaping their own destiny. In truth, the white population of South Africa acquired most of the land (roughly 87 per cent), the best land and the high-value resources (such as minerals, fertile agricultural land and infrastructure built by black labour), and then literally forced millions of black people, often against their will, to live in one of ten designated homelands or Bantustans, like Transkei, based on their perceived tribal origins. Except for the purposes of work, white people did not want black people in their vicinity. They wanted them in designated areas only, where they had limited autonomy over their lives. As a result, the Transkei was forced to accommodate many newly dislocated black people, irrespective of whether they wanted to be there or knew the area, or whether there were adequate facilities, infrastructure and jobs when they arrived.

It seems barely credible now, but shortly before apartheid was set in stone in 1948, Umtata received a royal visit from none other than King George VI, Queen Elizabeth, and Princesses Elizabeth and Margaret. The main purpose of their tour had been to open the South African parliament in

Cape Town a few days earlier and reinforce bonds with Great Britain. However, on 5 March 1947, Thembu, Xhosa and Mpondo chiefs and their numerous followers, from all over Transkei, marched into town, in festive mood, to present their esteemed foreign visitors with a gold-embossed scroll, to take home as a memento. Sepia photos, in the Royal Collection Trust, catch the moment the British royal family met the crowds and chiefs in the town square and the Fort Gale area. These images convey a time and a world that feels so utterly different from the early 21st century.

The Tomlinson Commission, compiled for the South African government in the early 1950s, recommended what was needed for Transkei and the other Bantustans to survive and prosper as 'reserves' for the black population. Little or no heed was paid to these recommendations. By 1980, Bantustans represented a significant proportion of the South African population, but only a small amount of the country's overall wealth, as measured by gross domestic product.

In addition to a growing population, the Transkei had to deal with soil erosion, the prevalence of malnutrition, high levels of disease, poor levels of education, unpopular land and stock management practices,

King George VI, Queen Elizabeth, Princess Elizabeth (HM Queen Elizabeth II) and Princess Margaret meeting Transkei's dignitaries outside Umtata Town Hall in 1947. [Photograph by permission of Royal Collection Trust / © Her Majesty Queen Elizabeth II 2020]

and insufficient commercial investment to provide jobs. The situation had deteriorated to such an extent that by the early 1960s, thousands of people in Pondoland, in eastern Transkei, were hostile and in open revolt, with the dissent suppressed only after the security forces killed eleven people and injured many more in the Ngquza Hill Massacre.

As part of South Africa's ruse to convince the outside world of the merit of apartheid, they granted the Transkei what they called internal self-government in 1963. With the Thembu Chief Kaiser Matanzima at the helm in Transkei, there was a push for an independent Transkei, which they celebrated in 1976. It even had a nice national flag and an anthem.

The Transkei coat of arms proclaimed *Imbumba Yamanyama* – unity is strength. But Transkei wasn't independent in any meaningful way. The real power and the purse strings were still controlled by politicians sitting in a Whites-only parliament in Cape Town and Pretoria, promoting the best interests of the white population. No one was hoodwinked, except Kaiser and his entourage, who celebrated their achievement at home and abroad. The United Nations, African states and the rest of the world were certainly not convinced. It was pseudo-independence, a sham, and one that failed to convince the black resistance movement in South Africa, particularly the ANC. The Transkei had been turned into a dumping ground for two and a half million black people by 1976 and an easy source of cheap labour for white industry. This was the pseudo-morality of separate development, and the symbols of sovereignty were only veneers.

After the Matanzima brothers fell from grace in 1986 and 1987, Stella Sigcau succeeded them. She'd barely got her feet under the table when General Bantu Holomisa elbowed her out, using military force. By 1994, with the arrival of multiracial elections and a new constitution, all the Bantustans were dissolved, and Transkei was fully integrated into South Africa as a region of the Eastern Cape. Strange as it may seem, many Transkeians had been very proud of their pseudo-'country' and even mourned its loss, as the flag of white, green and red ochre was lowered for the last time.

I find the history of this small part of Africa epic and quite tragic, detailing the decline of a once great people by the ruthless imposition of white rule and law. The spirit of the people was never entirely crushed, as is evidenced in the huge contribution this region made to the struggle against apartheid, with many of its original leaders being Xhosa people. There was a buoyancy, a pride, and a strong sense of community amongst the Transkeian people, aligned to reserves of deep spirituality which I got to glimpse, but never quite understand.

15

The Great Kei River

Many readers will have travelled internationally one way or another. Some may have caught a local bus from Botswana to South Africa, or flown to a sunny destination to relax on a beach in Spain, for example. Some of you may be big shots, frequently flying first class to glamorous business destinations like Chicago or Hong Kong. Whether you're the backpacker, the wheeler-dealer or the beach lover, most of us have had the pleasure of going through border checks and passport control. Seldom is this an uplifting experience.

South African border officials were zealous users of passport stamps as I travelled frequently in and out of Transkei.

What is it about people who check your passport? They're always so serious, suspicious, scrutinising you as though you've done something wrong, even when you're innocently returning to your home country. You may have attended a conference at which you explained how to save millions of lives, cure cancer or prevent global warming, but do they care? Not a sausage.

I must confess to having pinched the in-flight magazine once or twice, which raised my guilty look. And I once accidently brought a rogue banana into the United States. It was either Houston or Los Angeles, I'm not sure which. This resulted in me being immediately diverted out of the normal passport processing system, through several clinical glass-walled corridors to see uniformed administrators for questioning about the source of the errant fruit, before being escorted to the deviant fruit removal area where the offending yellow object, now bruised, was placed in a plastic container by a cautious uniformed woman wearing blue disposable gloves. There weren't too many smiles en route through this fruit eradication maze, which I shared with a group of confused Latinos, mainly from Honduras, El Salvador, and Mexico. I'm not sure if the banana was incinerated or consumed, but we were never going to enjoy each other's company again.

In my experience the world over, border control folk are not the most charming or welcoming. I give them some latitude by assuming they've recently had a family bereavement or are in the middle of a messy divorce. It's as though in this profession they're never given the 'customer service' part of the training. They all have to complete the 'how to look severe and menacing' part of the training course with distinction, leaving no time for learning how to make people feel comfortable as they arrive after a long and tiring journey.

Things were no different at the Great Kei Bridge border crossing between Transkei and the Republic of South Africa. Transkei may have been a puppet state to the rest of the world, but it suited the South African government to treat it as a separate nation, and so a hard border existed. A border crossing that spoke volumes.

Not only is the Great Kei River historically symbolic as the border of the area over which many of the Xhosa were finally pushed, but it is also scenically spectacular. The river flows in a deep gorge, the road in and out of the valley surrounded by craggy rocks, amazing views and lush vegetation. This is important, as I was to see more of it than I planned or wanted to.

Fortunately for me, and unlike the Xhosa people of the previous century, I made this crossing without having to wrestle with arrogant

Driving speeds were regulated by the sudden roadside appearance of cattle, goats, sheep, dogs and horses.

19th-century British Army officials such as Lieutenant-General Sir Harry Smith and Major-General Sir Henry Somerset, belligerent European farmers or angry displaced Zulus – only the South African border guards. These border patrol chaps were as neat as a whistle, with short hair, crisply ironed shirts and occasionally a peak hat. Whichever way I was travelling, the suspicious and earnest young men of the South Africa border patrol would make an inspection of the vehicle, ask to see the passports of my Transkeian and South African passengers and invite me inside to a glass-fronted booth to answer the same questions every time about what I was doing and where I was going. Stickers were applied to my passport and the obligatory rubber stamp thumbed down and I was good to go. I did not warm to them, nor they to me. They were forever suspicious of a young white guy choosing to work in a Bantustan with black people.

On 29 January 1980 I was still a fresher in this neck of the woods. Doug and I were in one van with a couple of the children and their luggage, and Sister Genevieve was in another van with a couple of children we'd picked up in and around East London. We were now returning to Ikhwezi. It seemed like plain sailing.

We drove down the valley in tandem to the South African border crossing on the Great River Kei. As soon as we came to a halt, Sister Genevieve hopped out of her van looking a little flustered, and came over to Doug and me. Apparently, we were missing the passport of one of the children in my van. My suggestion that we might negotiate with the border officials, explaining our unfortunate predicament in order to continue our journey, was rejected in the blink of an eye by the good sister as 'not a good idea'. The ever resourceful, pragmatic and action-orientated sister had an alternative plan and she was already implementing it before the noses of the South African border guards could smell mischief.

Sister Genevieve's idea was to hide the poor passport-less child under a mountain of luggage, out of view of the border staff, thus negating the need for his passport. Before Doug or I could object or challenge the wisdom of this approach, she was taking suitcases and string bundles from the rear of my van and stacking them over the hapless child. While there was plenty of luggage to do the job, the biggest obstacle to this cross-border escapade was the child himself. He was a willing party to the ruse, but his body posed a significant obstacle to its success, being as stiff as a board. The unfortunate teenager had a dreadful disease where his whole body was gradually becoming more rigid, so bending limb joints was not possible. It was therefore very difficult to get him to hug the contours of the van seat and the rapidly encroaching luggage. Did

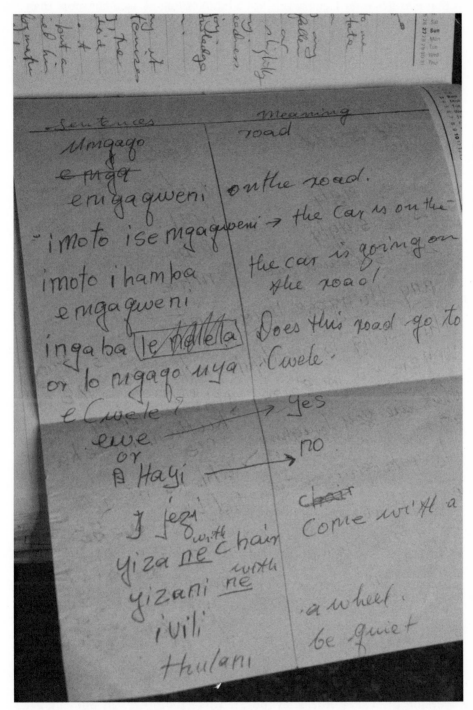

After getting horribly lost en route to Cwele, my isiXhosa lessons included practical phrases such as, 'Uh … does this road lead to Cwele?'

that perturb Sister Genevieve? Not a bit. Nothing pleased her more than cocking a snoop at authority, black or white. When it came to getting one over on someone with a uniform she was colour blind. I thought she was a very fine woman then, and I still do today.

Her deception worked a treat. However, whilst our passport-deficient boy went undetected by the prying eyes of the eager border custodians, we did not know that the exciting part of the day had not yet begun.

As I started up the van with a couple of children and my smuggled passenger in the back and Doug in the front passenger seat, a very smiley and mischievous Sister Genevieve drove up parallel to us, window down, and shouted, 'I'll race you to Butterworth!'

While I was a little confused at the prospect of racing a nun, I accepted the challenge. No need to engage the brain here. So, much to her surprise, Team Doug, hidden passenger and Treive were off, stealing a march over the bridge and starting our ascent out of the valley. Delivering two pints of milk and three strawberry yoghurts to the doorstep of 23 Wisteria Crescent in Godalming now seemed like another universe. I had my foot to the floor of an Ikhwezi-branded van, racing a nun up a steep valley to a town 35 kilometres away. What's more, we were winning. Or so we thought.

The road was getting steeper, twisting and turning, exposed rock on one side, a steep ravine on the other. In my wing mirror, a healthy distance back, I caught sight of the other Ikhwezi van in hot pursuit. We were feeling pretty pleased with our lot when, like an exhausted donkey flogged one time too many, our van started to run out of steam. She was making a lot more noise and going a lot more slowly. Pressure on the accelerator made no difference. Desperate verbal coaxing from us made no impact either, amazingly. Our mechanical donkey had had enough; our engine was giving up the will to live. Of greater concern was not so much our mechanical fragility but the fact that our race competitor was now overtaking us. Our competitive and mischievous ecclesiastical adversary smiled as she cruised by, adding to our growing sense of failure and vulnerability.

We literally ground to a halt, exposed on the slope of the Great Kei River Valley.

The humour of the occasion ebbed away rapidly. This was not a good place to break down – halfway up a steep valley 30-odd kilometres from the nearest town. Thoughts of beating Sister Genevieve, in a Transkei version of *Wacky Races*, evaporated like the power in our engine, switching instead to eliciting her urgent help. By flashing the headlights and sounding the horn of my moribund vehicle, we caught her attention just before she disappeared round the next bend.

While she returned to see what was up, I made a cursory inspection of the engine, finding that we had no oil in the sump. Not a drop. Nada. Rien. Zilch. It was the equivalent of our proverbial donkey without hay. This van was going absolutely nowhere and so our collective thoughts turned to what we should do next. Smiles were thin on the ground – that is, until we heard a muted cry for help from inside the deceased vehicle. In all the excitement of the race and the unfolding drama we'd forgotten about the smuggled boy, still covered in miscellaneous baggage. Realising our dreadful oversight broke the tension and we excavated the young man, who offered a smile of relief as he came up for air.

A plan was hatched. As much of the luggage as possible and our passengers were to be transferred to the sister's van. She would drop Doug at Butterworth to find help while she pushed on to Umtata with all the children. I was to remain with the crippled vehicle. And so, the Great Kei River caper unfolded.

I was now alone on what was then a quiet road, with wonderful panoramic views down to the Great Kei River and a succession of steep overlapping valleys and ravines. On the passenger side of the van, not more than a metre away, were bare cracked boulders rising up several metres, decorated by coarse roots, bushes and the ubiquitous aloes of

Waiting to be rescued with my broken-down Ikhwezi van in the Great Kei River Valley as a proper Transkeian thunderstorm approached.

the area. From my spectacular vantage point, dark, churning clouds were distinctly visible on the horizon, with an undulating opaque curtain of rain close behind. If I'd been on a top-dollar tourist trip I'd have been getting my money's worth, but I wasn't on a comfortable guided tour; I was alone and stuck in an unfamiliar location, with little understanding of how I was to get home. All my hopes were pinned on Doug returning with the metaphorical cavalry.

Exhausted by the excesses of the day so far, and feeling secure at the prospect of the imminent return of my travelling partner with rescuers, I lay on the back seat of the van and fell into a deep sleep before you could say 'racing nun'.

I had very little idea of how long I slept, but I was deep in la-la land when I was woken suddenly by the ear-splitting sound of thunder and the vibration of the van, literally shaking in the explosion of a Transkeian thunderstorm. Not only was my tin-can protection shaking to the roar of thunder, it became a cacophonous cell as sheets of rain bombarded it. I rose, groggy from my deep sleep, to peer out of the window, and could see no further than a few metres. The spectacular panoramic views were completely obscured by low cloud and the heavy downpour. It all felt rather claustrophobic and unnerving. My sinking feeling sank a little more, but I told myself that Doug would be back to rescue me soon. All was not lost.

Time was hard to judge. I wasn't wearing a watch and the sun was blocked by cloud. I don't know how long Doug took, but come eventually he did, pleased as punch to be the rescuer. The cavalry had arrived, or so I thought. But my euphoria was short-lived.

Doug hopped into the front seat from out of the rain, mumbling something about the difficult trip he'd had. I wasn't interested. I'd been trapped in a tin can with Armageddon going on around me. Sympathy was in short supply.

So where was the tow truck? There *was* no tow truck! What had he done? Proudly he pulled a pint of engine oil from his shoulder bag. One pint! One tiny, measly pint of oil! Was that all? Our van engine was thirstier than a bull elephant at a dry watering hole. One pint of oil would barely touch the sides of the engine. We needed gallons of the liquid gold to breathe life into our dilapidated mule.

It would be fair to say that there were a few tense moments as I realised that there would be no cavalry rescuing us and Doug explained that there was little else he could have done. He'd had almost no money, he explained, and just getting back to me with the oil had been a challenge in itself.

Shit. We were now in a right fucking mess. Bollocks, bollocks, bollocks! Thumping the steering wheel only exacerbated the situation and ratcheted up the tension another notch. I didn't want to spend one more minute stuck on the side of this valley shaken by thunder. The atmosphere was tense in more ways than one.

It was time for a clear head. Stick together and put your best foot forward, I thought. 'Cometh the hour, cometh the man' and all that. Time for fewer profanities and more action.

Step number one: thank Doug. Step number two: put one pint of oil in the engine. Step number three: let the oil settle. Step number four: cross my fingers. Step number five: turn the van ignition key. Voila! The mechanical old beast started. She actually started! Unbelievable! A miracle! She sounded troubled and feeble, but she had been resuscitated, just. If it had been a human operation, we'd have heard the cardiac monitor pinging again as a green line peaked and troughed on the oscilloscope screen. She continued to judder and splutter but she didn't give up the ghost yet.

The mood changed in an instant. Doug was now a hero! It looked as though he had saved the day. It was nervous smiles all round in the front seats of our Ikhwezi van. Keen to be anywhere but on this steep slope of the Great Kei River valley, I gingerly engaged the clutch, using more carrot than stick, and we crawled forward, Doug and I looking at each other in surprise and delight – 5 kilometres per hour, 10 kilometres per hour, 15 kilometres per hour. To improve matters the rain started to abate, so we could see where we were going and we were now doing nearly 20 kilometres per hour! After a few bends the road started to level out and we'd reached the top of the river valley, with undulating road ahead of us.

Dare I think of supper or a cup of tea? No. Our unplanned adventure was not over, not by a long chalk …

Before long the patient was losing the will to live again, and our van got slower, and slower, and slower. We knew the signs and we ground to a halt. The good news was we weren't far from the town of Butterworth now. The bad news was the rain had resumed in proper African style. It wasn't a gentle English spring shower. The traffic on the road was quiet, but we frantically flagged down a passing truck, hopped in the back and were soon in Butterworth, where we tracked down Charlotte, another Project Trust volunteer who worked in the local hospital.

Our spirits rose significantly at the prospect of calling Sister Dolorata or Sister Mary Paule back at Ikhwezi and her sending someone to collect

With very little money, getting out of Butterworth proved difficult. Doug's attempts at hitchhiking drew a blank, so we tried our luck at the bus station.

us. But that wasn't going to happen – all the telephone lines were dead. So we resigned ourselves to spending the night at Butterworth Hospital, sleeping in the staff quarters, before calling for help the following day.

Matters were not much better in the morning, as telephones were still down. We got a garage to tow the Ikhwezi van off the road into the repair shop, where the diagnosis was poor and several days of mechanical work were forecast. I didn't fancy having to report that back to Sister Dolorata, but there were more pressing problems to solve.

As money was low, we tried hitchhiking out of Butterworth, which drew a blank. Next we located the bus station, but to us rookies it looked like a piece of muddy open ground and all very chaotic. People were milling about, seeming to know what they were doing, but we were at sixes and sevens. We couldn't see any signs, postings or boards communicating which buses were going where, and there was a distinct lack of buses. To the local people we must have looked like a right couple of lemons standing there. Which we were.

Then the whole place gained a greater sense of urgency and collective momentum, affecting everyone except us, rooted to the muddy spot, still looking and acting like lemons. A huge, grunting articulated bus barged into the open ground and before it was even stationary a semicircle of local people many rows deep surrounded the entrance door. We had absolutely no idea where the bus was going, but everyone else did. Our hearts sank and our spirits ebbed away as it became apparent that this was the bus to Umtata. Umtata, our destination! This should have been our means of escape. But we were two penniless blokes in a muddy patch further from the bus than anyone else. As there were many more people hustling to get on the bus than seats, we didn't stand a chance.

Our faces told how dejected we felt and we exchanged a few words. What should we do next? Go back to the hospital or start hitchhiking? While we were licking our wounds, the bus driver, a young white guy alongside his black co-driver, beckoned to us. At first Doug and I looked around trying to fathom who they meant, until the penny dropped that it was us being summoned. The local people crowding the bus realised before we did, and parted, forming a path through the crowd to the drivers. We were more conspicuous than a bacon sandwich at a bar mitzvah. Everyone's eyes were on us as we walked to the front and the driver's cabin.

I assumed they wanted to know what two young white people were doing in Butterworth, but instead they were offering us the first two seats on the bus. We looked at them in surprise and concern. They explained that we had two options: return to the back of the crowd and not catch a bus for at least another six hours, perhaps longer, or take up their offer to jump the queue. By this stage the whole crowd had worked out what was being said and we could feel their reproachful gaze. What a dilemma. I thought the previous day had been challenging, but things were not getting any easier. At that moment I'd have swapped my predicament in Butterworth for my mundane milk round in Guildford.

As Doug and I procrastinated, the drivers opened the bus door and showed us in. We rapidly secreted ourselves at the very back of the bus, making ourselves as small and inconspicuous as possible as everyone else, chickens and all, clambered on board. They knew where we were hiding. They knew what had gone on.

In all my time in Transkei I encountered very little animosity or hostility from local people. In fact, I was constantly surprised that there wasn't more demonstrable resentment towards me because of my race and British background. If I had been black and had to live with apartheid I would have let a couple of arrogant young whites know what I thought about them and their privileges. This reticence to confront was not shared by the Xhosa gentleman of about sixty years old in the seat in front of us, who told us in no uncertain terms, during our three-hour journey, what he thought of us, our behaviour and our stinking privilege. We couldn't move away, nor could we disagree with a single word he said. He had a few points to make, and of course he was right. To start with, he objected to white people being in Transkei. It was a place for black people, he insisted. There was the rest of South Africa for people like us.

As a man of sixty-ish in age, he would have been born in the early 1920s, when family members would have had memories from the late 19th century of white settlers coming from the west, taking their ancestral land by force. He may have been taught how many of the great Xhosa chiefs and their followers had been killed or subdued by repeated waves of settlers, their commandos and military force. He'd as likely as not have experienced the worst of apartheid and the deteriorating circumstances of his people: Pass Laws, Bantustans, the migratory labour system, the banning of any meaningful representation or protest. He had every right to tell Doug and me what he thought of us and what we represented. But it did make for a long and difficult journey.

We arrived back at Ikhwezi rather hoping to be treated like the prodigal sons, but we were in for a rude surprise. Failing to check the van's oil level before leaving for East London was going to cost the mission over eight hundred rand in repairs. In her no-nonsense Dutch accent, Sister Dolorata laid the blame firmly at my door. She demanded better in future.

And if I expected to lounge about recuperating after our self-enforced hardship, I was mistaken. She'd already called Mr Gray from our local repair garage in Umtata. He'd be picking me up in the next day or so to return to Butterworth to collect the resuscitated van. I'd had enough of Butterworth for a lifetime. I'd just escaped. Even now the mention of the town grates.

And so, reluctantly, I found myself returning to Butterworth in Mr Gray's pickup truck. The place was proving a trap for me. Mr Gray was of slim build, medium height, white, probably in his thirties, with a moustache and longish hair in a style that had been fashionable in Europe in the early 1970s. He was casually dressed, as you might expect a garage supervisor to be.

He wasn't a natural conversationalist, and neither was I, but we had a few hours on the road together and, besides, our forced companionship was a novelty for both of us. He didn't get to meet a British teenager often, if ever, and I hadn't met many white working men from Umtata. We were a bit awkward at first, but he ended up explaining how he admired Ikhwezi and the work done to help the unfortunate children. To my utter surprise, he confessed that he couldn't come into the mission to see the children as he found it too upsetting. Here was a man who looked and sounded like a typical white South African alpha male and he was telling me that the sight of disabled Bantu children made him upset. I tried explaining that he should overcome his natural inclination, as Ikhwezi was an unusually happy place where children received an opportunity many in southern Africa could only dream of. He confessed that he was aware of all this and preferred to show his respect through donations and by discounting his garage work to the mission.

At the same time, like many white people I came across in South Africa, he had deep-rooted racial prejudices that he wanted to express, whether I wanted to hear them or not. Firstly, he disliked Afrikaners. In his hierarchy of prejudices I think he may have disliked them the most, but I chose not to quiz him for fear of causing offence, especially as he was buying lunch for me and ensuring my safe return home. He didn't elaborate on why Afrikaners incurred his displeasure, but he insisted on calling them big hairy rock spiders, and this was not as a term of endearment.

I expected him to tell me what he thought of black people in a similarly derogatory style, but I suspect the fact that I was living and working with black people persuaded him to think better of it. But his attitude to the black population became abundantly clear when we stopped for lunch at a Golden Egg fast food restaurant. Up until this point I'd enjoyed his company; we'd been two blokes having a conversation about this and that, laughing at his description of big hairy rock spiders and discussing the vagaries of life in Umtata. In the restaurant, in the company of black waiters and waitresses, his whole demeanour changed. He started playing the big-man role, snapping orders without the common courtesy of a please or thank you. His behaviour in this situation spoke volumes and I didn't like it. I did not want to be sitting with someone who was so blatantly rude to other people because of their race. You can point the finger at me, though, since Doug and I had accepted a seat on the bus ahead of everyone else at Butterworth station only a few days earlier. We'd been rude and discourteous in our own way.

A couple of days after returning the repaired van to Ikhwezi, I bumped into Sister Genevieve, the instigator of the Great Kei River caper-cum-farce. After explaining the various troubles Doug and I had been through, she laughed loudly in an uninhibited way, amused at our protracted return, and confirmed with delight that she'd still won the race to Butterworth as mechanical failure was no excuse on our part. It was a rude awakening and valuable lesson. Ikhwezi and the sisters were not as soft as I'd expected.

After this little incident I made sure Monday became van oil inspection day.

16

Mr Bidla and the Various Mrs Bidlas

Mr Bidla, or 'Driver' as he was sometimes known, was a character. He was frequently intoxicated at work, often grumpy, belligerent and cantankerous. And those were just his good points. I liked Mr Bidla, and so did Sister Mary Paule – some of the time. Cantankerous was a description I used to describe my late Granny Phyllis and I loved her a great deal.

My friend, the incorrigible Mr Bidla, outside his township home.

Mr Bidla wasn't always easy to like. He was often hard to find in the extensive grounds of Ikhwezi, especially as he knew every quiet secluded place where he could keep a low profile or sleep. Because of his drinking and general unreliability, he was transferred from driving duties to heading up the gardening team. He didn't like taking instructions, particularly from the nuns, and always had a ready answer when things hadn't been done, which was often. I think he thought that a gentleman like him shouldn't be taking directions from women. But the place was run by women, from top to bottom, and extremely efficiently, too.

As I'd sussed out most of his hiding holes, I would sometimes seek out Mr Bidla during my lunch break to pass the time and chew the fat. He was of slim build and medium height with very dark skin, creased from working outdoors in the blazing Transkei sun. The strong light appeared to have taken a toll on his eyes, too, as they had various distinctive blemishes, and his teeth were a little worse for wear. I'm not painting a very flattering picture am I? He was distinguished by a battered trilby-type hat that he wore frequently on his greying head, and a blazer or sports jacket that had seen better days many years earlier.

While he often wanted to complain to me about the nuns and his workload, I preferred to steer the conversation towards his life and background to learn more about life in Transkei. It didn't take much for him to start talking about his wife in the country. He stressed 'his wife *in the country*' in a way that led me to believe he must have others, which of course he did.

Mrs Bidla clearly had the measure of her husband. While he lived in Ngangelizwe township with his town wife, she lived in the country on their smallholding. I was unclear about how the country Mrs Bidla felt about the town Mrs Bidla. I think she just tolerated the situation, but the country Mrs Bidla knew how to manage her husband and constrain the ambitions of her counterpart in town. At the end of every month, on payday, the country Mrs Bidla would schlep into Umtata to take her cut of the wages before Mr Bidla frittered it on non-essentials, as she saw it, like alcohol. Smart woman, I thought. Once she'd sequestrated her portion of the pay she was off, pronto, preferring not to hang around longer than necessary, leaving Mr Bidla and town Mrs Bidla to drink and party as they chose, which is what they did.

My understanding of this sequence of monthly matrimonial musical chairs wasn't based only on Mr Bidla's word. I witnessed it first-hand. I got to know Mr Bidla well enough to be invited to his residence in the township (or 'location' as townships were also known), and I visited the

Left: One of Mr Bidla's drinking circle who enjoyed home-made mielie meal beer or *umqombothi.*

Below: Umtata's Ngangelizwe township, situated close to Ikhwezi, where poor-quality houses were jam-packed.

area frequently enough so that on other occasions I might call unannounced and receive a warm welcome. I use the word 'residence' for his home deliberately as it wasn't a house as most people might perceive a house to be. Like many residences in the township, it was small, always crowded, and fairly flimsy in structure, made partly of brickwork, partly of wood board, dried mud, corrugated iron and other miscellaneous materials. The small yard at the front consisted of hard or soft bumpy earth depending on the weather. An ad hoc fence of sticks and wire defined the boundary, beyond which rested a smashed-up abandoned car. Many of the township's houses were like this, sandwiched shoulder to shoulder, without a cigarette paper's gap between them, and lacking basic amenities.

There were many higher grades of residence in the location, but Mr Bidla and town Mrs Bidla's was towards the bottom end of the scale, in the less salubrious area. Rent for his humble dwelling was about eleven rand per month. Even in and around his own home he was a little nervous, slightly on edge, with one eye on the street. Thieves were always a worry, but not his principal concern. That privilege was held by the debt collector, who was a constant bane in his life, as a game of cat-and-mouse was played out.

Mr Bidla was never happier than when drinking locally brewed mielie meal (crushed maize) beer from a large tin container, holding court with his entourage of mates. Mielie meal beer, known as *umqombothi*, had an unusual consistency for beer, and was unlikely to win the admiration of any beer appreciation society that I knew of. It was thicker than Guinness, like a thin gruel or porridge in consistency. As for the taste, it didn't hit the spot for me either. Nevertheless, in the interests of cultural exchange and the broadening of my horizons, I sat down with Mr Bidla, accompanied by a huddle of his buddies, and drank *umqombothi* from the communal tin can. It was apparent that my friend had some authority among his companions, who listened attentively to him. I was polite enough in my praise of the beer so as not to cause offence, but not so insincere as to create a false impression of delight. *Entente cordiale* won the day.

I got to know the ins and outs of the township pretty well and was sometimes recognised by residents as a helper from Ikhwezi. I got to meet and chat with the township's *tsotsis* or gangsters on one of my very early morning forays to take photographs. They were so shocked to see a white man in shorts walking the streets of the township alone at 6 a.m. one Sunday that they approached me to find out what I was doing there. Our curiosity was mutual. As their English was poor and my Xhosa even worse we used the universal language of smiles and hand signals to communicate and defuse any tension, which there was at first. Strange as the encounter

I often walked around the township by myself or with a Transkeian friend, meeting other residents and chatting. To my surprise, I never encountered any animosity.

was, we gently and safely allowed our two distinct and separate worlds to collide as we exchanged goodwill through the lens of my camera.

That said, I had a rule of always leaving the township by nightfall and never drinking too much alcohol while there. On payday and on Friday nights in particular the township was not a safe place to linger for anyone. It could get a little lively and violent. While most people ignored, tolerated or even enjoyed the novelty of a naïve white teenager in their midst now and again, I didn't want to overstay my welcome nor make myself a target for those harbouring understandable resentments. So after sharing a few beers with Mr Bidla and his buddies, I would slip away up the slope to Ikhwezi, perhaps dropping in at the home of one of the teachers or the school secretary's family en route.

One day at lunchtime, when Mr Bidla and I were having one of our chats in the mission grounds, he was noticeably grumpier than usual, which was pretty grumpy by any measure. After some gentle probing it emerged that his foul mood was not caused by the usual suspects of nuns, fellow gardeners or his town wife. I deduced that country Mrs Bidla might be the root cause of his displeasure. Bingo. Indeed, country Mrs Bidla was the cause of his angst. More precisely, money – his money and the lack of it – were the root cause. It was becoming

Above: Many Transkeians were quite religious. A group of Zionists out celebrating and recruiting.

Below: This Ikhwezi gardener, who enjoyed the occasional drink, was always hospitable when I turned up.

abundantly clear to me that country Mrs Bidla was *way* too smart for our head gardener. He was out of his depth when country Mrs Bidla was on the scene.

I should say at this point that Sister Mary Paule had read the tea leaves correctly many weeks earlier and shared with me her view that Mr Bidla was no match for his rural wife. And so it proved.

Not only had country Mrs Bidla arranged a robust system to get her share of his wages, but she had also got her paws on the *lobola* (dowry) money paid to the family recently by a young man's family just prior to the marriage of their daughter. While my grumpy friend had designs on entertaining himself, his buddies and town Mrs Bidla on the *lobola*, his shrewd and persistent wife in the country had other, more sensible ambitions for the money. Mr Bidla was feeling poor and outsmarted, which on reflection was a pretty accurate assessment of his situation.

During my extended conversations on more mundane matters with Mr Bidla, I learnt about rural life in Transkei, including how to grow mielies, the staple food. Like many farmers, he grew his *dagga* among the mielie crop so it would be less visible to nosey police officers. *Dagga* had been successfully grown in the Eastern Cape for centuries as a drug for recreational and spiritual use by the San, Khoikhoi and Bantu tribes, including Xhosa speakers. Even today, Lusikisiki Green from Pondoland in Transkei is regarded as the champagne of weed by some seasoned potheads in South Africa, or so I've been told.

Opportunity knocked for Mr Bidla.

In response to his probing, I confessed to not having tried *dagga* or any other recreational drug. This he found amusing and smiled. Where I came from, I explained, recreational drugs were the preserve of middle-class people and hippies, who were often the same people. I would have to confess to having hippy tendencies by virtue of my hair length, my peace badge and predilection for progressive rock music. Mr Bidla was now grinning in a knowing, predatory manner.

That I had never tried recreational drugs may actually be slightly inaccurate. Aged thirteen I'd been to a Pink Floyd concert at the Liverpool Empire where the hippy density had been at the maximum level achievable. It had been a hippy epicentre. The air had been full of smoke that had a very distinctive smell, sweeter than cigarettes, and everyone was mellow. Based on the fact I had sat through a two-and-a-half-hour show, I can only assume I had enjoyed the benefits of the fragrant weed for the

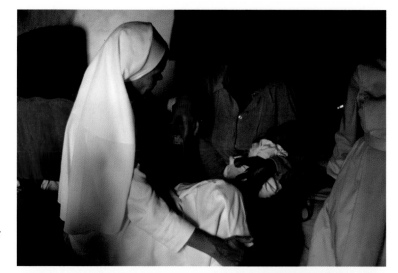

1. Sister Mary Paule, doing what she often did – providing care to a vulnerable mother and her malnourished infant.

2. Out and about, visiting Ikhwezi workers settling into their new homes, Sister Mary Paule always cut a distinctive figure.

3. Dusty in winter but muddy in summer, the long straight road from Umtata to Ikhwezi.

Above left: 4. Doug, from Scotland, and Babs, from Switzerland, were my work colleagues and friends at Ikhwezi.

Left: 5. Villages hugged the contours of a typical Transkeian landscape.

Below: 6. The silhouette of traditional Transkeian huts (*amakhaya*) at sunset.

Above: 7. Much of Transkei was rural, where mielies (maize) was one of the main crops grown near the home.

Below: 8. *Amakhaya* with thatched roofs often extended for miles across the undulating Transkeian landscape.

Left: 9. Collecting Ikhwezi students meant driving many miles to remote villages on dirt roads. Sometimes roads were non-existent and the trip quite an adventure.

Below left: 10. Even in 1980, many rural Transkeians needed to live close to a river to access water for themselves, their crops and their livestock.

Below: 11. Tranquillity in Transkei – a morning view across the misty valley from a village kraal.

Above: 12. In the racially divisive world of apartheid, the sight of a white man helping a blind black athlete run around a cinder track in Durban momentarily restored my faith in human kindness. It was a sight I've never forgotten and never will.

Right: 13. Many of Ikhwezi's students were packed, ready and happy to see us when we arrived to collect them from their homes.

Above left: 14. An Ikhwezi student by candlelight, at Easter.

Above right: 15. Ikhwezi students, all of whom had a range of severe physical and mental disabilities, received care from a wonderful team of nurses.

16. Sister Maria Corda lighting candles in the Ikhwezi chapel for Easter celebrations.

17. After-care students joined the younger Ikhwezi Scouts and Guides on our musical fundraising day.

18. Kirri Philiswa Maqume, an Ikhwezi after-care student, was a fine young Transkeian woman with an inquisitive mind, wonderful personality and great determination. She introduced me to many friends and family in Ngangelizwe township.

19. Out in Transkei's villages, disability and poverty were a common sight. Mothers looked forward to the day their disabled children could go to Ikhwezi for treatment and an education.

Left: 20. A pensive look on the face of an Ikhwezi student, shortly after we returned him to his home in rural Transkei.

Below: 21. Umtata, the capital of Transkei, was a real mix of old and new – the colonial-style town hall and a modern office block stood side by side.

22. In 1980s Transkei, fields were still ploughed by hand with oxen.

Above left: 23. My long-suffering Xhosa teacher, or more accurately, my isiXhosa teacher.

Above right: 24. This woman could still raise a warm smile after we'd worked hard for the day harvesting mielies together.

Above: 25. Women wearing white face clay were a common sight, particularly away from Transkei's towns.

Below left: 26. Frequently, Transkeian women in traditional dress were eager to be photographed.

Below right: 27. Beads, braids, facial markings and cloth colours distinguished different Transkeian clans.

Above left: 28. Elaborate headwear in traditional colours was a common sight in rural areas.

Above right: 29. At dawn, Transkei's rich flora framed the landscape.

Right: 30. Sunrise in Umtata.

31. While fishing at the Wild Coast, we shared the beach with a group of Bomvana women who were harvesting shellfish.

32. While shellfish cooked on a wood fire, one of the Bomvana women proudly displayed her arm rings and pipe.

Above: 33. When the sun set behind the mountains of Lesotho, temperatures plummeted, and Jack Frost appeared in Mariazell, near Matatiele.

Below: 34. Three shepherd boys wrapped in warm blankets found me floundering about somewhere in Lesotho's mountains.

Left: 35. In winter, the dirt roads of Transkei were so dry and hard that car tyres polished the ochre-red clay until it shone.

Below: 36. The light at Camps Bay, Cape Town, reminded me of the light back in Cornwall, around Sennen Cove and Nanjizal.

Right: 37. At dawn I got to meet *tsotsis* (bad guys) in Umtata's township of Ngangelizwe. We got on just fine.

Below: 38. Many parts of Umtata's township of Ngangelizwe had shoddy, flimsy houses, but other neighbourhoods were colourfully decorated.

Left: 39. When I returned to Ikhwezi in February 2020, forty years after working there, I handed Sister Maria Corda (right) the farewell card she had given me the day I left. Sister Raphael Buthelezi was my companion for the visit. (Sister Maria Corda passed away in June 2020, a victim of Covid-19.) [Photo taken in 2020]

Below: 40. Bethany Home, next to Ikhwezi Lokusa, was started by Sister Mary Paule to protect vulnerable and abused children. Here, in 2020, I had the great pleasure of meeting Project Trust volunteer Jenny Walshe. [Photo taken in 2020]

entire duration. None of this I relayed to Mr Bidla, for fear of boring him senseless. He was still grinning intently, ready to lay his trap.

As part of our cultural exchange, I thought it polite to say that while recreational drugs were deeply frowned upon by the UK Home Counties set, their use regarded as criminal and deviant, drinking alcohol in large quantities was positively encouraged. I had thought of mentioning to Mr Bidla that in my school rugby team excessive drinking was normal, a rite of passage in fact, especially when accompanied by tribal chanting and singing, such as 'Drink it down, you Zulu warrior' on the team bus, but on balance I thought it best to keep quiet, for fear of mixing confusion and racial insult into one heady, undiplomatic cocktail.

I provided a timely opportunity for Mr Bidla to make his proposal. Still grinning, he suggested that if I would like to try some *dagga* as part of my cultural experience then he would happily supply it from his mielie plot in the country. He stressed its quality as part of his pitch. As though I would have known the difference.

In exchange, all he wanted were bottles of peppermint liqueur from a particular off-licence in Umtata. Simple. There it was, a bartering trade proposal in both our interests, as he saw it. As we now say in modern Anglo-American business spiel, a 'win-win' situation unfolded. Mr Bidla was happy because he had secured a reliable supply of peppermint liqueur in exchange for the *dagga* he already had. The Greek chap running the off-licence in Umtata was happy because a green-behind-the-ears British teenager from the mission was now popping in regularly to boost his peppermint liqueur sales. Babs, Doug and I were happy to be enjoying the cultural benefits of *dagga*, as were the numerous new friends we started to acquire. Word got out pretty quickly about our new mode of recreation, and people were popping up from everywhere, from as far afield as Natal. I even had bus drivers rolling up, every now and again, in their large articulated vehicles, for their batch of prime Transkeian weed. The arrival of these conspicuous vehicles opposite our modest accommodation did raise one or two questions from other members of staff from time to time. Apart from that, our little *dagga* ruse was running nicely.

Even the students benefited from our new recreational activity, as Babs, our Swiss colleague, soon had the pottery class making a variety of traditional Transkeian clay pipes. They looked fabulous and quite authentic. As well as reinforcing the students' cultural heritage, the pipes were put to good use for our *dagga* smoking.

What could possibly go wrong?

Well, we ended up with so much *dagga* it was hard to hide the stuff in our room. It was everywhere and became quite a nuisance. We stored it in drawers, stuffed it into our rucksacks under the bed and in the end even hid some in the loft space above our room. It all got a little out of hand. Were we taking a risk? I suppose we were, and it did occasionally weigh on my mind. Having seen Umtata prison more than once, I certainly didn't want to end up in residence there. I'd found the local police station unpleasant enough, and I was in there only fifteen minutes.

And then there was Mr Bidla, our co-conspirator in all this. I expect you're wondering what happened to him. Despite the best efforts of Sister Mary Paule not to dismiss him for numerous misdemeanours, the axe eventually fell. He was caught having 'relations' with a female gardener, not for the first time, in the grounds of the mission. He hadn't helped his cause a few weeks earlier when he was found drunk just before the arrival of a government minister and the Bishop of Umtata for the official opening of the new Ikhwezi workshop and accommodation. The whole thing had been getting messy. In the end, I think everyone was relieved at the dismissal, including the incorrigible Mr Bidla. Country Mrs Bidla, however, may have had a word to say to her husband on his return.

17

Transkei Heart

There aren't many regions of the world with a serious communicable disease named after them, but that was one of the dubious privileges held by Transkei. Transkei Heart may sound like a term of affection or a romantic consequence of cupid's arrow, but is in fact the name of a nasty disease, widespread in the country. The medical term for it is tuberculosis pericarditis, which I think you'll agree lacks even a hint of romanticism. There were a fair few other types of tuberculosis (pulmonary, abdominal,

A mother with her malnourished child, listening intently to Sister Mary Paule's advice.

bone, lymphatic) in Transkei too, but this Transkei-branded version of TB infects the heart lining, causing a severe deterioration in health, frequently leading to death if untreated.

As part of my job at Ikhwezi, I often visited Transkei's hospitals and clinics, both in Umtata and in the smaller towns and rural settings, so that the children could receive treatment or be collected, and meet various medics. Sister Mary Paule would sometimes effect an introduction to local experts, so I got to visit the local TB clinic to hear first-hand about the disease and its causes from the very knowledgeable and earnest Dr Strang. Time at any one of these medical centres offered a direct and uncompromising view of life and death in Transkei. It became clear that these two were never far apart in this region of South Africa, and I had to learn to put aside some of my personal sensibilities and squeamishness.

On the life-affirming side of the balance sheet, these medical centres were busy, bustling places. Female visitors, who often had to walk miles from rural villages to get there, were conspicuous in their tribal clothing, armbands, large headscarves and beads. Some wore a traditional, coarsely woven cream cloth decorated with black bands and beads stitched into them, while others adorned themselves in striking red ochre clothes. Dark blue and sky blue dresses, cloaks and headscarves were prevalent elsewhere. These dye colours, their combinations and hues, the presence of arm or leg decoration, and their facial markings differentiated them as members of the many different clans or groups, such as the Thembu, Mpondo, Mfengu and Bhaca. If it weren't for the medical setting and obvious discomfort of some patients, it looked at times like an exhibition of Transkei's diverse and distinctive rural dress styles.

Inside, the smaller clinics were not always very nice and sometimes the level of sanitation and hygiene could have been much improved. They seldom had air conditioning and were cramped and overcrowded, so that in warm weather wards might smell dreadfully. That was my experience of the hospital in Butterworth in the rainy season, when the wards had numerous patients recovering from horrendous burns as a result of lightning strikes. One poor soul had up to sixty per cent burns. I'd been under the mistaken impression that being struck by lightning was a rare occurrence, but in Transkei it was evidently quite common. If lightning struck the rondavel where a family took shelter, all huddled together, several people could be horrendously burnt in one strike.

Polio was common, too. A number of the pupils at Ikhwezi bore witness to its debilitating effect on young lives.

In rural clinics, mothers in maternity wards frequently helped each other, particularly women unable to feed their babies.

Out in rural Engcobo, where there was still a great deal of faith in traditional medicine, herbalists, healers and other practitioners, a lot of effort was being made to improve the health and wellbeing of mothers and their babies by overcoming concerns about modern medicine and encouraging antenatal visits. Ensuring that births took place in the clinic, rather than at home in the village, was one simple but crucial change medics were attempting to implement. One of the doctors I got to know had recently received a grant that enabled him to pay for pregnant rural women to buy a bus ticket so they could visit the clinic for at least one antenatal examination and to give birth. He explained that the simple act of providing a free bus ticket to expectant mothers, so they wouldn't have to walk long distances, was one of the most effective ways of ensuring a successful delivery and a positive outcome for mother and child.

Inside the maternity clinic at All Saints in Engcobo, it was wonderful to see and hear about the supportive ethos among the new mothers. As one of the mothers was unable to breastfeed her infant, all the other mothers expressed a small quantity of breast milk into a cup and gave it to her to feed her newborn child. This was genuinely heart-warming, another example of Xhosa generosity and communal spirit, but I was quite surprised when eight young Xhosa women insisted on demonstrating the breast milk expressing process to me at close range. This wasn't a

Above: As Sister Mary Paule drove around Ngangelizwe township helping struggling families, residents would recognise her temperamental white VW Beetle – the Pig, as we named her.

Below: In the township several generations of a family would live in a few crowded rooms.

discrete demonstration, but a conspicuous en masse display, just for me. And, they wanted me to take their photograph. What should I do? I felt very uncomfortable, but the mothers were standing right in front of me, so proud and enthusiastic about what they were doing to support each other that I hid my foolish embarrassment and watched, listened and learnt about the collective and caring nature of Xhosa family life, particularly among the women.

When I arrived in Transkei, bright-eyed and bushy-tailed, I had no medical knowledge except from my Boy Scout days and from watching the occasional TV hospital drama, where more attention was given to the fractious and amorous relationships of the medical staff than the suffering patients. Despite this woeful ignorance and paucity of experience, I quickly got to know the signs of malnutrition that were many and varied in Transkei. Much of this I learnt from Sister Mary Paule.

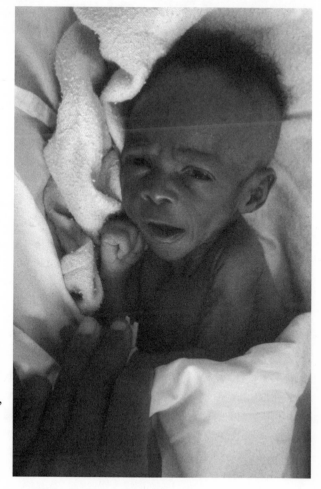

Accompanying Sister Mary Paule to clinics and homesteads around Transkei, one would sometimes encounter sick infants, desperately in need of medical help and nutrition. Some survived no more than a few days.

Sister Michael was a close companion of Sister Mary Paule.

People suffering from malnutrition would be thin, wouldn't they? Wrong. Many were in fact quite bloated and puffy in appearance, while others had the telltale signs of skin lesions and blemishes.

Malnutrition was what you saw in infants and children, wasn't it? Wrong. While there were many malnourished children, it afflicted numerous adults too, especially the elderly.

Malnutrition is what you saw in the country, not the towns, right? Wrong. In addition to rural malnutrition, it was prevalent in towns, too. In fact, some of the worse cases of malnutrition and child neglect I saw were on the local township of Ngangelizwe, right under our noses. Often, these personal tragedies reflected much bigger social ills such as the break-up of the family structure due to migrant work, alcoholism, limited healthcare and the adjustment from a rural to an urban lifestyle. Whatever the causes, the effects were difficult to witness.

One unforgettable morning I was doing various odd jobs about Ikhwezi when Sister Mary Paule asked for help, which I thought meant I was needed for some extra teaching or to go to the post office in Umtata. She was serious in tone and looked worried, explaining that we had to find Sister Michael, although I did not know what for. The lack of information was slightly worrying, but for once I thought it best to be patient and keep quiet. Sister Mary Paule and Sister Michael were very close, very supportive of each other, and did not exchange many words once we were all together. I drove them down to Ngangelizwe in one of the vans. The Pig had been playing up recently and it was clearly not a day for unreliable automobiles.

We were in Ngangelizwe in less than five minutes, navigating our way through familiar roads and less familiar side alleys. Using basic Xhosa to communicate with residents, we honed in on a shack that was run down and ramshackle, even by the standards of the location. We were in the same part of the location as Mr Bidla's home, only this shack was even cheaper, with a monthly rent of nine rand. The Sisters got out first, and without being asked I followed them towards the closed front door.

A neighbour was nervously hovering around outside, as though expecting our arrival. Maybe she was. Lots of things happened in the township that everyone seemed to be aware of except me. I knew there was an invisible network that operated, but I certainly didn't have access to it. Sister Mary Paule most certainly did. She was tapped into the whispers, rumours and goings-on of the township, one step ahead of likely issues. Before I left Ikhwezi I had worked out how this network operated and who passed the discrete messages to Sister Mary Paule. It was the aunties, teachers, gardeners and nurses who worked at Ikhwezi and who lived in the township that served as a non-digital information superhighway, faster and more reliable than many of today's WiFi networks.

As we approached the tatty door, the neighbour and Sister Mary Paule exchanged a couple of words in Xhosa. Without knocking, the two nuns entered purposefully, me in tow, slightly behind, bewildered and nervous

A similar dwelling to the one where we found the emaciated infant who was christened Michael just hours before he died. [Photo taken in 2020]

about what was to come. There on a makeshift mattress, wrapped to the waist in a dirty stained sheet, was an infant of indeterminate age and gender, dying of hunger, gastroenteritis and pneumonia in front of our eyes. Put more brutally, the infant was a victim of gross neglect. It was sickening.

I didn't shed a tear. I suspect I was too taken aback by the awfulness and futility of it all. I struggled for words then and I still do now, but the image of the emaciated, starving infant helpless in front of us, with no mother, father or carer in sight, was quite simply pitiful. Just pitiful.

Evidently this is what Sister Mary Paule had been expecting to see, though perhaps she had hoped things wouldn't be so bad. I just kept quiet, struggling and lacking the emotional hardware and software to process what I was witnessing. On numerous future trips accompanying Sister Mary Paule, I was to visit other malnourished infants, often in the arms of their distraught mother, but in most cases they were to be saved by care, food supplements and rehydration. Not this time. The nameless male infant in front of us had hours to live and there was a heavy stillness as we invisibly shook our heads in sadness and despair.

Sister Mary Paule knew who the mother was. She had a serious drinking problem, she didn't want the child and simply neglected him. I didn't glean anything about the father.

One or two neighbours were now milling around outside. They knew something was wrong.

I remained quiet and tried to stay small. I was superfluous in this tragedy.

I have had the misfortune to have experienced a handful of acute and dreadful circumstances in my life, and on these occasions I have found myself noticing the oddest and least relevant things vividly. Maybe it is a defence mechanism against the trauma or simply a way of coping with the onslaught of too much horribleness. But it is a strange and recurring experience at times of great shock and adversity.

Faced with this sudden and intractable human tragedy, I found myself thinking about the light in the tiny shack. It seemed perverse to focus on the ambient light when an infant's life was visibly ebbing away. There was no internal light, only the insistent, piercing shards of sunlight streaming in uninvited from the open door and many gaps in the walls. The rays were razor sharp, purposeful and uncompromising, real mid-morning Transkeian sunshine, in extreme contrast to the dwindling light in the life of the child. It was obtrusive and cut the stagnant, dusty air in the shack, where the gloom robbed everything of its colour, and our eyes struggled to make sense of our surroundings. Almost motionless, the fading infant lay just outside the light in a morbid shadow.

The atmosphere in the tiny room was heavy and still. Muffled and detached, the sounds of township life went on outside. Sister Mary Paule and Sister Michael communicated with looks, as only those who know and trust each other can.

Sister Mary Paule was in the bright light staring at the baby. Sister Michael was in the dusty filthy shadow looking on. I was just to the side of the door. Someone still hovered outside knowingly. Without a word, Sister Michael stepped forward and gently christened the fading infant where he was. For the few remaining hours of his wasted, neglected life, he had a name: Michael.

With very few words, we left, the neighbours' eyes following us to the Ikhwezi van.

Driving up the slope out of the township I was told, in low tones, that there was no hope for Michael. He had been neglected so badly and for so long that there was nothing we could do. Hearing the word 'nothing' hit hard. It sounded terminal, and it was.

We felt a collective shame.

By the time the sisters returned, later that afternoon, Michael had died, alone and abandoned in a pathetic shack, barely fit for a farm animal.

The next day Mr Bidla was given the responsibility of digging his grave and burying him in the township. By then the bright skies had become cloudy. In a way that was so fittingly Transkeian, Michael was buried in the rain.

18

Dignity and Dust
(an Adventure in Lesotho)

When I explained to Sister Mary Paule that one weekend I wanted to visit the north-east parts of Transkei called Griqualand East, near the borders of Natal and Lesotho, she was good enough to arrange a lift for me with one of the parliamentary chiefs who would be returning from parliament in Umtata to his home near Matatiele at the end of the week. Because Sister Mary Paule had started her Transkeian missionary work in this neck of the woods, she knew a number of the chiefs and was confident she could pull the necessary strings. Perfect, I thought. What could be better than a free lift and a chat with a Transkeian chief for a few hours as we traversed the wintery landscape? I'm not sure how the chief felt about this prospect, but I was as keen as mustard, eager to have a chat and excited to see the stunning scenery I'd heard about.

The plan was scuppered, however, much to my disappointment, as the chiefs decided to leave parliament early that week. That sounded like a good wheeze to me, but not one I could swing at Ikhwezi. While an early end to the week was hunky-dory for the chiefs, I still had a class to teach on various aspects of electricity.

So instead of a comfortable and informative car ride with a parliamentary bigwig to the mission station at Mariazell, near Matatiele, Sister Mary Paule and the capricious Pig took me, my rucksack and camera to the Umtata bus rank for public transport. Now, as any of you seasoned travellers will know, it is a universal truism that wherever you are in the world, taking a bus with the local people is not as comfortable as a ride in someone's private car, but it is invariably more interesting, where 'interesting' has a broad and flexible definition.

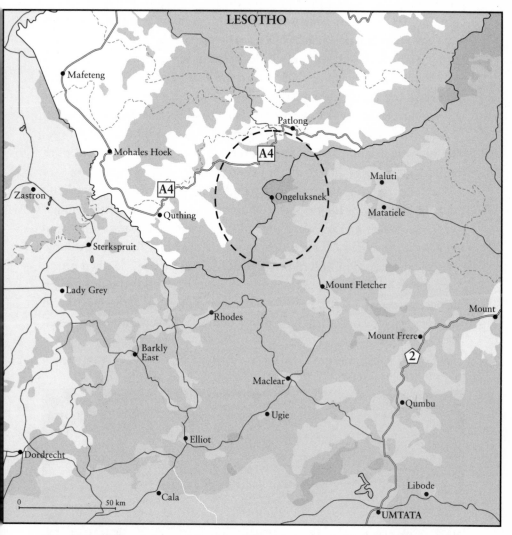

Map 3. Ongeluksnek in south Lesotho, Matatiele in South Africa, and Umtata.

This bus journey to Kokstad and Matatiele in rural west Natal was to be largely in the company of young men coming and going to work at the platinum mines up in the northern parts of South Africa. There was an obvious loose camaraderie among them that I was not a part of. I was the conspicuous white bloke unsuccessfully trying to blend in and feeling the cold, just like them. In fact, that's the most obvious thing we had in common. To a man, we were wrapped up in several assorted woolly layers and sporting thermal headgear of various types to keep the bitter, dry cold at bay. The winter sun had very little warmth. Several fellow passengers wore mirrored sunglasses, which served the dual purpose of making them look cool and keeping the piercing light down to acceptable levels. The temperature plummeted as we travelled first towards Kokstad, and then on to Matatiele, only a short distance from the stark mountains of Lesotho. The sun was bright, casting long wintery shadows at all times except at midday, but it felt as though all the energy had been sapped out of it.

My fellow passengers mostly carried their possessions in synthetic holdalls, zip bags or flimsy plastic shopping bags, and had little enough to carry, considering they were going away for months or returning from months on the mines. More conspicuous than their luggage were the large cassette tape recorders and radios several of them carried, clearly a prized possession and the centre of their attention as they huddled in groups on the bus, listening to music. I could relate to the pleasure of gathering around a cassette tape recorder listening to my favourite music with mates, even

Travelling by bus to Matatiele in the north-east region of Transkei, with migrant mineworkers for company.

when the batteries were tired and running out of power, as several of them audibly were. Listening to music on cassette tape distorted by old batteries hadn't stopped my mates and me, and obviously did not perturb them either, as the noisy and fumy old bus gingerly ate up the miles heading north-east.

In Kokstad we disembarked to await the connecting bus to Matatiele. A crowd of us hunkered down on cold benches in the bus station, having little idea of when the bus might arrive. 'Soon,' I was told on the few occasions I asked, and I left it at that. In fact, we waited a few hours. There were no shops and no street vendors, just us few cold souls waiting, all quiet except for the lively rhythms from their cassette tape players. In juxtaposition to this serenity, some groups of travelers would spontaneously start singing loudly in Sotho. These songs, including wailing sounds, were captured on the tape recorders and then played out aloud, giving the singers a break before a repeat performance commenced.

Occasionally there was the spiralling breezy flutter of ochre-coloured road grit, powdery and desiccated from the parched air. It was that time of year when the dirt roads were as hard as the bench I was sitting on, and much of the vegetation had the complexion of anaemic straw. It was as brittle as dried spaghetti to the touch. There wasn't a single sign of a green leaf on trees or on the veld. Winter had sapped colour from all living plants. Everywhere and everything was dry, desiccated even, and covered in a layer of pale dust, including everyone waiting for the bus to Matatiele. Finally, our bus pulled up and we clambered on, reaching

Waiting on a cold bench with fellow passengers at Kokstad bus station, listening to their radios and tape players.

our destination by late afternoon. The peaks of Lesotho now formed a conspicuous backdrop as the sun dropped low and the temperature again began to plummet. Jack Frost was eager to chase us all indoors.

I was the guest of a number of priests at the Mariazell mission and so spent the evening answering questions about life in late 1970s Europe while playing chess very badly with them. It was obvious that they had a lot of spare time on their hands in the evenings and had honed their chess skills sufficiently to take on challengers quite comfortably. However, humiliation at the hands of a strategically placed rook and a cavalier knight did not stop me sleeping soundly that night in this very quiet, scenic part of South Africa.

One of the best things about staying in these missions, which I did quite often during my sojourn at Ikhwezi, was the quality and quantity of food you were always offered. I seldom saw a thin priest! It was no different at the Mariazell mission, where breakfast set me up for the whole day – fortunately, as things turned out. Having planned my trip to Mariazell for some time, I soon realised that I hadn't planned *what* to do when I got there, as though arriving were good enough, which it clearly wasn't as I'd already had enough of chess for some time. So after a hearty breakfast, I left the mission on foot with little idea of where I might end up; I just sauntered off down a dirt road, vaguely heading north towards the magnificent distant Drakensberg mountain range that was high, vivid and imposing. The sky was clear and it was cold and fresh, with a gentle

The mission station at Mariazell, near Matatiele, where I stayed a couple of nights and lost badly at chess to my enthusiastic hosts.

breeze generating small twisters of reddish dust that would suddenly appear, zigzag sprite-like down the road, and disappear. Apart from the rustle of dry, brittle grasses, all was quiet. Few vehicles passed, and I had only wandering livestock for company in the form of a goat, a horse or a mule. But things were about to change.

When an orange Isuzu truck trundled up behind me, kicking up a dust tail visible from miles off, I impulsively flagged it down and, without so much as a word to the driver, hopped into the open rear, with no idea of where I was going, how long I'd be or how I'd get back. The driver was a middle-aged white chap and his side passenger a younger black chap. Off we went, me exposed to the elements, heading north with the steep-sided mountain looming larger by the minute. Evidently, we were heading to Lesotho, despite the fact that I had no passport, no additional warm clothes and no money. I did have my camera tucked into my side for comfort.

Lesotho is an independent country, marooned in the middle of South Africa. It is about the size of Belgium and largely mountainous, with the land varying from about 1,400 metres to 3,400 metres above sea level. In short, it is small, landlocked and high. It is home to the Basotho people, another branch of the Bantu. Its status as an independent country had a great deal to do with the canny and tenacious King Moshoeshoe (1786–1870), who shrewdly combined military force and diplomacy to repel waves of pressure from the Boers, the British and the Zulu. That was no small achievement at a time when many indigenous people in southern Africa were being brutally displaced, their leaders undermined and thousands of them massacred. Without King Moshoeshoe, it is likely that Lesotho would not exist today. I have more than a passing admiration for this fine chap. He was quite the diplomat.

Part of me was alarmed to be heading God-knows-where and the other part was equally excited at the adventure unfolding before me. Either way, things were quite out of my hands now. I wanted to see more of South Africa, and I was most definitely getting to see it *and* Lesotho, from the back of a pickup.

Before long, we were at the base of Lesotho's mountains at a South African passport control post, which is where I assumed I'd be kicked out either by the driver or the SA passport inspectors. Instead, the driver asked me to keep a low profile while he went in to clear things with the passport people. A few days later I was to deduce that this was an isolated post called Ongeluksnek. Anyway, the next thing I knew, an official barrier was raised and we were off, heading up a hideously rough

The view of South Africa and Transkei from the back of a pickup truck as we ascended the cold, remote mountains in south-east Lesotho.

track that one could hardly describe as a track at all. It had boulders the size of footballs littered all over it and was bristling with bushes, some halfway up the vehicle. At times, it was hard to make out the way ahead. The track was steep and getting steeper, to the point where the vehicle was stalling and struggling to make progress. We crawled at 1 or 2 kilometres per hour to manoeuvre around obstinate rocks and coarse flora. The gritty substrate meant the tyres sometimes failed to grip and the wheels spun, kicking up dust and making one hell of a din, but without propelling us forward. I could smell burnt rubber.

There was no other traffic save for one man on a horse, and there were no huts nearby. It looked and felt extremely remote, becoming more so by the minute. Ongeluksnek had consisted of only a few buildings, as far as I had made out, and was soon lost from view. There were no trees, just mountainsides and valleys of low dry grass and hemi-spherical bushes, as obdurate as heather and gorse. Boulders were everywhere. I was getting shaken about in the back of the truck like a stick in the mouth of an overexcited dog and becoming colder, too, as we climbed higher up the zig-zagging track of Lesotho's foothills. This is not what I had envisaged earlier in the morning as I ate my porridge and toast. Served me right for not planning my trip.

Offsetting my encroaching trepidation at the foolhardiness of my unscheduled, unplanned, un-everything trip were the vast panoramic views of Transkei and Natal unfolding below as we hit new heights. I could see for miles and miles – east, west and south – with mountains, valleys, riverbeds and plains formed over millions of years cutting this way and that, as far as the horizon. What bound this magnificent ancient geomorphology together was the blended colour of dust and tinder-dry vegetation, framed above by a vast, cornflower blue sky. Green was nowhere on the palette.

These absorbing panoramas had the additional benefit of offsetting the increasing discomfort of my bruised buttocks and cold fingers, but I was getting to the point where I really didn't want to endure much more physical abuse on the back of a grizzly Isuzu pickup. Finally, the track levelled out onto a plateau of low, grassy pasture, tough grassy tufts and dry riverbeds, flanked by the ubiquitous boulders. Some of the hillsides appeared roughly terraced, partitioned by stone walls. I felt on top of the world, literally and figuratively – I was king of the castle. Nothing within view now seemed higher. After that bone-shaking slog up the mountain I felt a huge sense of relief, despite the fact that I still had no idea of where I was going, how I would get back or what my driver had planned.

At altitude, Lesotho was bitterly cold, grassy, rocky and bleak, showing few signs of human existence.

Now we motored ahead at lofty speeds of 20 kilometres per hour or so. We didn't even stop at two huts in the middle of the plain that seemed to serve as Lesotho's customs checkpoints. A man came out of one of the huts waving vigorously for us to stop, but the driver ploughed on until presently a host of huge yellow and orange bulldozers came into view. Ahead was a scar on the plain where they had ploughed through soil and rock to carve out the foundations of a new road. On either side were large, conspicuous soil spills, littered with more rock. Remote Lesotho mountain pastures were colliding headlong with the industrial 20th century. Diesel grunt and grind looked so out of place in such a remote, untouched landscape where the most conspicuous evidence of human intervention was the flock of sheep and goats nearby.

While I was pondering this juxtaposing view of mountain pastures and bulldozers, we came to a halt and the driver and passenger got out to see how their external passenger had fared. They weren't men of many words and it was obvious they were more comfortable with drive shafts, gearboxes and oil sumps than non-functional chitchat with a bewildered tourist. They explained succinctly that they had come from Pinetown in Natal to fix some of the bulldozing machinery and that a new road was being constructed to help connect the remoter reaches of Lesotho with the rest of Lesotho and South Africa. They had no desire to stay up in

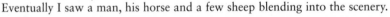

Eventually I saw a man, his horse and a few sheep blending into the scenery.

Above: The Isuzu driver had come to repair machinery used to bulldoze a new road through the south Lesotho landscape into South Africa.

Below: Suddenly three shepherd boys ran down a grassy slope towards me.

this Godforsaken place longer than they needed to and were returning home as soon as they were done with the bulldozer repairs. If I wanted a lift back, as though I had an alternative plan, then I shouldn't stray far. They'd give me a shout when they were ready.

There is no doubt they were more than a touch perplexed about what I was doing and why I had chosen to accompany them to the middle of nowhere. I tried to explain a bit, in a way that sounded coherent, but in the end I admitted I had not the slightest clue what I was doing, and was just savouring every minute of this trip into the dark side of Lesotho, thanks to them. Our conversation couldn't continue for long, as they were impatient to attend to their mechanical patients and I had some exploring to do.

It was rocky, remote and bitterly cold. For the first time all morning I could now see far north, a view extending for miles of high peaks and sculptured valleys – the vast panorama of Lesotho. I was gazing about, soaking in the vastness and stillness, when suddenly the carpet of grasses and rock in the mid-distance came to life, seeming to crystallise into three young shepherds, rushing down the hill towards me. Evidently, they'd

The young shepherds were all wrapped up against the biting cold.

Lesotho's rugged landscape formed a stunning backdrop to my new shepherd companions.

abandoned their flocks. Turned out they were coming to take a closer look at me, a curiosity. They may not have met many white people up there in the mountains, and I, of course, had met no Basotho shepherds. Having looked at each other in a friendly but slightly distant way, we progressed to pointing and gesticulating to communicate. Once comfortable, they agreed that I could take their photograph. I took some marvellous shots of the three of them wrapped in their thick blankets and woolly hats, framed by the sweeping, stark mountain and deep blue sky. They were so relaxed you might have thought they were professional models.

It was all so very surreal. At breakfast time I'd intended a brief amble around Mariazell and Matatiele town; now here I was atop a high mountain peak in Lesotho, chatting to young shepherds as their flocks ambled about us. Some hundred metres away a man, also wrapped in a blanket, slowly descended the valley on a horse, curiously looking back now and again. I wondered what he made of us.

Suddenly the deep, guttural rumble of monstrous combustion engines damaged the stillness, signalling to Mother Nature that normal, brutal business was about to be resumed. The impatience and realities of the 20th century rudely returned. The men from Pinetown were done with the bulldozers and beckoned me back to my personal deluxe space in the pickup. The young shepherds, now standing in a close huddle, looked on as we returned the way we had come. Soon they were an ill-defined speck camouflaged against the vast canvass of grass, rock and hillsides.

The return trip was far less traumatising than the ascent, as I got an upgrade. Instead of being exposed to the elements in the back of the pickup truck, I sat in the driver's cabin, sandwiched tightly between the driver and his colleague. Besides, I knew there would be a warm meal ready for me back at the mission. With as few words as we had begun our day's journey, the men dropped me off on the roadside, where they'd found me hours earlier. Then off they sped to Pinetown, rays of low-angled sunlight cutting sharply through the voluminous mushroom trail of dust behind them.

What a crazy day!

I must have been a dishevelled sight as I strolled into the mission covered in a thick layer of dust from two countries, exhausted, thirsty and bruised. Inside I felt a mixture of deep fatigue and exhilaration, brought on by the spontaneity of the high-altitude adventure. Moreover, the mission priests were incredulous when I explained, as succinctly as I could, where I'd been and what I'd seen. I retired early to bed that evening, sidestepping the chessboard.

The next morning, I awoke still tired, and decided on a slow, unadventurous day. Mundane was what I was looking for, not high-

A local netball game near Mariazell, close to where I fell asleep on a grit path.

octane gallivanting. I was delighted when one of my hosts invited me to join him for an amble around the local village in a pastoral capacity. We set off after breakfast but soon parted company, as he was eager to cover a lot of ground while I was still stiff, drowsy and drained.

As the priest strode off, I sat down on the side of a small gritty path overlooking fields and a small collection of rondavels. This was the quiet, uneventful day I'd wanted; it was five-star mundane. The next thing I knew I was waking up, my head resting on my arm on the gritty soil. I'd literally fallen asleep on the spot, out in the open, and I didn't have a clue for how long. Had I been asleep for three minutes, ten minutes or half an hour? Had anyone seen me prostrate on the ground? I didn't dwell on the matter and was about to return to the mission when my attention was caught by an impeccably dressed man striding confidently out of his stone-and-thatch rondavel. He paused, surveying his surroundings in a well-fitting dark suit, radiant white collared shirt and black polished shoes, his posture perfectly upright and commanding. The scene was striking and I was mesmerised; here was a man beautifully dressed and perfectly at ease in an environment with so much dust and without the electronic cleaning and ironing conveniences of city life. I watched him as he strolled off, unaware of the impact he had just made on me.

That sight of a dignified, well-dressed local man emerging from a village hut in rural Transkei has remained with me over the four decades since. During my professional life, wearing a smart suit and tie was the required corporate uniform, and whenever I looked dishevelled or below par I used to chastise myself, mindful of the man who strolled out into the country that winter's day near Mariazell, looking as though he had just paid a visit to a fine gents' tailors in Cape Town or Johannesburg.

19

Save Water Drink Wine

Are you the sort of person who likes to get home from work, kick off your shoes and crack open a chilled bottle of wine before heading for the TV remote control? If I'm not mistaken, you're probably partial to a crisp white or a flirtatious rosé. Perhaps not; maybe you're more of a 'fire up the BBQ' type, in which case a robust bottle of red might be your tipple of choice. I say bottle, but you may go the whole hog and have one of those three-litre boxes. That way there's less danger of running out of drink if the evening gets lively.

Clouds tumbling over Table Mountain suggested a tablecloth flowing over a table.

Well, if any of my voyeuristic foresight is remotely accurate, I'll go a little further and suggest you've enjoyed a few bottles of South African wine along the way. You know the sort I mean, often costing less than ten quid and with evocative names like Quirky Bird or Porcupine Ridge. Names like Stellenbosch, Paarl and Franschhoek pop up on the bottles too, to stress their heritage. To be honest, after the second glass all this is normally lost on me and I can't tell the difference between the grape, the town or the vineyard. Either way, I think we can agree that a glass or two of South African wine goes down rather nicely.

If you *do* enjoy the occasional bottle of South African wine then you will be surprised to hear that in a vicarious way you have Martin Luther to thank. That's right, I'm talking about Martin Luther, the irate German monk who nailed his ninety-five complaints, or theses, to the door of a church in Wittenberg in 1517. His indignation against the excesses of the Roman Catholic authorities not only started the Protestant Reformation but set in train a series of events leading to the establishment and growth of the wine industry in the Cape region of South Africa. The Huguenots, who were French, emerged as a distinct group of Protestants who particularly incurred the displeasure of the Catholics. So, when the Edict of Fontainebleau (1685) was decreed, persecuted Huguenots scattered far and wide across the known world, including the Cape region. They took with them their grape-growing and wine-making expertise. Many prospered in their new home, which is why many white South Africans today have surnames of French origin.

So, thank God for Martin Luther, the Edict of Fontainebleau, the Huguenots and that chilled glass of white wine you're enjoying on your sofa!

I didn't know about Huguenots in August 1980, but as I sat in a posh restaurant in Stellenbosch drinking copious amounts of red wine, I wanted to thank someone. I had gone past the squiffy phase, and was well and truly sozzled. As I'd been wine 'tasting' since mid-morning, knocking back whites, reds, rosés, brandy and liqueurs, it wasn't too surprising. What was great to my nineteen-year-old self was that I hadn't paid a bean for any of it.

Hitchhiking out of Cape Town to Stellenbosch that morning had gone better than expected, as I was picked up by a middle-aged Rhodesian couple who were down in the Cape for a holiday. They took me under their wing, showed me various vineyards and then invited me to lunch. Best of all, I didn't have to endure a lecture about Robert Mugabe, apartheid, communism, black people, or the state of the nation as was so common when discussions unfolded with white people from southern Africa. Instead, we compared thoughts about wine. I didn't have a clue. I was more a beer-drinking kind of bloke. But I made it up as I went along, commenting on the wine's colour, its body, the hint of citrus or oak, the delicate aftertaste of fresh lawn clippings or whatever, and then I necked it back, ready for the next one. The optional glass of water, to cleanse the palate, seemed surplus to requirements.

With its immaculate, centuries-old European architecture, Cape Dutch gables, abundant oak trees and acres of long, straight vines, Stellenbosch was a place of tranquillity and beauty to the casual observer like me. Signs of its Dutch and French heritage were everywhere, and it did not feel like Africa at all. The contrast with Umtata and Transkei could not have been greater.

Anyway, there I sat in an elegant Stellenbosch restaurant, tucking into my third course of haute cuisine, making great efforts to polish off another bottle of wine, and chuckling to myself as my Rhodesian hosts engaged in a little gentle domestic bickering. The wife had caught the husband paying undue attention to one of the female restaurant managers. The wife herself had been so busy watching everyone coming and going, she hadn't engaged much in conversation with either of us. Their bickering was all a little vague and hazy to me. I don't think it came to blows. We'd all had a bit to drink, and the mood was mellow and forgiving, as the mood so often is when the food and drink are plentiful.

And I'm pleased to report that the generous couple did not abandon me among the vineyards of Stellenbosch, but drove me all the way back to Cape Town, to the youth hostel I was staying at in Muizenberg.

I had not been expecting a visit to Cape Town, as I'd used up my leave allowance at Ikhwezi. But at short notice, and with Sister Dolorata absent, Sister Mary Paule suggested that I take a few days off to visit the Cape. So, after giving a demonstration of the Wonderbox, a fuel-saving cooking device that Sister Mary Paule was promoting among residents of the new Ikhwezi houses, I was driven to the bus station in Umtata to catch the overnight bus to Cape Town. My fellow passengers were mostly black or coloured women, returning to the Cape to work, almost certainly in domestic roles. They made quite a contrast with the young black men who had travelled with me to western Natal and the foothills of Lesotho – those huddled, silent migrant workers heading north and east to industrial and mining towns. These young women were talkative and jovial, and quite a sense of community developed among us as

Hitchhiking in the morning rush hour on the outskirts of Cape Town, after an overnight bus ride from Umtata.

we traversed the 1,200 kilometres to Cape Town – an afternoon and overnight bus trip.

By the time the morning sun rose over the horizon, the vast outline of Table Mountain loomed into view. It was a relief to know the journey was almost at an end. Then, without any warning, the bus stopped at a busy dual-carriageway junction, and the driver, ably assisted by the other passengers, insisted I get off, even though Cape Town city centre was miles away. I was still bleary-eyed from a broken night's sleep, but the thrust of the message from several people was that I could not go on to the next stops. The bus was going to the black and coloured areas of town, and they thought it best if I got off here, even if it was at the side of a busy highway. So off I stumbled and there I stood, somewhere outside Cape Town, my rucksack by my side and swathes of commuter traffic rushing by, as it does at 7 a.m. in any major city.

Despite being slightly disorientated, I did the only thing I could do, and stuck out my trusty hitchhiking thumb, not expecting much. However, Lady Luck was shining down on me. Within minutes, a rather swanky car stopped fifty metres down the road, in the *outside* lane of the dual carriageway. At first I assumed it had broken down. Why else would anyone stop in the outside lane during rush hour? Then a well-groomed white chap hopped out and waved vigorously at me over his car roof. Was he nuts? Was he seriously suggesting I join him? This meant I had to run the gauntlet of the swiftly moving river of cars, with passing drivers

Cape Town nestled below Table Mountain. Robben Island was conspicuous a few kilometres offshore.

in no mood to assist some wally who was stupid enough to try to weave through rush-hour traffic on a dual carriageway. Taking my life into my hands, I plunged in, recalling my side-stepping moves from rugby training as I danced my way around boots and bumpers to my waiting carriage. Perplexed but relieved, I shook the driver's hand and we were on our way, with Table Mountain straight ahead.

My driver was a trendy young executive working in the centre of Cape Town, and was giving me a lift because, he said, so many people had helped him when he'd travelled in the UK a few years earlier. His friendly questions revealed, once again, how ill prepared I was for my trip.

'Where do you plan to stay?'

'No idea.'

'What are you planning to see?'

'Not sure.'

'How long are you staying?'

'Not really given it any thought.'

'What do you know about Cape Town?'

'It has a large mountain.'

'Would you like some help?'

'Yes, please.'

At 7 a.m. I'd been hitching a ride into Cape Town. By noon I was near the summit of Table Mountain.

Based on my planning ineptness, a short but necessary partnership was forged, and soon I found myself in the plush offices of a corporation's marketing department, where my driver worked. Here I drank buckets of coffee and scoffed my way through a plate of biscuits while twirling in an executive chair. For the record, the biscuits were even better than the ones served at the Bishop of Umtata's residence. While I marvelled at my good fortune, my smart executive friend was planning my stay in Cape Town, phoning numerous contacts he seemed to have at his fingertips and writing down names, places and transport routes. I honestly don't know what I would have done without him.

Just from staring out the office window onto the streets below, I could tell this city was very different from other places I'd visited in the country. Pretty soon I was handed my itinerary for the next few days on a sheet of paper, complete with the name and telephone number of someone who would give me a personal guided tour. Then I was back in my benefactor's plush car, whisked off to a youth hostel high on the slopes of Camps Bay where I signed in, dumped my stuff and was taken to the base of Table Mountain to catch the cable car. I thanked him profusely, but he was now in a hurry to get back to his executive lifestyle, and off he sped. The next thing I knew I was at the top of one of the world's most famous mountains with a view to die for. Three hours earlier I had been half-asleep on a busy dual carriageway gazing at Table Mountain in the distance. Now I was on top of it.

This was 1980, so there were only four or five people with me on this iconic landmark, which really is as flat as a table on top. It was quiet, too, except for the sound of a gentle winter breeze moving through low vegetation. What was most remarkable was not just the grandeur of the views, the mountains and sea, but what the views said about South Africa. Within the 360-degree panorama spread out before me, I could see the Cape Flats – a semicircular swathe forming the distant outskirts of the city, where huge townships housed thousands of non-whites. These included Crossroads, Nyanga, Langa and Gugulethu. Closer to the mountain, and reaching into the lush forests at its base, were the luxurious suburbs of professional whites, the hustle and bustle of the port, Cape Point reaching out to the horizon, the beaches of Hout Bay and, a few miles offshore, what looked like a large aircraft carrier. It wasn't a ship, however; it was Robben Island, or simply The Island, as this notorious place became known to many Xhosas over the last couple of centuries. While it is a high-volume tourist destination today, I was only vaguely aware of its use back then. I'd heard it was a prison, but I wasn't sure whether Nelson Mandela and other ANC members were incarcerated there. In fact they were; Nelson Mandela served twenty years there from 1963, and was only transferred to a mainland prison in 1982, two years after I left Transkei. So as I stood inhaling the bracing winter air and gazing out to sea, he was no doubt hewing limestone or suffering any of the innumerable hardships he and others endured on the island not far from where I stood. No one in South Africa talked about this, and probably few were even aware of his presence so close to their daily goings-on.

By late afternoon I'd made my way back to the beautifully situated Camps Bay hostel ready for a much-needed kip. But that wasn't going to happen. Some nasty little Nazi was about to spoil my day – my week, to be honest. Every time I think about him, I loathe this piece of shit even more. So I try not to spend a nanosecond more than necessary with him pinging around in my grey matter. I've trawled up my memory of him just because he was central to my Cape Town tale and I thought you needed to hear it. These sorts are best avoided.

When I got to the dormitory of the hostel, there was a white lad in his mid-twenties milling around. As we were going to be sleeping only a metre apart from each other for a few nights, I introduced myself and explained my job working at Ikhwezi and our collective efforts to help disadvantaged Transkeians. So far, so good, a harmless bit of chitchat,

The Cape Flats in the distance, home to several of the Cape's large townships for 'non-whites'.

I thought. I was curious what he was doing in this neck of the woods. My roommate explained, in a thick accent, that he was from Germany and South West Africa (now Namibia), and that he was waiting to catch a ship to stay with his German uncle in Paraguay. German uncle in South America? Alarm bells sounded straight away. I'd heard about these sorts of uncles before, on TV documentaries. Shortly after the Second World War, a number of German officials hotfooted it out of Europe to hide in South America in case their past was investigated. At that time, investigative reporters were often tracking down these sorts in remote Argentinian towns to expose their history.

Who was I to judge? What did I know? There must be a hundred and one other good reasons why his uncle chose to reside in Paraguay. But my doubts accelerated, and my alarm flared with every word he spoke.

After explaining the objective of his stay in Cape Town, the young man launched into a tirade about how much he hated black people. I wasn't aware I'd said anything to prompt this outburst, but it got worse. From his personal possessions next to his bed he got out what looked like a martial arts weapon, comprising two thick wooden poles connected by a flexible metal chain (nunchakus, I believe they are called). Using considerable force, he beat the mattress of his bed to punctuate a torrent of vile opinions about black and coloured people, using inflammatory and derogatory terms as shorthand. Every vicious word and the violence

193

of his beating nunchaku left me in no doubt as to what he would do if provoked more than he already was. It was disgusting to listen to, hideous to watch and the combination of the two was scary.

He calmed himself down slowly by re-emphasising that he would soon be in Paraguay in the company of his uncle and would no longer have to endure the people he so abhorred. Was I really going to share a dormitory with this terrifying psycho for a few days? It wasn't written on my itinerary.

The idea of an afternoon nap passed. I just needed to get out of the dorm and away from Herr Angry Psycho as fast as possible. I meandered down the sloping road to Camps Bay beach, relieved to be heading for a beautiful sandy beach and among more normal people. The bay was so picturesque, framed by the slope of the Twelve Apostles, stretching off Table Mountain. The boulders near the shore had a very distinct curvaceous shape, and wouldn't have been out of place at a Henry Moore or Barbara Hepworth sculpture exhibition. But most striking of all was the light. It reminded me of the light I experienced on sunny days in the Isles of Scilly and Penzance, back in Cornwall. It appeared saturated in colour, containing the whole spectrum, and the sand and the frothy sea lapping the shoreline contrasted wonderfully.

Much later, I made my way back to the dorm and, avoiding the psycho as much as I could, slipped into bed.

A view of Camps Bay from the youth hostel, where Herr Angry Psycho was spoiling my day.

The next morning I was up and out early, noting the comprehensive itinerary prepared for me by my high-flying executive friend. It told me I that I had a personal guided tour of Cape Point with the Park Ranger lined up. Walking through Cape Town city centre to get to the railway station, I was struck again by how different this city was from all the other South African towns and cities I'd visited. It looked and felt cosmopolitan, and a touch more multicultural, for a start. In addition to blacks and whites, there were many more coloured people, those of mixed race, and people whose heritage was from South East Asia and the Indian subcontinent. This included a distinct Malay population. Many were the descendants of slaves, imported and sold to build and grow the Cape Colony in its nascent days.

There were vendors on the streets, predominantly selling large floral spreads of glowing colours. Here and there were boutiques selling Western and indigenous art, and the occasional tourist shop selling the ubiquitous T-shirt. I succumbed to temptation and bought one with the logo 'Save Water Drink Wine'; I wore it for many years until it was threadbare. Weaving in between all this were double-decker buses, the sort you might see in London, emblazoned with bold advertising for products like Pepsi. Colonial buildings, an old fortress, modern office blocks and dock warehousing all sat shoulder to shoulder as I explored the streets. More than once I looked around to see where all the other tourists were. There

In Cape Town, old colonial buildings and modern commercial office blocks stood cheek by jowl.

Above: Fynbos plants were unique to the Cape and made wonderful floral displays at street corners.

Below: Was I back in London? Double-decker buses displaying international brands were conspicuous across the city.

were very few, but I'd never visited a city more suited to tourism. Perhaps it was the time of year – winter. More likely, though, it was the impact of the international embargoes that subjected South Africa to quite serious cultural and economic isolation in protest against apartheid.

A couple of hours later, I was collected at Simon's Town railway station by the Cape Point Park Ranger in his 4x4 Land Rover. My itinerary was going like clockwork. We drove through a sea of fynbos, vegetation unique to the area and dotted with exotic protea flowers, to arrive at the Cape of Good Hope, also known as the Cape of Storms, right at the very bottom of Africa. It was exposed and buffeted by a firm, steady wind. The peninsula I stood on was only a few tens of metres wide, with exposed steep cliffs on either side, tumbling into the sea. Behind me was a vast continent of many countries, diverse people and contrasting geographies, covering more than 30 million square kilometres. The tip of North Africa was some 8,000 kilometres behind me. In front were an ocean and a fully hemispherical bright sky, barely touched by cloud. The only land south of where I stood was Antarctica, more than 4,000 kilometres away. To the east lay the warm waters of the Indian Ocean, the East Coast of Africa, India, South-East Asia and the Orient. From the 12th century AD, Arab traders had toiled against the cruel elements to pass Cape Point, heading east to west

The bottom end of Africa: the Cape of Good Hope, a place of huge historical and strategic global significance.

East from the Cape of Good Hope, the warmer waters of the Indian Ocean would have been a great relief for European mariners in previous centuries.

on their way to West Africa and the Northern Hemisphere. To the west was the cooler Atlantic Ocean, the route to the Americas, North Africa and Europe. By the late 15th century the Portuguese had also sailed past Cape Point, but in the opposite direction, heading West to East in search of trade in luxury goods and slaves. For the mariners of these disparate cultures, and the sponsors of these high-risk maritime ventures, the spot where I stood had huge symbolic value as a landmark on their arduous journey. Centuries ago, traveling in ships of very modest construction, they would have been taking their 'one small step for man' into the unknown world. The risks and dangers would have been horrendous. They were, so to speak, the Neil Armstrongs and Yuri Gagarins of their day.

Even Adam Smith, the great moral philosopher and economist, recognised the importance of this part of the world in his famous *Wealth of Nations* (1776):

> The discovery of America, and that of a passage to the East Indies by the Cape of Good Hope, are the two greatest and most important events recorded in the history of mankind.

You cannot deny that is praise indeed!

It would be fair to say that the history and symbolism of this narrow piece of land, surrounded on three sides by two oceans, was not lost on me. Neither was the generosity of my South African hosts.

As we made our way back to Simon's Town, a more taxing issue usurped my thoughts – how would I avoid the vile Nazi in the Camps Bay hostel? His views and behaviour were a nagging worry. I loathed the prospect of his nunchakus thudding on his mattress as he spewed out more racist diatribes. And who was this so-called 'uncle' in Paraguay? Herr Angry Psycho was spoiling my trip, even when I wasn't in his company. My dark thoughts about his ship sinking somewhere off Argentina weren't helping either.

I realised that for my own sanity, I had no other option but to move out of the Camps Bay hostel. That afternoon I found a perfectly good hostel in Muizenberg, another relaxed, seaside suburb on the slopes of the mountain, much favoured by surfers and hikers.

I'd always chosen to travel alone around southern Africa so that I didn't have to make any compromises. Selfish, I know, but I was pragmatic and hungry to see a lot. During that week, however, I began to feel lonely for the first time. I'd had many experiences and was feeling the need to share them with someone, so I decided, soon after my day trip to Stellenbosch, to hitchhike back to Transkei. The journey through the lush and beautiful Garden Route along the east coast was beautiful, but much of it was lost on me. I just wanted to get home. Two days later I ambled up the dusty dirt road out of Umtata and through the familiar gates of Ikhwezi Lokusa Special School. There was the reassuring sight of the Pig parked outside reception, to welcome me home.

Later that week, Sister Mary Paule had me take some of the students for their orthopaedic treatment in East London. On this occasion I had Nadiwe, one of the young teachers, for company. She was smart, with a sharp mind and a wicked sense of humour, and we had always got on famously. In the big city of East London that lunchtime, we made a point of sitting together in the middle of a busy shopping mall, sipping our cokes in full sight of everyone. We felt dreadfully conspicuous – a young black woman and young white man sitting side by side in South Africa! It was almost unheard of. But we were determined to make it normal, and spent a pleasant half-hour chatting about the students, her educational aspirations and all the fascinating things I'd seen and done in Cape Town.

I'd stopped feeling quite so lonely.

20

Summons to Appear in Court K 504855

Have you ever visited a police station? They're not pleasant places in my opinion, though I don't have a long and exotic criminal record to back up this assertion. I have no hidden international banking fraud in my past, no shop heist or common or garden suburban murder to confess to, I'm afraid. But based on a few parking and speeding offences and the occasional lost passport or camera, I've had to visit one or two police stations in my time, in different parts of the world. They all seem to share a grim, overbearing atmosphere and unpleasant smells, ripe with the anticipation of human suffering and desperation. Perhaps in Scandinavia or some other socially progressive countries they're a little nicer, more like a McDonald's or a doctor's reception room, but elsewhere I've concluded that they're best avoided. In fact, being a law-abiding citizen, I've tried to keep my relationship with the police at smiling distance.

In Transkei, however, I got to meet the good officers of the law on several occasions. Sometimes I was guilty, sometimes, not.

Firstly, an admission of guilt. I failed to stand trial in Court C, at Umtata's Inferior Court, on 10 September 1980. I did a no-show. Bad form and disrespectful, I can hear you tut. Yes indeed, very poor form. What's the crime, you're thinking?

My offence: A defective hooter.

Fine imposed: Five rand.

The scene of my crime: Ngangelizwe Road, Umtata.

Date of offence: 3 September 1980.

Time at the offence: Circa 11.30 a.m.

Umtata town centre, where I was stupid enough to leave money in an Ikhwezi van. Guess what? It was stolen.

How do I plead? I *was* guilty, but let me explain.

It wasn't unusual for Transkei police to set up roadblocks in Umtata and adjoining areas now and again. Frequently, I could see them ahead and would take evasive action by taking an alternative route or enforcing a sharp U-turn. After a few months I'd sussed many of the local roads. It was a bit of a cat-and-mouse chase between the officers of the law and miscreants like me driving faulty vehicles. Their job was to fine people on the spot, for driving below-par vehicles. Some of the Ikhwezi vans were a little below par, with minor mechanical defects such as faulty hooters and damaged windscreen wipers. But as long as I could avoid the attention of the police I had little to worry about.

And so it was that on 3 September 1980, the day before I was due to leave Transkei for Johannesburg, the Umtata police set up roadblocks for vehicle inspections in Ngangelizwe. Normally this was no problem, as I knew the rat runs and could avoid detection, but on this day I slipped up. My stomach got the better of me, as it was approaching lunchtime, and my mind drifted. I began anticipating one of Sister Ignatia's lunches – my last one, in fact. With my mind focusing on a plate of cooked mielie meal and sardines, I suddenly found myself merging into a queue of traffic with police waving vehicles forward for a mechanical health check. A U-turn was not an option.

The entrance road to Ngangelizwe township, close to the site of the police roadblock that caught me.

A young officer of the law strode up to me, looking serious and in charge, and began gesticulating about which component of the vehicle he wanted tested. First, the headlamps – tick. Second, the windscreen wipers – tick, but only just. Thirdly, the hooter. Nothing sounded. He articulated again that he wanted to hear the hooter. For a second time I put pressure on a fractured plastic device, with the aim of eliciting a squeak, a hoot, a rumble or anything vaguely audible. Not a chance – my Ikhwezi van was hooter-less. I was still thinking about tinned sardines and mielie meal for lunch.

Now for the punishment. The young officer, replete with irrefutable evidence of my vehicular deficiency, came up to my open van window to extract a fine, there and then, on the spot. I felt vulnerable. He looked pleased. He started explaining that he wanted thirty rand from me. That was more than I was paid in a month. He was definitely trying it on. And so I thought I would reciprocate and politely refused to accept the fine. I know what you're thinking; how arrogant and cocky. But the reason I declined was that I was rand-less; I did not have my wallet with me. Nonetheless, the haggling continued, our conversation mixed with road dust and exhaust fumes from the numerous vehicles filing past. Many drivers were chastised, a few were not. The officer reduced his demands for immediate payment in increments of five rand, as though we were negotiating in an Arab souk, until we got to five rand. Then out came

My summons to appear at 'Umtata Inferior Court'.

the printed NOTICE TO APPEAR IN INFERIOR COURT, K 504855, signed by Officer 1869. I had a written summons, which I still have, to appear in court on 10 September 1980, when the judge would extract my fine. The young officer went off to catch his next victim. I went for lunch and then to my room, to pack my rucksack for my departure the following day.

Concerned that my court summons might reflect badly on Ikhwezi, I shared my morning's motoring mishap with Sister Mary Paule, knowing full well she took an absolute delight in flaunting all rules, and traffic rules in particular. Her dismissive chuckle suggested that I didn't have much to worry about.

Perhaps I have underappreciated my knack for avoiding traffic fines. The City of Durban police department wrote to me at Box 156, Umtata, Transkei on 15 April 1980 to explain that the Senior Prosecutor, Durban, had accepted my written explanation and was not going to levy the traffic violation charge I incurred while at the South African paraplegic sports championships. There you go, that's two fines levied and two dodged, and in neither case did I have to visit the actual police station.

Perhaps I'm just not a fine, upstanding citizen.

Back in February, I'd been a little greener behind the ears; in fact I'd been outright gullible, the new boy in town, more eager than a puppy with a bouncy ball. So when I was asked to do a series of errands in

Umtata Magistrate's Court, where I should have appeared on 10 September 1980, shortly after I had left the country. [Photo taken in 2020]

Umtata I was in there, bright-eyed and obliging, buying this, fetching that, off to the bank, into the post office and all done with a spring in my step. Parking on the main roads in downtown Umtata was easy and I could just about walk everywhere. Except I was being watched. I don't know by whom, but some bright spark was keeping tabs on me, because when I foolishly left some money in the van, someone was in there like a shot via a small side window. I hadn't left the van long, but someone had broken in and taken thirty-three rand of Ikhwezi money quicker than you could say, 'Why did you leave money in the van, stupid?'

To add to the ignominy of the theft, when I returned to Ikhwezi, I was told by Sister Dolorata that the money would be deducted from my very modest monthly payment. Ouch, that hurt. I knew she was right, it was a fair punishment for an act of gross stupidity. Who leaves money in a vehicle in the middle of any town? Furthermore, I had to go to the Umtata Police Station to report the crime. So, off I trotted, tail between my legs.

I'd already visited the Umtata prison on a couple of occasions, soon after I'd arrived in Transkei, and even from the outside it was ominous. Knowing I was keen as mustard to get to know the real Transkei, Sister Mary Paule had thought it appropriate to take me there. One visit was

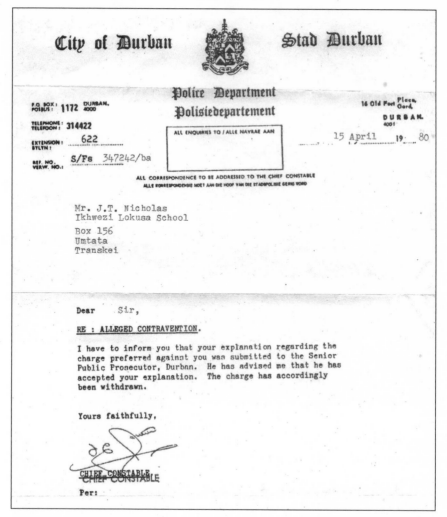

Alleged Contravention letter from City of Durban Police Department, Ref. No. S/Fs 347242/ba.

bad enough, but maybe she thought I was vulnerable to straying from the righteous path and needed a second visit to serve as a deterrent. I liked Transkei a lot, but the prison was not a favourite spot. It gave me the heebie-jeebies. I was soon to add the Umtata Police Station to this list.

To my surprise, there was no queue at the police station when I arrived. It appeared that I was the only person there, except for a tall, imposing policeman. Standing behind a tatty counter, I think his aim was to intimidate people and I was most certainly intimidated. The room wasn't warm, it was hot and sweaty. The air in the room was still and stale. The sweat patches started appearing on my T-shirt in the seconds it took me

An ambulance driver at
Umtata Hospital.

to walk from the door to the counter. I felt that I was interrupting him,
although I had no idea from what, as there was no one else about, or so
I thought.

Then I heard the distinct sound of crying and heavy sniffling coming
from somewhere in the room. As far as I could make out, we were the
only two present and we were now staring at each other, silently not
acknowledging the whimper from somewhere underfoot. He was waiting
to hear what I wanted. I was waiting to log my story of woe.

I started to recount my mishap with the money and the insistence of
Sister Dolorata that I log the crime. The officer sighed, took up a pen and
an official document, and began writing. Again, I heard the crying and
sniffling, a little louder this time. A small boy, tears streaming down his
face, peered out from under the counter and tried to make a dash for it.
His escape was stymied by the heavy boot of the officer and then another
kick as the officer shoved the boy back under the counter. Understandably
and alarmingly, the crying and moaning raised a few notches as the small
boy caught my eye and retreated to the sanctuary under the counter. The

A Transkeian soldier.

officer put in another couple of kicks for good measure. I stood there motionless, speechless and shocked to the core.

Seeing my distress and unable to deny the existence of a sobbing third party, the officer nonetheless carried on writing, and without so much as a pause or a glance at me, said in a matter-of-fact way, 'He stole some pens. This is for his own good.'

He'd provided an explanation, but there was no comfort in knowing that a boy of a similar age to my Ikhwezi students was being beaten while cowering under a desk by a bloke who would not have looked out of place in a rugby scrum. I was trying to reconcile the explanation and the event, completely thrown. I pretended it was some sort of accepted local custom.

The whole thing was torturous, and I did not have the balls to do or say anything about it. I carried on relating the details of my petty incident while the sobbing continued. God, it was dreadful. I can't believe I did nothing. I was a rabbit in the proverbial headlights and I couldn't log the crime quick enough to hurry outside. Was this really local justice?

I've recalled this awful event and my appalling cowardice on many occasions since then, just hoping that a beating under a police station counter in Umtata might have put that child off stealing for life. But who am I kidding? Myself. I was a dreadful coward, and I should be called out as such.

Now you know why I have such an aversion to police stations.

I can only hope that that vigilante-style act of deterrence on the part of a man who was supposed to uphold the law served some long-term greater good. Who knows what further forces acted on the life of that small boy that might have nudged him toward the straight and narrow or, alternatively, deeper into a life of crime? For myself, the incident was a reminder of my own glaring flaws and how much growing up I still had to do.

The tearful boy hiding under the police station counter would be about fifty now.

21

Freedom Fighter or Terrorist?

Louis, his lovely wife and two children could not have been friendlier, more hospitable or more accommodating if they'd tried. I was sitting at their dinner table, enthusiastically eating their steak, with a cold beer in hand to wash it down. Before supper they'd pointed me towards their warm shower where, with some effort and generous dollops of shampoo, I had rinsed off the grime and bush dust I'd recently accumulated on the dry roads of Zambia, Zimbabwe, Botswana and South Africa. Their modest house was spotlessly clean and simply furnished, with nothing ostentatious on show. They were a traditional Afrikaans family, from Klerksdorp in the Transvaal, a good 800 kilometres north of Umtata by road. Louis was in the motor or tyre trade. I'd gleaned that from the company's regional newsletter he proudly gave me. It included a black-and-white head-and-shoulders shot of him looking at the camera. He appeared to be in management and a respected man in his community, which led me to wonder if he was a member of the local *Broederbond*, the secret male-only network to promote Afrikaans causes, particularly in commerce and politics.

I was quite taken with Louis and evidently he with me, for we'd met only hours earlier and here I was, sitting down to dinner with him and his lovely family in a respectable neighbourhood and with the prospect of a warm bed before me. He had picked me up while I was hitchhiking outside the town of Mafeking soon after I'd crossed the border from Botswana into South Africa. Compared to many Afrikaners I met on my hitchhiking travels, he spoke good English and was comfortable talking

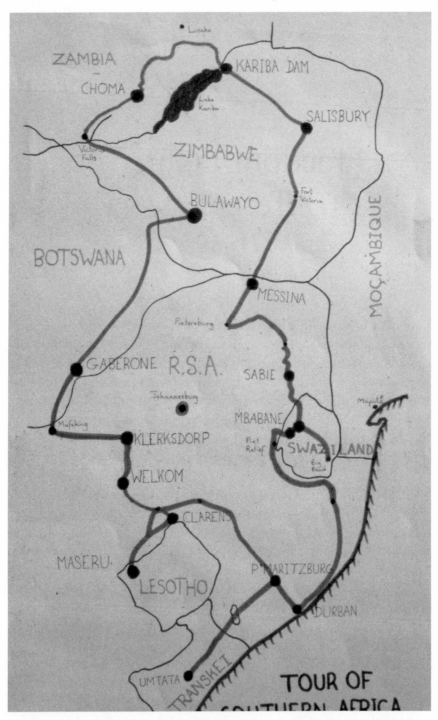

The map I drew of my 6,500-km hitchhike around southern Africa. (Harare was labelled Salisbury, to prevent confusion with audiences in Transkei and in the UK.)

to me in his second language. In fact, he was keen to speak to me. He had some opinions he wanted to share, and since he was giving me a lift, I was obliged to listen.

Travelling in various remote reaches of the Transvaal, I had already met many Afrikaners who were, firstly, surprised and curious to meet an Englishman (*rooinek*, or redneck) in their midst, and secondly, mostly uncomfortable speaking English, although everyone was courteous, albeit abrupt, which seemed a general cultural trait. The Anglo-Boer War of 1899–1902, or the Second War of Independence, as the Boers called it, came up in conversation more than once, but I feigned ignorance so I could hear what they thought. For many of these people the scars had not healed and the atrocities of the British were not forgotten, particularly the use of concentration camps. Some even recounted the suffering and death of their own relatives, particularly women and children, at the hands of their colonial enemy. Whilst the Boers had frequently humiliated the British army in the veld and from the kops, for much this bloody war, the cost in lives was high on all sides – at least twenty-five thousand Boers, twelve thousand Africans and twenty-two thousand British perished in less than three years of conflict.

Thankfully, Louis did not want to make me feel guilty for the wartime excesses of my forebears. No, he was much more contemporary and wanted to justify apartheid to me. But before he broadened my mind,

Setting out on my four-week mammoth hitchhike from Transkei to Zambia and back, living on biltong and dried apricots.

211

as he saw it, he wanted to hear about my mammoth 6,500-kilometre, four-week hitchhiking trip from Transkei to the interior of Zambia and back, via Natal, Swaziland, Western Transvaal, Harare in the newly independent Zimbabwe, Zambia, Victoria Waterfalls, Bulawayo in Zimbabwe, Gaborone in Botswana, the Orange Free State, Maseru in Lesotho and many small, glorious places in between. He was quite taken with my venture and so was I, truth be told. I'd had many more scrapes and hairy moments than I cared to admit. I don't think he'd ever met anyone who'd been to Zambia before and I don't think he had anyone on his Christmas card list from Transkei either. We had time to kill on the car journey between Mafeking and his home in Klerksdorp, so as we drove the long flat road he asked me questions about what I'd seen. We made quite an odd couple. He was large, smartly dressed in business attire, and I was thin by comparison, in rough, dirty denim clothes with only a tattered rucksack for company. My longish, hippy hair, though, was gone. That had been seen to by an overenthusiastic Italian barber in Harare, who seemed familiar only with military-grade hair shearing.

When I'd finished explaining my near encounter with guerrilla fighters in the bush of Zambia and other memorable events, he turned to the ubiquitous question posed by almost all white South Africans at the time:

'What do you think of South Africa, hey?'

The 'hey' was often included at the end of the sentence to make sure I knew a question had been landed. It was just a tiny bit confrontational – or assertive might be a better way of putting it. On the surface it was a reasonable question, one that you would be asked by the hosts of any country you visited. In Iceland, you might recall the challenges of trying the local fermented fish. Your proud Malaysian hosts may be eager to hear your impression of their magnificent limestone caves. In Rio de Janeiro, the experience of being mugged by feral street children on *Praia Vermelha* twice in a week, might colour your opinion about holidaying in Brazil. All very normal, I think you'll agree. But in 1980s white South Africa, the question was heavily loaded. It was often just a preamble to explain and justify apartheid. Being ostracised on the international stage hurt a great deal and felt grossly unfair to them, particularly as they viewed apartheid as a reasonable response to South Africa's diverse range of challenges. I found that there was a sort of ubiquitous assumption among the white population that if the history of the country could be explained and the complexities of racial differences articulated to outsiders, like me, we might see that apartheid wasn't so bad after all.

So, when Louis asked me for my opinion of his country I did what I always did when posed this question by white South Africans – I dodged it. I replied with great enthusiasm about how beautiful the country was, citing the majesty of the Drakensberg mountains, the views of the Blyde River Canyon, the beaches of the Wild Coast, and one hundred and one other fabulous landscapes. My reply was immaterial, an irrelevance. My hitchhiking host was already off, explaining about the arrival of Europeans at the Cape centuries earlier, specifically 1652, and the fact that black people had barely populated South Africa at that time. As there were so few black people back then, he explained without fear of contradiction, it had been fair for the white man to colonise the wild, open country that stretched out for hundreds of kilometres. Louis then got onto the plight of the Boers. He felt the need to explain, in some detail, about the desire of the Boers to get away from the control of the British in the Cape, and the suffering they subsequently endured, from the elements, the topography, infighting and myriad African people, not least the Zulus. After all, the *volk* were God's chosen people.

He had just started on the trouble with the black man, the irreconcilable differences between the regions' races and the impossibility of different races living together when we pulled into his driveway. An explanation of Mandela and his band of communists and terrorists would have to wait until suppertime.

And so it was over a steak and cold beer, with Louis at the head of the table, that he continued his sincere and heartfelt explanation of why apartheid was necessary, and why Transkei and other Bantustans, with their separate development strategies, were good for black people. Apartheid, I was told, helped the black man develop as he wanted to in his home territory, while still having access to employment in mines and the like. Without the white man, the non-whites would be lost, the situation would be hopeless, the country a mess. Besides, where were the likes of him and his family to go? He stressed repeatedly that he was African and that he had a right to be in South Africa. Over many generations, his family and others like his had endured many hardships to take an empty, hostile country and turn it into the most prosperous in Africa. So why was the outside world so hostile to white South Africa, he wanted to know? He was emotional and passionate about the issue.

For the first time, and not the last, I started to form an image of the Afrikaans people as a distinctive white tribe. Were they a tribe of Africa like the Xhosa-speaking people of Transkei or the Zulus in Natal? That

The granite Voortrekker Monument commemorating the Great Trek made by Afrikaners in the 19th century, including Louis' ancestors. [Photo taken in 2020]

was the picture Louis and his wife were trying to paint. They were African, they insisted, Afrikaners with a right to live and prosper in South Africa. The shores of Europe, they explained, were now alien to them and certainly no place of refuge if things turned bad locally.

I need not have worried about getting embroiled in answering him as he now moved on to the 'Mandela' issue. The family were listening attentively to the head of the house. I suspect that some of Louis' comments were designed to reinforce their views, as well as to challenge mine. I hadn't offered a single view about South Africa except about the landscape, but as a teacher of Bantu children in Transkei, in his mind I no doubt had reservations about his people's treatment of Blacks. He thought that I did not understand the Afrikaans community and their views. Indeed, I did not, but I was listening quite sincerely.

Soon the theme of the one-way conversation was communism, terrorists and 'Mandela'. The word 'Mandela' was extremely loaded, a generic shorthand for all bad things associated with undermining apartheid and white rule. The threats, the risks and dangers from the likes of 'Mandela' and his anarchists were repeatedly stressed. As communism was creeping through Africa with the liberation of each new country, he needed me to know that this, too, represented a danger to both the white and the black man. His views about communism were similar to those expressed by the Bishop of Umtata. Everyone was at risk. He was proud that his country was being vigilant and that the armed forces were doing a good job, patrolling the national borders and dealing with Russian-backed guerrillas and terrorists in Angola, Mozambique and the like.

Ordinarily, you would say that this was a lot of opinion and information to take in, but I'd heard similar sincere and earnest arguments from white South Africans many times before. In truth, I genuinely felt for the dilemma facing Louis and his family. I thought the future for white South Africans looked bleak, although I kept such views well under wraps and took no pleasure in my conclusions. How could I *not* have sympathy for a man who had shown such warm, open hospitality to me, a complete stranger? Without him I'd have been stuck on a cold, dusty roadside somewhere in the Transvaal or the Orange Free State. I was actually concentrating less on his talk about apartheid than on the delicious steak and cold beer, and the prospect of a warm, clean bed. The night before, I'd failed to get much sleep as my improvised bed had been a few loose blankets on a chilly concrete floor of a school somewhere in Botswana. By comparison, my bedroom in Klerksdorp looked homely, warm and inviting. I couldn't wait to wrap up in the clean sheets and fall asleep.

What I knew, and Louis fortunately did not know, was the fact that there was communist and revolutionary black freedom fighter literature right under his own roof that night, tucked away safely in my rucksack, away from prying eyes.

It was time for bed.

At this point, I suspect you're asking *why* and *how* on earth was I carrying in my rucksack this incendiary political material, and in the heartland of conservative white South Africa of all places? I think you deserve an explanation, so let's backtrack and fill in some of the gaps.

A couple of weeks or so earlier, and using only my outstretched thumb, I had hitched rides for more than 2,300 kilometres from Transkei to Harare, the recently renamed capital of the new Republic of Zimbabwe. The former name, Salisbury, had been binned, confined to the past, as had the country's earlier name, Rhodesia. It was only two months since the country exuberantly celebrated independence, to the music of Bob Marley and the Wailers, after decades of white rule. Robert Mugabe and Canaan Banana were the new democratically elected Prime Minister and President, respectively.

The halo effect of black independence was palpable in Harare, particularly among the many young black people I met. As far as they were concerned, the future looked bright and opportunity beckoned. In their minds, things were about to get way better, and in conversation they were bubbling with excitement for their future, for everyone's future. Now the war was over, now Robert Mugabe was in power, a fairer, multiracial society would prosper, they thought. I listened, touched by their optimism and hunger to build a new and better country. Trite as it may sound, at that specific time and in that specific place, I sensed a level of optimism, hope and excitement for a country that I had never known before, nor felt since.

I did not find these upbeat views and aspirations shared by most whites, or Rhodesians as they called themselves. They were largely bitter, with anger seething just below the surface. In fact, their resentment often verbally spilt over; they couldn't keep it contained. One or two white people did confide in me that they were sticking around, not fleeing to South Africa or the UK, to help build a new multiracial post-colonial country. One white person who gave me a lift in the Harare area said he had voted for Robert Mugabe, although he would never admit it to friends and family.

Part of the Zimbabwe independence celebrations included a large art exhibition in central Harare that I happened upon quite by accident. As well as displaying regional black art, which was stunning, it also celebrated the black liberation movement and the partnership between the freedom fighters of Robert Mugabe's Zimbabwe African National Union – Patriotic Front (ZANU-PF) and *Frente de Libertação de Moçambique* (FRELIMO), the communist-backed government of Mozambique. Numerous bright posters and leaflets around the exhibition space conspicuously promoted black power, the armed struggle and the role of Marxist–Leninist philosophy to build a better future for the workers. For me, coming from a conservative suburban British background, this was all very unfamiliar and a touch unnerving. I was in a hall that was unambiguously celebrating communism and revolution, and I was just a tad out of my comfort zone. These were not the usual topics of celebration back home in the leafy streets of Guildford, where local political parties usually wrestled with the challenges of new one-way traffic systems and bus timetables. I'd read about the French and Russian revolutions, and I knew that both had got a little out of hand with the Sans-culottes and Stalin's 'Great Purge' causing more than their fair share of misery. The messages and themes of black liberation were bold and undiluted. While the sacrifices of those lost in the armed struggle were reflected upon, the main focus of the posters and leaflets was on a prosperous future for black people, led by ZANU-PF and FRELIMO. Who was I to challenge the wisdom or otherwise of revolutions? I didn't even know what Marxism really meant.

Sensing that I was witnessing a piece of African political history, I politely requested and received a handful of the communist-themed leaflets and bright posters, stuffing them into my rucksack and forgetting about them. After a few days I headed north to the border of Zimbabwe and Zambia.

With my arm and thumb outstretched, rucksack on my back, I left sophisticated, bustling Harare. Every driver who gave me a lift wanted to talk about the years of war, the impact on their families, the country and the future under Robert Mugabe. These were often very harrowing personal stories ending with an uncertain future. But it soon became clear that for some people the war still wasn't over.

After several hours on the road, I was stranded for a while in an unmarked part of the bush, with no villages or towns in sight, when a smart Mercedes car pulled over to offer me a lift to Lake Kariba, my destination. Before setting off, the driver, a slim white businessman in smart short sleeves and stylish aviator sunglasses, asked me if I knew how to fire a gun. My silence and blank face spoke volumes. At which point, he leant over to my side of the car to open the glove compartment and produced a large handgun with a shining steel barrel. I'd never seen a handgun before, except in Hollywood films, but this was a whopper! This was no popgun. This monster weapon meant business. My surprise was probably visible, as he explained that there was still the realistic risk of trouble from 'fucking terrorists' in this part of the country and that I would need to use the gun if we were attacked. Evidently, this was all very normal stuff for him, so he gave me a one-minute lesson on how to use the weapon: the grip, stance, aiming, etc. I failed to absorb one bit of my ballistics training session, except that I'd have to follow his instructions and use the gun should the worst occur.

The owner of the Mercedes, a manager at the Lake Kariba fisheries, then went on to advise me that I should take more care where I hitchhiked in future. Pointing his finger over the steering wheel, he showed me where a pride of lions had passed through the previous day, some 200 metres from where I'd been standing all bright-eyed and bushy-tailed, trying to cadge a lift. Now, I wasn't sure whether to be more frightened of a chance encounter with wild lions or human assailants. My jolly adventure around southern Africa started to feel a little less jolly and a lot more serious.

I hadn't given too much thought about how my hoard of black liberation literature might be received when I got back to South Africa.

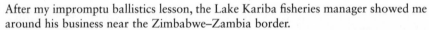

After my impromptu ballistics lesson, the Lake Kariba fisheries manager showed me around his business near the Zimbabwe–Zambia border.

Not well, I suspected, but I ignored the issue, hoping my nagging doubts might subside. After I'd walked over the huge Kariba Dam, overlooking the legendary Zambezi River on one side and a vast lake on the other, the magnitude of my problem was brought rapidly into focus by the border guards at the Zimbabwe–Zambia crossing.

When they searched my rucksack, they swiftly pulled out my political contraband and were immediately taken aback by the communist and black liberation nature of the material, and insisted on asking me more than once if I was serious about taking it with me back to South Africa. Three border officers now crowded around my rucksack, unfurling the posters and reading the political brochures. Their earnest tone of voice and animated body language suggested that it would not be a smart thing to do. They were quite incredulous, and suggested I ditch it all there and then. What if I were caught with it in South Africa, they asked? Did I really want to take this stuff back to Transkei via the South Africa border post? While I had no intention of offloading my valuable revolutionary booty, I was now acutely aware of how inflammatory it would be considered if found in my possession by authorities in South Africa.

In particular, the officials wanted to know what I was going to do with my politically sensitive material. Why, they wanted to know, did

Crossing the mighty Zambezi River from Zimbabwe into Zambia at daybreak. Border officials were alarmed at the black liberation literature they found in my rucksack.

I need to risk taking it into the heartland of conservative South Africa? If you're expecting me to proclaim a conversion to the revolutionary cause or to communist ideals for the masses, you'll be sadly disappointed. I was doing it mainly to put two fingers up to apartheid. Smuggling this ZANU-PF and FRELIMO material across the border, in front of all their guns, uniforms and snivelling looks, would be my small way of registering what I thought of the security services and state apparatus that underpinned white South Africa. I saw it as my personal act of defiance, a pathetic form of resistance, which no one would know about except me. Well, that was what I intended.

So I needed a Plan B if I was to avoid the attention of the South African border guards and the likely consequences of my hoard being discovered.

My Plan B was simple. After feeling around, I discovered that I had a tight lining to my rucksack that went all the way down the frame side and underneath. I carefully slid the inflammatory literature into it, as far down as I could push it without causing damage. Now it was tidily out of view and accessible *only* if you knew how to get into the lining. I felt rather pleased with myself, and hoped I wouldn't have to experience a personal search by the South African security forces as I resumed my hitchhike around southern Africa and back to the safety of Transkei.

As it transpired, it was a good job that I did implement Plan B.

My next few days of travel from Lake Kariba through rural Zambia to Victoria Falls and then Bulawayo were to be challenging if not outright traumatic at times, covering a distance of some 1,300 kilometres.

A black guy and a coloured guy had watched and listened to my fraught conversation with the Zambian border officers, and were curious what a British bloke working in Transkei was doing in these parts. I was beginning to ask myself the very same question. So I ended up answering their questions in the driver's cabin of the grain truck they were taking north to Zambia. Besides asking about my motives for hitchhiking alone in southern Africa for several weeks, they were bursting with enthusiasm about the new Zimbabwe after experiencing years of war in the liberation struggle against the Rhodesian government. Like the white people I met in Harare and on the road, they shared personal stories about the horrific impact of the war on their friends, family and communities. Instead of hearing about war in some vicarious way, through television or a book, I was learning about it in a very visceral fashion, face to face with the people whose lives had been seriously blighted, and in some cases ruined.

After traveling north through Zambia for quite some time, they were keen to show me the expansive bush areas, adjacent to the road, where

Just before dropping me off, the driver showed me the sites in the Zambian bush occupied by freedom fighters, or 'fucking terrorists' as many white Rhodesians called them.

many of the freedom fighters of either Robert Mugabe (Zimbabwe African National Liberation Army – ZANLA) or Joshua Nkomo (Zimbabwe People's Revolutionary Army – ZIPRA) had hidden and were still encamped. The freedom fighters of these liberation armies had used Zambia as a base to train and launch attacks on Rhodesia during the many years of the armed struggle. I'd assumed the freedom fighters would have disbanded now that the liberation struggle was over, but I was assured that thousands were still living in the bush close by, not yet integrated into the newly liberated Zimbabwe. These 'freedom fighters', I reasoned, were the same 'fucking terrorists' I'd heard the white Rhodesians refer to. So, 'freedom fighters' and 'fucking terrorists' were evidently the same people described by different individuals. That gave me some food for thought.

More concerning for me was that, soon after passing the bush area that the driver had identified as the freedom fighters' camp, he dropped me off at the side of the road, as he would be travelling in a different direction. I immediately felt uncomfortable. Besides an uninterrupted expanse of wild bush, there were only a handful of makeshift roadside stalls selling fruit and vegetables. In fact, I wasn't sure what they were selling, and was keen to get out of the area as soon as possible. A handful of locals were milling around, but no one spoke to me. They seemed to avoid me. Being a lone, naïve white guy not far from freedom fighter camps did not feel smart in 1980. Added to which, it was now late morning, the sun was high, the air was hot, and I had very little water on me. No vehicle was in the slightest bit interested in giving me a lift, so I was stuck in the wrong place at the wrong time, feeling mighty uncomfortable. I did not know exactly where I was, but it was somewhere in rural Zambia, a long way from anywhere.

My concerns for my safety weren't ill-founded. After an hour or so, a local man walked from the fruit stalls towards me, making sure he did not stop or come closer than two metres to me. It was clear that he did not want to be seen talking to me. He warned me to get out of the area as some men were coming to 'get' me. 'Get' was unspecified but

Hitchhiking somewhere in Zambia, but I hadn't a clue where. Somewhere near Mazabuka, I guess! I was told to move on quickly to avoid trouble, so I did.

sounded concerning. He said something like, 'Mister, you must go from here quick, the men are coming to get you.'

After warning me, he carried on walking as though oblivious to my presence.

Which 'men' was he referring to? The freedom fighters? In truth, it didn't really matter who they were; apparently they didn't like me, which was bad news and all I needed to know.

I didn't doubt his warning and started to panic. If anything happened to me here, no one in the world would know where I was, as I was effectively off the radar. Why, I asked myself, had I strayed so far, to somewhere this unsafe? But there was no time for self-pity and indulgent analysis; I had to get away, urgently. I picked up my rucksack and stood in the middle of the road, waving my arms as soon as the next vehicle came into view. It was an open-back pickup truck that was forced to stop or run me over. It stopped. Two Czechoslovakian guys were in the driver's cabin, but there was no time for pleasantries. We exchanged the fewest of words before I hopped into the back, mighty relieved to be moving on, although I had no idea where to.

In addition to my relief, I felt a huge sense of debt to the local man who had warned me. He had no obligation to. Then, as now, I wanted to show my thanks and appreciation.

After sunset in the Zambian bush, I listened to local people discussing geopolitics around a wood fire – should they trust the Russians or the Chinese?

I remember feeling a very long way from Umtata and the security of Ikhwezi.

The next twenty-four hours travelling through Zambia to get to Victoria Waterfalls on the north-western border with Zimbabwe did not go much better. When my Czechoslovakian rescuers dropped me at a Zambian railway station that evening, I accidently fell asleep on the platform floor, only to be woken by a young man trying to rob me of my camera. The fear of another assault kept me awake until the train arrived. The train left the station but broke down in the middle of the night, midway to Livingstone, surrounded by trees and bush. It was so cold everyone got off the train and huddled around campfires. The passengers made one fire for each carriage, using nearby branches and logs. Overhead, the mahogany-coloured dome of a pristine African sky, radiant with vivid stars, crowned us.

The whole experience was very surreal. Congregated around the impromptu fire for the basic human need of warmth, with a rail carriage and steel track on one side, and the outstretched African bush on the other, I listened to my fellow passengers sharing their thoughts. They were not talking about their sports team, the rail service or trivial domestic matters. Instead, they were asking each other whether they should trust the Russians or Chinese to develop Zambia. They were serious and passionate in their debate, taking it in turns to offer opinions, in English. Notably, the USA, the UK and other European countries did not feature in their future plans as regional development partners. I could only assume that their experience of colonialism had tainted their views, and that the promises of new communist partners had won their confidence and given them hope for their future.

I metaphorically had to pinch myself as I heard local Zambians articulate their thoughts on geopolitics in these unlikely circumstances. The 'third world' and 'first world' were colliding and synthesising in front of me, around an open wood fire, somewhere in the bush, late at night.

Despite the traumas of the previous day, I did eventually get to the spectacular Victoria Falls, where I was quickly soaked to the skin by the spray of the River Zambezi, and deafened by the guttural sound of water crashing down more than a hundred metres into a brooding aqueous cauldron. Following the euphoria of that truly great natural wonder, I returned to the more mundane task of hitchhiking south to Bulawayo, Zimbabwe's second city.

After mentally and physically refuelling in Bulawayo for a few days, I set off on my travels with my rucksack and camera still my faithful companions. I was now going to meander my way back to Transkei over

Above: Victoria Waterfalls. The deep guttural resonance of the Zambezi River, layers of rainbows and sheets of spray made for a truly exhilarating experience.

Below: Hitchhiking through Zimbabwe, Zambia and Botswana, lorry drivers gave me a few Zambian Kwacha and Botswanan Pula in exchange for biltong and biscuits.

the next week or so, covering 2,400 kilometres, via Botswana, South Africa, Lesotho and miscellaneous small towns and cities. On the one hand I wanted to see more of these uncompromising and contrasting regions. On the other hand, I wanted to return to the security of Ikhwezi.

There was still one obvious issue though. Was I going to be able to smuggle my contentious political material into South Africa without being caught? And what if I got caught? It all played on my mind a touch. Would Plan B be sufficient to outsmart the might of the South African security forces if challenged?

My journey west out of Zimbabwe and south through Botswana to Gaborone, its capital city, went smoothly enough, courtesy of a grain lorry driven by a black guy from Natal. We got on famously. A couple of days later I was in the back of a pickup van, driven again by a couple of black chaps who took me to the Botswana–South Africa border post in the town of Mafeking.

Mafeking was a significant place, or more accurately, a significant *event* for the British in the Second Anglo-Boer War of 1899–1902. It was the location where Robert Baden-Powell, founder of the Scout Movement, made his name as commander of the British forces, holding out against a long siege by the Boers. He and his troops were supported by the Tshidi branch of the Rolong, who'd lost their land to the Boers. So, in the end the Boers did not take Mafeking and the British moved north to the Transvaal, to face a new and even more challenging phase of what was erroneously called 'a white man's war'.

It would be fair to say that my transit through the Botswana–South Africa border post did not go well, starting with my arrival. As we pulled up, I could see the border guards eyeing me.

Mistake #1: I was in the back of a pickup driven by black men, not the other way around as was customary in these parts. Furthermore, this mistake was already drawing attention to me, when I really wanted to be inconspicuous.

Mistake #2: I went to the wrong passport counter. Without a word, the border officer who stood on the other side of the counter slowly moved his head from side to side to indicate something was wrong. He deliberately did not say what was wrong and was terribly agitated, refusing to take my passport from me. Then I realised that I was at the counter for black people, so I stepped one metre to the left to the counter marked 'Whites'.

Mistake #3: I was British. The pugnacious border officer was now very clearly my adversary. He was short and stout, with a crisply ironed uniform, and was obviously uncomfortable speaking English, so he did not. He must have been a local Afrikaans lad, with a few historical grudges weighing heavily on his chipped shoulders. For the most part he stared at me, not saying a word. Not one. A colleague in the office watched us. This must have been good sport for him. But it was all extremely awkward and tense for me.

Mistake #4: My passport was replete with stickers showing multiple entries in and out of Transkei, as well as border stamps from Swaziland, Zimbabwe and Zambia. He smelt a rat and wouldn't return my passport. In fact, he wouldn't stamp it for re-entry into South Africa. I tried to stay calm, conscious not to goad him.

Mistake #5: He could see my rucksack in the back of the pickup van. His eyes honed in on it, his suspicions raised. Now my concerns shot up, too. Although I didn't know a word of Afrikaans, I understood the instruction he bellowed at a tall young soldier standing guard at the border post. Still keeping a firm grip on my passport, he instructed the soldier to search my rucksack. Shit. This was getting serious. This wasn't supposed to happen. I never really thought Plan B would come into effect. More to the point, I wondered if it would work as I tried to keep my anxieties hidden from the arrogant little fascist who switched his glare from me to the soldier and back again, not uttering a word.

The soldier, in beige field fatigues, got to work pulling open the straps of the rucksack. My pulse nudged up a few notches. Stay calm, I told myself. For God's sake, don't look stressed and give the game away. Would he find the rucksack lining? The rucksack was now fully open. Shit! In went his arm and out came three soapstone figures from Swaziland, sweaty T-shirts, a dusty fleece, underwear that had endured two stomach upsets, a pair of boots, biltong, toothpaste, crusty socks and quite a bit of dust. The ripe odour must have served as a repellent, as the soldier stopped, shook his head and roughly stuffed everything back inside. He'd seen enough to convince himself that it was just travel stuff.

Could I relax? No.

The passport officer still wasn't satisfied. He disliked me a lot and was convinced I was hiding something, so he went from staring at me in silence to bluntly asking me, in his very thick accent, why I had travelled to South Africa from Transkei so many times. He insisted this was not normal. He seemed fond of normal. The five-foot-nothing gatekeeper was bristling, his agitation visible. My passport lay open on his side of the counter, his piggy fingers leafing the pages. And why had I gone to Swaziland, Zimbabwe and Zambia recently? Who would want to go to these dreadful places? Everything I'd done represented irregularity and deviance. Without inflaming the situation, I explained my job at Ikhwezi and a desire to see southern Africa, emphasising the natural beauty and landscape. He was most certainly not happy with my explanation. For him, there remained the distinctive whiff of a rat in the air. He knew I was talking bullshit and he really didn't want to give me an entry stamp, but he couldn't nail me, and reluctantly caved.

Thump! He stamped my passport and slid it across the counter. Plan B had worked. By the skin of my teeth I'd got away with my subterfuge. His glare, his stiff, upright posture and his tight lips did not mellow, even as I hopped into the back of the pickup van with my rucksack at my side. Through the dust I could see him still watching intently as we drove off. For him, the smell of rat still lingered.

That had been way too close for my liking.

For all its historical significance, Mafeking looked much like any other rural South African town, with its assortment of supermarkets, car parks, Whites-only city centre and black township circling its edges. We did not stop, which was a relief.

Only a couple of hours later I found myself accepting a lift with Louis before being invited back to join his family for dinner in Klerksdorp. His genuine hospitality and the offer of a warm clean bed were just what I needed after the stresses and strains of my previous week's adventures on the roads of southern Africa. Besides, I was soon to learn from Louis and his family about a new African tribe, the Afrikaners – one, I learnt, that had been created in South Africa.

22

Sister Mary Paule Tacke (MP)

After four weeks traversing the roads of southern Africa, I felt the pull of Ikhwezi and the comforts of my Transkeian home. Before heading back, I spent a few days roaming the mountains of the Orange Free State and north Lesotho, enjoying the spectacular Golden Gate gorge and its caves, where I marvelled at primitive rock paintings by San people who'd passed through many generations before. But I could not be sustained on biltong

Sister Mary Paule's grave in the simple but pretty Glen Avent cemetery, literally a stone's throw from Ikhwezi Lokusa Special School and Bethany Home. [Photo taken in 2020]

and dried apricots forever. After spending another restless night on a bare concrete floor, this time at the YMCA in Pietermaritzburg, I snuck out at 5.30 a.m., when it was still cold and dark, to begin the long hitchhike back to the undulating hills of Transkei. For the final 2 kilometres of my 6,500-kilometre hitchhike around southern Africa I walked from Umtata town centre up the long dirt track to the gates of Ikhwezi. I'd made it, and it was a huge relief to arrive home, in one piece, with my rucksack and camera still in my possession. I was smelly, hungry and tired, but a great deal wiser than when I'd left.

More than anything, I was bursting to tell Sister Mary Paule about the trip; whom I'd met, what I'd seen and what I'd experienced. I was excited, with a real need to talk through the journey. It was Sister Mary Paule who had nurtured my enthusiasm to explore southern Africa during our many hours of conversation in the sanctuary of her office in the school library. Now I could bring our National Geographic map to life, based on my personal experience, and later with the aid of my photographic slides. Places with wonderful names like Welkom, Piet Retief, Maseru, Sabie, Choma, Gaborone and Clarens weren't 2-D cartographic annotations anymore but places I'd visited and explored. The Limpopo and Zambezi Rivers were no longer squiggles from left to right across lines of longitude and latitude. Zimbabwe wasn't just another independent African country. Robert Mugabe was no longer just a news item to me. I'd seen the glow in people's eyes as they spoke from the heart about their personal hopes *and* fears for the future of their new nation. The words 'freedom fighter' and 'fucking terrorist' now had more nuanced meanings to me.

Late that afternoon, after refuelling, washing and changing clothes, I found Sister Mary Paule quietly studying in the Ikhwezi library. I did not wait to be invited in. I sat down opposite her desk, and in response to her casual comment about it being good to see me back, started talking. I talked non-stop for a full four hours, with no convenience or coffee breaks. Sister Mary Paule listened intently, out of interest, I think. Frequently she asked questions, I'd reply as best I could, and on I would go, galloping through the kilometres of roads, countryside, towns, people and events – north, south, east and west. I did not miss a thing.

By the time I had told her all, it was evening and the room was dark and still. Twilight had set in. A few light bulbs illuminated the external open-air school corridors outside the office, decorated by excited orbiting insects. After recollecting my entire journey, I pulled out of my pocket the bishop's letter of introduction that Sister Mary Paule had advised me to take, so that wherever I found a Catholic mission, I might get a free night's lodging and a meal. It was now tatty, dog-eared and stained with grit from several countries. If you'll excuse the dreadful pun, that letter of introduction was a godsend. It was better than any Hilton Hotel loyalty card or Marriot Hotel membership scheme. The bishop's beautifully crafted letter had literally opened doors everywhere, enabling me to stay in a host of Catholic-run institutions, all the way up to the Zimbabwe–Zambia border. I thanked Sister Mary Paule for her foresight in arranging this.

I recalled that before I left, as the bishop personally handed me the letter, he took me by surprise by asking if he could bless me. Perhaps he thought I needed protection and guidance in advance of my foolhardy adventure. Did he have ecclesiastical foresight? I don't know, but to my own surprise, I accepted his offer, and stood quietly before him and Sister Mary Paule as he invoked divine protection with a few kind, holy words and a gentle hand on my head. It felt a little strange, but reassuring.

During the weeks of my travels, there were several times when I had felt fear, disorientation and regret at my rash actions. I wondered if it was the bishop's blessing that saw me through these scrapes and got me back home safely to Transkei. Whatever the role played by his divine intercession, I made sure to thank him on my return. When my photographic slides of the trip were processed I synchronised them to music, and with Sister Mary Paule acting as my promoter, I screened them in Umtata, starting with the bishop's staff in town. 'Treive's slide show' did the rounds, from the nuns in Glen Avent Convent to the British medics in town.

Sister Mary Paule Tacke came from Cottonwood, Idaho, the potato state of the USA, as she used to say with a wry chuckle. She had a gentle, rich American accent that made her stand out a little bit; the last thing I had expected to find in Transkei was an American, let alone an American nun, so at home and so dedicated to her adopted country. I'd known many Americans, expats in the oil business and the like, but the good sister was a bit different to these, that was for sure.

On more than one occasion, I told her that her move to Africa was America's loss and Transkei's gain, at which point she would tell me that the country of her birth was as much in need of missionary work as was this part of Africa. Not for the last time, she got me thinking. Fortunately, Transkei won this hypothetical international tussle.

In her next life, she enthusiastically and repeatedly insisted, she would be filthy rich, marry a Polish farmer and rear horses. Lucky chap,

I thought. I was neither Polish nor in possession of strong equestrian credentials. Back in 1968, a lame donkey unceremoniously threw me off its back at the Rosudgeon village fete near Penzance, so my chances of usurping the farmer were slim at best. She repeated her desire to marry the horse-loving Polish farmer more than once and with considerable conviction. It sounded like a plan or objective that was temporarily on hold while she did God's work and made Transkei a better place.

As far as I could tell, she had several brothers, sometimes speaking with a heavy heart about the loss of one in the Vietnam War, in a plane crash, if memory serves me correctly. The look on her face and tone of her voice spoke volumes about the pain of the family's loss; her whole demeanour would change and she'd shake her head slowly from side to side whenever the subject was mentioned. So many years after this tragic event, the pain was still close to the surface. I wondered if having Doug and me about as her companions reminded her of her brothers. Perhaps it was just coincidence, but she was certainly quieter and a little maudlin after Doug's departure. We both missed him after he left and so we supported each other.

She once showed me a black-and-white photograph of herself as a young girl back in Idaho. A homely, provincial girl stared out from that frozen moment in time. She seemed so different then, carrying a little more weight and of course wearing normal clothes, so that I saw her more fully, as a normal human being rather than as a 'nun'.

When I knew her, Sister Mary Paule Tacke was forty-eight years old, and she wore those years. Life had taken its toll on her physically. She was tall and slim, and stood upright and walked purposefully, never drifting along. She had a notable air of gravitas, her long, greying hair sometimes escaping her starched wimple and giving her an air of vulnerability. She was always easy to spot in a group, which was handy as she often attracted a small crowd when visiting various schools, clinics and social events.

She started out my boss and became a friend. But then, she was also everyone's friend. By the end of my stay, I was even allowed to drive the temperamental Pig! As you can imagine, this was a mixed blessing, but a privilege nonetheless.

Some people thought her saintly, but I thought she was way better than that. She was a first-rate human being at a time and in a place where race discrimination and chronic deprivation afflicted all areas of life, sickness and death. Yet it was her humanity that made her attractive and loveable. She had many human frailties, which she was only too pleased to flaunt and joke about, all wrapped in a sprinkling of self-deprecation and modesty. Any frailties and human weaknesses she had were swamped by her love of people and her dedication to improving the lives of impoverished Transkeians.

Her particular passion was for education and welfare, and for offering practical help to the poor, the sick and the disadvantaged. Nowhere was this more evident than at the crèche or junior school in Ngangelizwe, or out in a rural clinic with distressed single mothers and malnourished infants. As far as I could make out, she was liked by all and adored by many. Even the cantankerous and work-shy Mr Bidla, whose tricks and deceptions Sister Mary Paule could anticipate and foil, had a grudging respect for her. I never heard a bad word or derogatory comment made about her, which was a small miracle considering the challenges and social pressures she faced at the school and in the surrounding areas.

By any measure or yardstick, Sister Mary Paule Tacke was no ordinary person. She seemed to be made of different stuff to you and me. I was pretty certain of that. In the last forty years I've never met anyone like her, despite much global travel and work which brought me into contact with all sorts of fine people, including Amazonian Indians, eminent scientists, caring families, charity fieldworkers and CEOs of large corporations. I knew within days of meeting her that she was unlike anyone I had met before, although I had neither the experience, the intellect nor the emotional capability to know why. It was not just her selfless dedication to others that marked her out. There was something simply wonderful about her personality and temperament, which I came to know over time.

She was sensitive, sincere and listened closely to people. She was open-minded, intelligent and disarmingly witty. Even at times of distress, when faced with distraught mothers and dying infants, she had an air of deep calm and unflappability that imparted to others a sense of confidence and assurance. That included me.

Despite her inner strength and strong religious faith, it was obvious that she had a degree of vulnerability and genuine modesty. Many times we could see that the burdens she carried were too heavy and that she needed our kindness and support to help carry the load. Simply by the look on her face, as she walked the corridors of Ikhwezi, we could tell when she was unhappy, pensive or troubled. It upset us to see her so. Doug and I would remark to each other about it and then inject some of our youthful tomfoolery or humour to help her out, in our clumsy but well-meant way. We felt like her Huck Finn and Tom Sawyer, so we hammed it up, joking about, testing the rules and everyone else's patience.

A Nun and the Pig

I don't know what your expectations are of Catholic nuns, but I had always thought they were austere, with a serious, pious air, maybe a little sanctimonious. The prospect of having a nun as a boss and work colleague had been more than a little disconcerting. My previous boss had been a foreman called Ted, who wore a flat cap and a Co-op branded overall. Ted had a limited but rich and earthy vocabulary, and certainly hadn't been sanctimonious or pious, except about dairy products. But I need not have fretted. Sister Mary Paule's enduring trait was humour; even at the gravest of times, it seldom deserted her. She laughed at herself most, and instead of sniping or criticising the failures of others, she would chuckle, accepting their weaknesses and seeming to embrace the whole person. Outright laughter and ridicule was reserved for people in authority or for pompous types with an overinflated opinion of themselves, such as government ministers, church bigwigs and civic dignitaries. These were considered fair game for her amusement. Sometimes we would be in tears, secretly giggling at them. If only these big cheeses had known how much fun she poked at them and their egos.

Where I come from, we would say that Sister Mary Paule was 'down to earth'. She did not expect too much of anyone, and used humour with a generous serving of empathy when disappointed. A gardener found drunk in the grounds or a teacher returning late from her rural home at the beginning of term could expect a sympathetic hearing. But no one deceived her. No, ma'am. She was way too canny for that. She always preferred a cheeky sinner to a saint, a rule breaker to a rule keeper. Rogues and chancers were considered much more interesting than goody-two-shoes. In her book, the fallen were better company and would be more fun to redeem.

Doug failed his driving test in Umtata so many times we all lost count, and it became a source of collective amusement. So when he did eventually pass, Sister Mary Paule spontaneously arranged a celebration of tinned soup from her personal stash. She right royally burnt the soup and Doug arrived late for his own celebration, on account of the Pig refusing to start. When he did turn up, a little flustered but proud, we laughed over a prized tin of peaches instead. At other times the good sister might take us to the Golden Egg fast food restaurant in town, for burgers and chips, served with an abundance of jokes and good-humoured banter, normally at our own expense. These were special, intimate moments, where unlikely friendships were forged. Her humour and generosity of spirit bonded us together to tackle the many day-to-day human challenges we faced in and around Umtata.

A bottle of wine could also ease our collective pains and lubricate our humour. Over a cheap bottle of rosé Sister Mary Paule once declared quite indignantly, 'I don't dislike getting drunk, only not on this wine.' Several of us spluttered into our own glasses at the declaration, impossible to refute.

With a nun for company I might have expected to be tested on theological doctrine, but instead, with the aid of a bottle of wine for company, Sister Mary Paule and I spent one evening earnestly discussing *Peanuts*, the American cartoon series by Schulz. I spared no detail describing the comedic roles of Linus, Lucy and Charlie Brown in the sketches, which were always predictable and often repetitive. On the other side of the kitchen table the good sister strenuously refuted my assertions, claiming that *Peanuts* was simply unfathomable and lacked real humour. By the end of an entire bottle of wine no agreement had been reached but we had laughed out loud a lot, rocking in our chairs as we did so. We had started the evening a little sad, having waved goodbye to Doug a few days earlier. Debating the merits or otherwise of facile cartoons was a gentle distraction and provided a warm, caring environment in which to console ourselves.

We did fall out once, but only for five minutes and it was over President Jimmy Carter, of all things. A newspaper cartoon I showed her portrayed the luckless president, a former peanut farmer from Georgia, as one of the muppets. He looked a right fool, quite in keeping with the jovial puppets. I laughed insensitively. She didn't chuckle as usual, but frowned, and told me he was basically a nice man who needed a break. I'd hit a nerve, so I hastily pasted the cartoon in my diary and left it at that. We moved on, giving the 39th President of the USA a wide berth for a while.

I didn't realise it at the time, but my American companion had been deliberating feeding my appetite to see as many diverse aspects of Transkei and South Africa as possible. My Transkeian baptism, on arrival, was overseen by the caring nun, who threw me in at the deep end, taking me to meet all the ecclesiastical glitterati at the bishop's residence, and the impoverished residents of several homes in the Ngangelizwe township down the hill. She made sure I visited the local dam, the prison, the new University of Transkei, the small nature reserve, several rural mission stations and the remotest parts of Transkei, including the empty beaches of the Mkambati Reserve in eastern Pondoland and the ancient rolling hills of Cofimvaba, in western Thembuland.

After a thorough immersion in Umtata and these various Transkeian attractions, she introduced me to her 'little people', as she called the pupils at various schools in Umtata and neighbouring towns, where she was popular among the children, the teachers and their families. Trips to all manner of clinics, hospitals, factories, wholesalers, retailers and the East London docks followed in rapid succession. Emboldened by my interest in the new University of Transkei, she sent me off to South Africa with her journalist friend, Brenda, to understand why the black students at the University of Fort Hare were striking and protesting. She encouraged my mammoth hitchhike to Zambia, and later almost insisted that I travel to Cape Town and back, which I duly did within a week or so. Under her guidance, meeting medical experts, chiefs, local dignitaries and civic leaders all started to become the norm.

When she wasn't expanding my mind through introductions to new people and places, she was doing so through books; she encouraged me to read Chinua Achebe's *Things Fall Apart* and Alan Paton's *Cry, The Beloved Country*. Local newspapers were pointed out to me so that I could learn what various communities in Transkei, Durban and East London were thinking and doing. To add to my informal education, I was given tickets to see the play *Lobola*, in Umtata, about the traditional practice of bridal payment. Space in my head previously reserved for milk and juice delivery instructions was now occupied and expanded by weightier matters concerning the plight of Transkei and South Africa.

Everything I saw, read and experienced in Transkei and South Africa, good and bad, swirled about me in a maelstrom of emotions and thoughts that were conflicting and frequently contradictory. Often I felt upset, vexed or both. Ikhwezi, Umtata, Transkei, South Africa and southern Africa were concentric circles of rich experiences and points of view that were so varied, and often so at odds with each other, that my nineteen-year-old self simply could not process it all. I tried, but could not synthesise everything into coherent thoughts and opinions. These weren't just abstract or academic facts I'd gleaned; they were extremely real, often visceral, involving *real* people, with *real* lives, in *real* places. For many people, of all races, I thought life looked pretty uncompromising and binary.

What did I know for sure? For the most part, I was disorientated and unsure.

I knew that apartheid was wrong. I was no moral philosopher, but reference to any moral compass I knew told me something was seriously out of kilter in white South Africa. Whenever I crossed the border from

Transkei to South Africa, I was suddenly made aware of my whiteness, made to feel different from my black friends and colleagues, and treated differently by law. Immediately we approached a restroom or counter, my colleagues would have to step into a different queue to me. I'd be treated well, while they'd often be treated roughly and disrespectfully. How do people take a continual onslaught on their identity by every official person they meet? I hated it, and couldn't wait to leave South Africa to return to Transkei, even though it was a fabrication of apartheid and suffered hideous distortions.

Conversations with ordinary black people on the highways, on the buses, in the townships, at the hospitals, in theatres, in libraries, in churches and in universities gave me one perspective on the problems and what the potential solutions might be. Conversations with white people at their dinner tables, in their business premises and in their cars gave me a polar opposite view of the problems and their solutions. As far as I could see, the country was at absolute loggerheads, with all power and influence in the hands of people who had not the slightest intention of changing the status quo. Yet there was no way the status quo could be maintained. To my mind, anyone who thought it could was blind, stupid or bluffing. You only had to look at population growth rates by racial group, and listen to growing black aspirations, to see that the status quo was unsustainable. White South Africans were delusional, as far as I could see. Their neighbours in Zimbabwe showed the way the tide was flowing.

I had arrived in Umtata a naïve teenager, with no knowledge of the region and very little political understanding. After a few months, I was worried and anxious that South Africa, the Bantustans and all their many races and tribal groups were going to erupt in military conflict and massive civil unrest, with rioting, strikes and worse, leading to a meltdown, followed by anarchy. I thought the anger of the many oppressed people would, firstly, explode uncontrollably against the white population and then turn into conflict between tribal groups such as the Xhosa, Zulus and Basotho, and involve the coloured population, too. To me the future of South Africa looked bleak, very bloody and ultimately more divided. I saw a nation fracturing and buckling, pulled this way and that into a new jigsaw of territories, with everyone simultaneously protecting what they had while frantically trying to grab more for their own communities. I envisaged a conflict similar to that in the Middle East between Arabs and Israelis.

The Ikhwezi Lokusa library served as Sister Mary Paule's office and at the weekend I would often find her there, head down, beavering away at an academic assignment, modestly claiming she might not pass it. I gravitated there, too. It became a sanctuary, firstly to write a couple of reports and letters home, and secondly, as a place to help process what I was experiencing, either through thinking, reading or talking. I shared my bleak thoughts about Transkei and South Africa with Sister Mary Paule, who listened sensitively and empathetically to a young man with limited intellectual depth grappling with weighty issues that had no clear answers. If apartheid was wrong and impoverished Bantustans were a consequence, what was the solution? People were already so polarised, so damaged. Was a fairer way forward even achievable? Would Transkei ever properly share in South Africa's wealth? Would the mess I witnessed across these pseudo-national borders be resolved through bloody armed conflict, as I thought?

In response, my more mature and infinitely wiser friend would open up, sharing her thoughts, concerns and aspirations for her adopted country. While she saw the human and political challenges that I clumsily articulated, she was a great deal more hopeful. The bleak picture I had of South Africa's future was far from inevitable in her eyes. Like a couple of keen fencers with epées or foils, we intellectually lunged and retreated, challenging and rebuffing each other's assertions. Perhaps there was a way of untangling the Gordian knot. Her optimism was based on an unshakeable faith in the goodness of people and the benefits of education. Educated people, she reasoned, would be in a better position to manage the necessary changes, and good, strong leaders would arise to enable the transition. Faith in God and his hand in human affairs guided her thinking too.

My beautiful friend always won our verbal fencing matches, which was a source of comfort to me. And, as events in Transkei and South Africa in later years showed, her forecast about the transition away from apartheid was more accurate than mine.

I missed Sister Mary Paule's company dreadfully after I left Ikhwezi. Her companionship, humour and sensitivity were irreplaceable. We wrote to each other every few months, and I even planned a return trip to Ikhwezi in 1982, but that was scuppered by the Falkland Island conflict between Britain and Argentina. Instead, on her trip to Europe, Sister Mary Paule visited my family and me in Guildford during the summer of

Sister Mary Paule is cradled in the soil of South Africa, overlooking the convent and the rolling hills of the former Transkei.

1982. I resisted showing her the route of my infamous milk round, and instead took her to the theatre and Windsor Castle.

This remarkable woman dedicated most of her adult life and considerable gifts to the welfare and education of sick and deprived young people in Transkei. In 2014, at the age of eighty-two, she was hijacked at gunpoint while distributing food to a place of safety for abused children in Umtata. Two days later she was found dead, her body floating in a shallow river 30 kilometres outside the city. Her killers were arrested and one of the accused was sentenced to twenty-five years in jail for kidnapping and robbery, acquitted of her murder. She is buried at the Glen Avent Convent cemetery, by Ikhwezi, cradled in the soils of the Transkei, the region of South Africa she loved. Her grave is overlooked by Bethany Home, one of the sanctuaries for abandoned children she set up and cherished so dearly.

AFTERWORD

Shadows

I guess it's about time we brought *A Nun and the Pig* to a close. It feels like we're nearly done. But before you shut the book and shuffle off to make a cup of tea, I need to share with you a few notes from my February 2020 return to Umtata, now called Mthatha, and Ikhwezi, some forty years after I first arrived there. In some ways this trip was as important as the first. In modern parlance, I needed 'closure' on one

I returned to Umtata, now Mthatha, in February 2020, forty years after I'd left. [Photo taken in 2020]

or two things. There were too many loose ends still remaining from my departure on 4 September 1980.

Why did it take me forty years to return to Ikhwezi? I asked myself this many times. If the people, places and experiences meant so much to me, why wait so long to return? My friend Simon Mqamelo knew the answer, after I'd known him only a day.

Simon invited me to his rural home in Enkalweni, a village nestled among the craggy hills and sweeping grasslands near Ugie, a ninety-minute drive north-west of Mthatha. It was a beautiful homestead, comprising a couple of huts and a main house, surrounded by trees he'd planted himself, a vegetable garden and a small orchard. Insistent roosters, dotted all over the village, competed with their calls while industrious weaverbirds chattered incessantly in the high gum trees, constructing their intricate hanging nests. A steady breeze whispered through the eucalyptus and oak. Simon and I spent a day and a half chewing the fat together. One minute he lamented the corruption, crime and failing infrastructure of modern South Africa, the next he was discussing the meaning of his dreams and the day-to-day relationship he had with his ancestors. We pivoted between the industrial Western world and the spiritual world of his Xhosa heritage. Both, he insisted, made him the person he was – a modern South African, benefiting from and expressing the best of both cultures. When my guard was down, with my mind focused on his unconventional view of life, he slipped in with, 'Why has it taken you forty years to return to Ikhwezi and Mthatha, when you have such strong feelings for the place?'

Although slightly perplexed, I started to answer, fumbling for a coherent, honest reply. 'Well, I …'

Staring straight ahead, towards the mountainous horizon, he provided the answer.

'You were not ready.'

He still didn't look at me.

'You were not mature enough,' he said rather reassuringly.

There was quite a pause. The sound of the cockerels, weaverbirds and breeze filled the slightly awkward silence.

'Yes,' I reluctantly admitted, 'I was not ready. I was not mature enough.' Now, I insisted, I *was* ready and he nodded ever so gently, in an intimate, knowing way.

Above left: In 1980 people seldom mentioned Nelson Mandela. In 2020, I found his statue in the village of Mvezo, commemorating his place of birth. [Photo taken in 2020]

Above right: In-between discussing his ancestors, my friend Simon Mqamelo was insightful enough to explain that I had not been mature enough to return to Mthatha earlier. [Photo taken in 2020]

The long, straight, dirt road climbing out of Mthatha to Ikhwezi Lokusa Special School was still straight and climbing but replaced by a tarmacked dual carriageway. Assorted modern cars, vans and lorries rushed up and down, while workers and pupils in school uniforms bustled along the pavements and verges. Even after forty years, sights along the road began to feel familiar again – a sharp turn here, a bridge there and the main road into the Ngangelizwe township on the left. Information locked in my cerebral hard drive for so long was rapidly coming to the fore again. In minutes, I stood in front of the reception to Ikhwezi Lokusa Special School, unsure if I were in the present or the past. There were obvious physical differences, but 1980 and 2020 were coalescing for me. It was emotionally disorientating.

After getting the permission of the Principal, Archie Gulwa, I wandered around the school, observing the toll that time and some neglect had wrought. The school is no longer run by industrious and caring nuns but by the state. Despite its many dilapidations, I was transported back in time, my eye caught by shadows, the shapes of familiar friends from the past. I saw Sister Genevieve chasing small boys across the grassy quadrant, with

Above: In Mthatha town centre, road signs directed me back to places I'd last visited forty years earlier. [Photo taken in 2020]

Below: Forty years on, the dirt track from Mthatha to Ikhwezi was now a bustling dual carriageway. [Photo taken in 2020]

The sign that told me I'd finally found Ikhwezi after a long absence. [Photo taken in 2020]

Sister Mirriam giggling in alarm. Sister Ignatia's shadow marshalled staff around the canteen. The physiotherapy team pulled and stretched small boys and girls under the watchful eye of Sister Consolata's shadow. Dear Sister Dolorata was still alert to the tardy timekeeping of Doug and me. She need not have worried, though – there was Doug's shadow, sauntering down the corridor like the Pied Piper towards his class, with the Cool Gang in tow, laughing and playing practical jokes. But I couldn't see Sister Mary Paule's shadow, not in the corridors nor in the classes. Where was she?

The library, of course, but it was locked. Where was the key? There was no way I was leaving without going through that library door. Not a chance.

So I harassed some of the Ikhwezi staff until the key was found. By this stage, a number of teachers and the caretaker were curious and more than a little perplexed as to why a new visitor from the UK was so insistent on visiting their modest library. After I explained as briefly as I could, without being too impolite, the library door was ceremoniously unlocked. It was clearly a big deal for me and one or two staff watched me step forward to gingerly push the door ajar. For the first time since my return, I felt nervous, even anxious, as I entered this room where I'd spent so many hours in comfortable companionship with Sister Mary Paule.

The Ikhwezi Lokusa School library, where I glimpsed the shadow of Sister Mary Paule at her desk, and nearby, the shadow of my nineteen-year-old self. [Photo taken in 2020]

But I was right. Sister Mary Paule's shadow *was* sitting at the far end of the library, head down, quietly writing an assignment. I'd been right to get the library door opened, even if it had created a bit of a fuss. To my complete surprise, just to her left, in his usual place, I saw the shadow of my nineteen-year-old self, grappling with a report on the typewriter. As I looked on, rooted to the spot, they exchanged a few words, something about a good book to read or a local newspaper article. Then the moment evaporated, as did the shadows from the past. A teacher popped in and said she needed the room to do her marking, and I was back in 2020 again.

I sauntered out of the school, through the parked cars, but failed to see a shadow of the Pig. That said, I did catch a glimpse of a beige VW Beetle in Mthatha town centre during my stay. Since it was not running red lights or breaking down, I assumed that it was a poor imposter.

As many of you will know, travel often throws up the unexpected, and this trip was no exception. With the aid of Sister Raphael, one of the younger nuns of the Glen Avent Convent, I got to greet Sister Maria Corda, with whom I had worked in 1980. (Sadly, she lost her life to the Covid-19 virus in June 2020.) She and the other sisters still do wonderful work running the rehabilitation centre for handicapped adults and older students at Ikhwezi. To her surprise, I was able to show her the farewell card she had given me the day I left. After we'd recounted forty-year-old stories together, she invited me to lunch in the convent with the rest of the sisters, where I got to meet up with some old friends. Sadly, others I'd hoped to meet were no longer with us. I needed to visit the graveyard to reacquaint myself with them.

While writing this book I have been too cowardly to research much about how Sister Mary Paule met her end. I dodged it as much as possible, accumulating only the most basic details in order to tell you. In fact, I only found out about her murder less than a year before writing all of this down. But sitting in one of the quiet reception rooms of the convent, Sister Dominic, whom I had known all those years ago, told me the details about that fateful and dreadful day in 2014. It was obvious that the shock, pain and anguish had not dissipated for the sisters. The whole community still felt the loss deeply. It was also clear that I had not yet properly grieved, and so I listened, gently shaking my head from side to side, struggling to make sense of what I heard. I was grateful to be in her sympathetic company as I began to come to terms with the wicked events of that day. It was hard to bear, and it still is.

Still feeling numb and hurt, I ambled over by myself to the convent's beautiful cemetery, in the tranquil wooded enclave of tall eucalyptus.

Sinesipho Kohliso at Bethany Home, where some of the region's most vulnerable children, or 'small people', are protected and cared for.

Branches and leaves scattered fragmented shadows, animated by a lulling breeze. Soon, I found myself keenly focussed on the neatly kept graves of Sister Mary Paule and my other former colleagues, taken by time and illness. Simple white crosses with their names marked each resting place. Time slowed. My horizons narrowed and the outside world felt remote. This is why I had returned. There was a profound air of solemnity to the occasion, as I consciously reintroduced myself before talking to these wonderful, caring souls for a couple of hours. Sometimes I sat down on the gravel, at other times I meandered about, gently zig-zagging between the graves. I had a great deal to chat about, things I should have shared a long while ago. I told my lost friends that some of *their* story, *their* wonderful work at Ikhwezi and in Transkei, had been captured in this book and would be read, hopefully, by a worldwide audience, including people like you. So, you see, you too have been part of this journey that has been *A Nun and the Pig*.

We should finish here, but we can't. You need to know that the spirit of Sister Mary Paule lives on in the orphanage of Bethany Home, just over the fence from her grave. Here, abandoned and desperately vulnerable young children, some only weeks old, receive the love and physical care necessary to start building a life. The volume of the cheeky voices of the 'little people', as Sister Mary Paule called them, bore witness to this. It was here that I met Jenny Walshe, a Project Trust volunteer, and an active member of the caring Bethany Home team. I felt a bond between us, a sort of umbilical cord. Forty years ago, Doug and I had arrived as teenagers to do similar work, to help the vulnerable children of Transkei as best we could. Transkei may no longer exist, but many of the problems still do. I took a vicarious delight in seeing Jenny carry the same baton that we had first brought, all those years ago.

On 4 September 1980, I left Ikhwezi deeply moved by the beautiful harmonies of my students singing *Nkosi Sikelel' iAfrika* to me. This time there was no such musical fanfare. I quietly said my goodbyes to my friends old and new, and slipped out through the gate, mindful not to leave it another forty years before I returned.

Bibliography

Abu-Lughod, J. L., *Before European Hegemony. The World System A.D. 1250-1350* (Oxford University Press, 1989)

Beinart, W., *The Political Economy of Pondoland 1860-1930* (Cambridge University Press, 1982)

Brownlee, C. P. and Brownlee, W. T., *Reminiscences of Kaffir Life and History and Other Papers* (BiblioBazaar, LLC, 1896)

Burton, A. W., *Sparks from the Border Anvil* (Provincial Publishing Company, 1950)

Crais, C. C., *White supremacy and black resistance in pre-industrial South Africa: The making of the colonial order in the Eastern Cape, 1770-1865* (Cambridge University Press, 1992)

Crampton, H., *The Sunburnt Queen. A True Story* (Saqi Books, 2006)

Curtin, P., Feierman, S., Thompson, L. and Vansina, J., *African History from Earliest Times to Independence* (Longman, 1995)

Du Boulay, S., *Tutu. Voices of the Voiceless* (William. B. Eerdmans Publishing Co., 1988)

Elphick, R., *Kraal and Castle. Khoikhoi and the Founding of White South Africa* (Yale University Press, 1977)

Elphick, R. and Giliomee, H., ed., *The Shaping of South African Society 1652-1820* (Longman Penguin Southern Africa Ltd, 1979)

Fallon, I., 'Mandela and I wanted equality but our legacy has been betrayed', *Sunday Times World News* (5 May 2019)

Hamilton, L., *Are South Africans Free?* (Bloomsbury Academic, 2014)

Hamilton, L., *Freedom is Power* (Cambridge University Press, 2014)

Johnson, S., *Strange Days Indeed: South Africa from Insurrection to Post-Election* (Bantam Books, 1994)

Johnson, S., *The Native Commissioner* (Penguin Books, 2006)

Jordan, A. C., *Towards an African Literature. The Emergence of Literary Form in Xhosa* (University of California Press, 1973)

Kavanagh, R. M., *Zimbabwe. Challenging the Stereotypes* (Themba Books, 2014)

Lamar, H. and Thompson, L., ed., *The Frontier in History. North America and Southern Africa Compared* (Yale University Press, 1981)

Magona, S., *Mother to Mother* (David Philip Publishers, 2013)

Marshall, P., *1517. Martin Luther and the Invention of the Reformation* (Oxford University Press, 2017)

Mbeki, G., *South Africa. The Peasants' Revolt* (IDAF, 1984)

McKenzie, B., 'Historical, Political and Sociological Factors Affecting Land Use in Transkei Today. An Ecological Interpretation.', *Carnegie Conference Paper* 307 (1984)

Mda, M., *Struggle and Hope. Reflections on the recent history of the Transkeian People* (African Sun Media, 2019)

Mda, Z., *The Heart of Redness* (Picador, 2000)

Meredith, M., *The State of Africa. A History of the Continent Since Independence* (Simon and Schuster UK Ltd, 2013)

Mertens, A. and Broster, J., *African Elegance* (Purnell & Sons (S.A.) Ltd, 1979)

Mlambo, A. S., *A History of Zimbabwe* (Cambridge University Press, 2014)

Mostert, N., *Frontiers: The Epic of South Africa's Creation and the Tragedy of the Xhosa People* (Alfred A. Knopf, 1992)

Nattrass, G., *A Short History of South Africa* (Biteback Publishing Ltd, 2017)

Norman, J., *Adam Smith. What He Thought, and Why It Matters* (Allen Lane, 2018)

Pakenham, T., *The Scramble for Africa* (Abacus, 1991)

Pakenham, T., *The Boer War* (The Folio Society, 1999)

Parker, P. M., 'Transkei', *Webster's Timeline History 1869-2007* (ICON Group International, 2010)

Peires, J. B., *The House of Phalo. A History of the Xhosa People in the Days of Their Independence* (University of California Press, 1982)

Peires, J. B., *The Dead Will Arise. Nongqawuse and The Great Xhosa Cattle-Killing Movement of 1856-7. A History of the Xhosa People in the Days of Their Independence.* (Indiana University Press, 1989)

Price, R., *Making Empire. Colonial Encounters and the Creation of Imperial Rule in Nineteenth-Century Africa* (Cambridge University Press, 2008)

Rogers, B., *Divide and Rule. South Africa's Bantustans* (IDAF, 1976)

Rose, E., Dowler, E., Daynee, G. and Westcott, G., 'Transkei and Ciskei Disease Pattern Survey'. Paper read at the Tacresoc Meeting, 15 March 1975.

Saunders, C. and Derricourt, R., ed., *Beyond the Cape Frontier. Studies in the History of Transkei and Ciskei* (Longman, 1974)

Simons, H. J. and Simons, R. E., *Class and Colour in South Africa 1850-1950* (Penguin African Library, 1969)

Sleigh, J. C., *The World of the Dutch East India Company* (Tafelberg Publishers, 1980)

Smith, K., *The Wedding Feast War. The Final Tragedy of the Xhosa People* (Frontline Books, 2012)

Stapleton, T. J., *Maqoma: Xhosa Resistance to the Advance of Colonial Hegemony (1798-1873)* (PhD thesis Dalhousie University, 1993)

Taylor, S., *Shaka's Children. A History of the Zulu People* (Harper Collins Publishers, 1994)

The Republic of Transkei (Chris van Rensburg Press Ltd, 1976)

The South African Tourist Corp, *Introducing South Africa. A Selection of Fifty-five Colour Pictures* (1964)

This is Transkei (Chris van Rensburg Press Ltd, 1978)

Thompson, L., *A History of South Africa* (Yale University Press, 2014)

Thompson, L., *Survival in Two Worlds. Moshoeshoe of Lesotho 1786-1870* (Oxford at the Clarendon Press, 1975)

Tropp, J. A., *Natures of Colonial Change – Environmental Relations in the Making of Transkei* (Ohio University Press, 2006)

Vigne, R., *The Transkei – A South African Tragedy* (The Africa Bureau, 1969)

Williams, W., *The Current Status of Land Rights in Transkeian Territories of South Africa* (FIG Working Week, 2016)

Wilson, M. and Thompson, L., *The Oxford History of South Africa. Part 1 South Africa to 1870* (Oxford University Press, 1969)

Index

abeLungu 121
Achebe, Chinua 236
African National Congress
  (ANC) 19, *59*, 61, 68, 137,
  192
Afrikaans 19, 32, 39, 62, 72, 79,
  209, 213, 215, 227
Afrikaners 60–1, 153, 209, 211,
  214, 215, 228
Alexandra 44
All Saints 165
amagogotya 134
amakhaya 29
amathamba 134
Anglo-Boer War 39, 211, 226
Angola 76, 215

Babs 20, 93–4, 103, 116, 122,
  123, 124, 161
Baden-Powell, Robert 226
Banana, Canaan (President) 216
Bantu 12, 36, 127, 153, 160,
  177, 215
Bantustan 11, *14*, 27, 49, 68, 78,
  144
Bay City Rollers 44
Bessie 121
Bethany Home *229, 239, 247,*
  248

Bidla, Mr 103, 154–8, 160–162,
  171, 233
Big, Mr 66–7
Biko, Steve 31, 78, 138
Black Consciousness
  Movement 31, 138
Boer 131, 177, 211, 213, 226, 131
Bomvana 13, *113, 115,* 116–17,
  122, 126
Botha, P. W. 31
Botha, Pik 31
Botswana *14*, 141, 209, 212,
  215, *225*, 226
Bovine pneumonia 132
Brezhnev, Leonid 32
British Kaffraria 132
Broederbond 209
Brook, Very Revd Bishop 30, 72,
  73, 75, 162, 191, 215, 231
Bulawayo 212, 220, 224, 132
Buthelezi, Gatsha 78
Buthelezi, Sister 7
Butterworth *15*, 28, 146–7,
  149–53, 164

Cabo do Boa Esperança 129
Camps Bay 191–2, 194, 199
Cape Frontier Wars (*see also*
  Xhosa Wars) 132, 136

Cape Town   7, 78, 100, 127, 129–30, 132, 136–7, 139–40, 185, 187–93, 195, 199, 236, 256
Caribbean   114
Carter, Jimmy (President)   32, 235
Cattle Killing   133, 135–36
Cerebral palsy   28, 105
Chinese   76, 119, *223*, 224
Coll, Isle of   33, *34*, *35*, 36
Consolata, Sister   23, 79, 245
Cool Gang   *102*, *104*, 105, *106*, 111, 245
Cornish   39, 81
Cornwall   39, 42, 77, 79, 81, 117, 194
Cottonwood   231
Court   200, *203*, *204*
Cripple Care   99
Crossroads   192
Customary laws 78

Dagga   84, 103, 117, 160–62
De Klerk, F. W.   60–1, 63
Dias, Bartolomeu   129
Dolorata, Sister   72, 79, 84–5, 98, 149–50, 152, 188, 204, 206, 245
Dominic, Sister   246
Doug   6–8, 11, 16, *20*, 26, 62, 79, *80*, 81, 83–5, 91, 93–4, 98, *102*, 103, 105, *106*, 107, 116, 122, *123*, 124, 126, 144, 146–49, 151–53, 232–35, 245, 248
Drakensberg Mountains   22, 29, 84, 108,176, 213
Durban   *14*–15, 17, 43, *45*, 47–53, 72, 78, 99, 203, *205*, 236
Dutch East India Company   129

Eastern Cape   27, 127, 130, 138, 140, 160

Eastgate   44, *45*
East London   *14–15*, 29, 97–99, 144, 152, 199, 236
Edict of Fontainebleau   187
Edwards, Trooper   39
Elizabeth II, Queen   39, 42, 109–10, 138, *139*
Engcobo   *15*, 28–30, 138, 165
EsiKhaleni   see also Hole-in-the-Wall   116, 122

Farraghers
  Lynette   54–5
  Joe   54–8
Fingo 132, *134*
Fort Hare University   28
FREMILO *(Frente de Libertação de Moçambique)*   217
Freedom Fighters   53, 217, *221–23*

Gaborone   *14*, 212, 226, 230
Genevieve, Sister   *18*, 26, 79, 96–7, 146, 153, 242
George Abbot comprehensive school   36
George VI, King   138, *139*
Girl Guide   72
Glen Avent Convent   25, *89*, *229*, 231, 239, 246
Great Kei River   *15*, 97, 99, 101, 134–37, 141–43, 144, 146–47, 149, 153
Great Disappointment   134
Grey, Sir George 135–36
Griqualand East   172
Group Areas Act   44
Gugulethu   192
Guildford   29, 36–8, 55, 151, 192, 217, 238
Gulwa, Archie   7, 242
Gxara, River   13, *15*, 133–6

Hani, Chris   138
Harare   *210*, 212, 216–17, 220

Hemingway   114
Herr Angry Psycho   194, 199
Hintsa, Paramount Chief   132
Hole-in-the-Wall   *see also*
     EsiKhaleni   113, *116*, 122,
     123, 124, 126
Holomisa, Bantu   140
Hotz, Mrs   50
Huguenots   187
Hut tax   138

Ignatia, Sister   79, 86, *87*, *88*, *90*,
     91–2
Imbumba Yamanyama   140
Immorality Act   122

Johannesburg   7, 12, *14*, 40, 42,
     44, *45*, *46*, 185,2 01
Johnson, Shaun   7

Kariba, Lake 217–20
Kemp, Jon van der   130
Khoikhoi   128, 160
Klerksdorp   209, 212, 215, 228
Kohliso, Sinesipho   *247*
Kokstad   *15* 147, *175*
Kuoni   121

Langa   192
Lobola   160, 236
London   28, 32, 35, 37, 42, 112,
     132, 195, *196*
London Missionary Society   130
Lesotho   172, *173*, 174–83, 185,
     212, 226, 229
Limpopo, River   127, 230
Ludwig   *43*, 48, 50, 116, 122,
     123, 124
Luther, Martin   187

Maclean-Bristol, Lady
     Lavinia   33
Maclean-Bristol, Major Nicholas
     Verity   33
Mafeking   209, 212, 226, 228

Maluti   15, 27, 173
Mam   18–20, *43*, 48–50
Mandela, Nelson   12, 31, 39,
     59–63, 68, 78, 137, 192, 213,
     215, *242*
Mandela, Winnie   28, 138
Maqume, Kirri Philiswa   49–50
Maria Corda, Sister   79, 246
Marimba   56
Mariazell   172, 176, 183, *184*,
     185
Mary Paul, Sister   4, *8*, 13, 20,
     22, 63, 69–70, 71, 85, 91–5,
     98, *102*, 103, 105, 108, 149,
     154, 160, 162, 164, *166*,
     167, *168*, 169–71, 172, 188,
     199, 203–4, 229–35, 238–9,
     245–47
Maseru   14, 212, 230
Masondo, David   *65*, 66
Matanzima, Kaiser   68, 78, 140
Matanzima, George   68, *69*, 78,
     140
Matatiele   *15*, 172–6, 183
Mazabuka   222
Mbaqanga   62
Mbashe, River   135
Mbeki, Govan   138
Mbeki, Thabo   137
McTell, Ralph   112
Mdawe, Lennox M.   62
Mfengu   *see also* Fingo   132–
     33, 164
Michael   171
Michael, Sister   18, 79, 122, 124,
     168, *169*, 171
Minister for Agriculture,
     Deputy   92
Mirriam, Sister   79, 97, 100–1,
     245
Mkambati   28, *118*, 235
Monica, Auntie   79
Moshoeshoe, King   177
Mostert, Annegret   43, 48, *52*
Mozambique   *14*, 76, 215, 217

Mpako, River 122–6
Mqamelo, Simon 241, *242*
Mqhekezweni 60
Mugabe, Robert 31, 45, 187, 216–17, 221, 230
Muizenberg 188, 199
Mvezo *242*

Nadiwe 199
Natal *14, 15*, 27, 45, 49, 79, 137, 161, 172, 174, 179–80, 188, 212–13, 226
National Party 27, 60
Ngangelizwe 50, 69, 74, *80*, 88, *90*, 92, 155–6, *166*, 168–9, 200–2, 233, 235, 242, 256
Ngquza Hill Massacre 140
Ngwenya, Moses 62
Nkomo, Joshua 45, 221
Nkosi Sikelel' iAfrika (God bless Africa) 18–19, 248
Nobel Peace Prize 59–61, 63, 78
Nongqawuse 13, 133–7
Nonkosi *133*
Nyanga 192

Ongeluksnek *173*, 177–8, 192
Orange Free State *14, 15*, 45, 212, 215, 229

Paraguay 193–4, 199
Paramount Chief of West Thembuland 92
Paraplegic Sports Championship 17, 43, 45, *47*, 203
Pass Laws 44, 76, 152
Paton, Alan 236
Penzance 36, *77*, 79, 81, 194, 232
Phyllis, Granny *77*, 79, 81, 154
Pietermaritzburg 230
Pig, The 20, 22, 24, 69–70, *166*, 169, 199, 234, 246
Pink Floyd 32, 160

Police 21, *53*, 100, 160, 162, 200–5, 208
Polio 26, 164
Pondoland *15*, 28, *118*, 122, 137, 140, 160, 235
Project Trust 33, *35*, 36, 149, 248
Protestant 43, 130, 187

Qunu 31, 60

Razzmatazz 44
Read, James 130
Reformation 187
Reginald, Sister 79
Rehabilitation Centre *19*, 25, 71, 246
Rhodesia 45, 48, *53*, 187–8, 216, 220–1
Robben Island 31, 68, 136, *190*, 192
Rolong 226
Rooinek 211
Russians 76, 133, *136*, 223–4

Salisbury *210*, 216
San 128, 160, 229
Sandile, Chief 136
Sarhili, Chief 136
Schulz 235
Scotland 81
Sekoto, Gerard 108
Shaka, King 132
Sigcau, Stella 140
Sihlali, Durant 108
Simon's Town 197, 199
Sisulu, Walter 54, 138
Smith, Adam 198
Smith, Ian (Prime Minister) 31
Smith, Lieutenant-General Sir Harry 144
Somerset, Major-General Sir Henry 144
Soul Brothers *59*, 61–5
Soweto 39, 44

Stellenbosch   187–8, 199
Strang, Dr   164
Swaziland   *14*, 212, 227

Tambo, Oliver   137
Terrorist   39, 218, 221, 230
Thatcher, Margaret   32, 39
TB   164
The Who   35
Tomlinson Commission   139
Transvaal   *14*, 22, 209, 211–12,
   215, 226
Tsotsi   26
Tuberculosis *see also* TB   26, 163
Tutu, Archbishop Desmond   59,
   78

Umkhonto we Sizwe (Spear of
   Africa)   59, 137
Umqombothi   156–7
Umzimkulu, River   *15*, 27, 49, 51
Umzimvubu, River   28, 55
University of Transkei   54, 235–6

Victoria Waterfalls   212, 224,
   225
Venezuela   36, 113, 115
Voortrekkers   131–2, *214*

Walshe, Jenny   248

Wedding Feast War   136
Wembley Stadium   35
Wild Coast   29, *55*, 99, 103,
   114–15, 117, 119, *121*, 122,
   213
Wittenberg   187
Wonderbox   91, 188

Xhosa Wars   132

Zambezi, River   219, 224, *225*,
   230
Zambia   100, 209, 211–12, 217,
   218, *219*, 220–2, 224, *225*,
   227, 231, 236
ZANLA (Zimbabwe African
   National Liberation
   Army)   221
ZANU-PF (Zimbabwe African
   National Union – Patriotic
   Front)   61, 217, 220
Zimbabwe   12, *14*, 31, 45, 61,
   209, 212, 216–17, *218*, 219–
   21, 224, *225*, 226–7, 230–1,
   237
Zionists   *159*
ZIPRA (Zimbabwe People's
   Revolutionary Army)   221
Zulu   19, 42, 51, 132, 161, 177
Zulu, American   62

If you've enjoyed reading this book and want to find out more about
A Nun and the Pig and the author, further information, images and
useful links can be found at www.treivenicholas.com.